In Conversation with Denise Ferreira da Silva

BLACK LITERARY AND CULTURAL EXPRESSIONS

Bloomsbury's **Black Literary and Cultural Expressions** series provides a much-needed space for exploring dimensions of Black creativity as its local expressions in literature, music, film, art, etc., interface with the global circulation of culture. From contemporary and historical perspectives, and through a multidisciplinary lens, works in this series critically analyze the provenance, genres, aesthetics, intersections, and modes of circulation of works of Black cultural expression and production.

Volumes in the Series:

Wole Soyinka: Literature, Activism, and African Transformation by Bola Dauda and Toyin Falola
Social Ethics and Governance in Contemporary African Writing: Literature, Philosophy, and the Nigerian World by Nimi Wariboko
The Birth of Breaking: Hip Hop History from the Floor Up by Serouj "Midus" Aprahamian

Literature of the Somali Diaspora: Space, Language and Resistance in Somali Anglophone and Italian Novels by Marco Medugno

The Decolonizing Work of Jessica Huntley: The Political Roots of a Radical Black Activist by Claudia Tomlinson

Afro-Centered Futurisms in Our Speculative Fiction edited by Eugen Bacon

Chinua Achebe: Narrating Africa in Fictions and History by Toyin Falola

Irony, Agency and the Global Imaginary in Contemporary Nigerian and Kenyan Literature by Penny Cartwright

In Conversation with Denise Ferreira da Silva: New Methodologies for Race, Ethnic, and Decolonial Studies edited by Julietta Hua and rashné limki

Revitalizing Decolonization through Dance Scholarship: Dancing the African Personality by Eric Baffour Awuah (forthcoming)

In Conversation with Denise Ferreira da Silva

New Methodologies for Race, Ethnic, and Decolonial Studies

Edited by Julietta Hua and rashné limki

BLOOMSBURY ACADEMIC
NEW YORK • LONDON • OXFORD • NEW DELHI • SYDNEY

BLOOMSBURY ACADEMIC
Bloomsbury Publishing Inc, 1359 Broadway, New York, NY 10018, USA
Bloomsbury Publishing Plc, 50 Bedford Square, London, WC1B 3DP, UK
Bloomsbury Publishing Ireland, 29 Earlsfort Terrace, Dublin 2, D02 AY28, Ireland

First published in the United States of America 2026

Cover design by Eleanor Rose
Cover image: "Fire Next Time" © Emma McNally

A catalog record for this book is available from the Library of Congress.

ISBN: HB: 979-8-7651-2128-3
PB: 979-8-7651-2127-6
ePDF: 979-8-7651-2130-6
eBook: 979-8-7651-2129-0

Series: Black Literary and Cultural Expressions

Typeset by Integra Software Services Pvt. Ltd.
Printed and bound in the United States of America

For product safety related questions contact productsafety@bloomsbury.com.

To find out more about our authors and books visit www.bloomsbury.com and sign up for our newsletters.

CONTENTS

FIGURES

Orientations: Interlocutors

1

Introduction

Julietta Hua and rashné limki

That moment … between the release of the trigger and the fall of another Black body, of another brown body, and another. … What is there to do? To capture, to resignify as one remembers, reconfigures, and disassembles what lies before those elusive moments.

— DENISE FERREIRA DA SILVA (*TOWARD A GLOBAL IDEA OF RACE*, 2007: XI)

In *Toward a Global Idea of Race*, Denise Ferreira da Silva laments how, despite experiencing a moment in the 1990s when critical thought looked on the verge of rupture—when theorists insisted on the "death of the author!" and universities opened Ethnic Studies programs—raciality[1] continued unabated. This is made manifest in the lack of ethical crisis triggered by the repeated murder of black people. When it comes to the unfolding of racial violence, this condition of change-without-change leaves us asking: "What is there to do?" The 2020 protests, triggered by a series of police killings of black people including George Floyd, Breonna Taylor and Ahmaud Arbery, appeared as a reaction to so-called extra-juridical killings for many of us observing, participating, and covering these events. Yet what Ferreira da Silva suggests is that such moments also lie *before*; the protests, as a practice

[1] Raciality is understood as "The ontoepistemic toolbox that has transmuted the spatial 'others of Europe' into historical 'others of whiteness' … as it places the 'others of Europe' before the horizon of death" (Chakravartty and Silva, 2012, 367).

of living memory, both represent and disassemble the ways of knowing and conditions of doing that precede instances of racial violence. In other words, for Ferreira da Silva the 2020 protests for Black Lives must be understood not just as an articulation of political grievance, but as occasion and action for exposing the architectures of knowledge that allow for the continued indifference to racial violence.[2] The fact that police killings of unarmed black people continue—despite protests or local efforts to reform policing—speaks to the power of knowledge about blackness itself. Ferreira da Silva's work suggests that in order to disrupt this continued ethical indifference to racial violence, the architectures (onto-epistemological tools and assumptions) that shape how we know blackness must be reconceived. In other words, to disassemble the world that understands the authorization of racial violence as inevitability, we need a reorientation of our shared knowledge structures and a critical undoing of the how-we-have-always-known.

As a philosopher of race, with institutional affiliations in Ethnic Studies and Gender Studies, Ferreira da Silva has made the case for why the untangling of our investment in modern ways of knowing (modern grammar) is necessarily a project of feminist Ethnic Studies. While the political and intellectual project of feminist, queer, trans and Ethnic Studies has importantly called to task "heterosexual cisman" inhabiting "the centre of dominant perspectives" (2018, 25), Ferreira da Silva pushes feminist, trans and Ethnic Studies scholars to think beyond heterosexual cisman's positioning, and focus instead on the very forces that, in positioning heterosexual cisman at the center, instantiates a subject as well as his other. Ferreira da Silva expresses that, "What is troubling is not that (in actuality) a cisman will occupy the position of the subject, but that the gender-sexual feature—referent of the patriarchal-form—requests both positions (a subject and an object)" (2018, 25). The project, then, should focus on that *request* for subject and object inherent in the gender-sexual apparatus. This insistence on the request necessarily engages us in deeply knowing *and* then un-knowing how knowledge itself is structured.

Ferreira da Silva's intervention in Feminist and Gender Studies follows from an understanding of the coloniality underlying modern ways of knowing, akin to the tradition set forth by feminists like Maria Lugones. Working through the philosophical architecture that shapes how we know the world—from our investment in rationality to our understanding of difference as dialectic and progress as natural—Ferreira da Silva presents the very European basis of thought as the first step to un-thinking. As she

---

[2] Put another way, requiring police to wear body cameras may or may not alter individual officers' behaviors. Body cameras may enable survivors access to evidence of abuse of power. Yet the requirement for police body cameras has neither ended questionable police enactments of racial violence (including continued killings of unarmed black people), nor has the camera requirement ended the broader ethical indifference to racial violence.

states in the *Global Idea of Race*, "Failing to grasp how the racial produces modern subjects (even though we have no doubt that it does so), I think, results from *how* we know it" (italics ours; 2007, 3). She therefore moves readers through modern philosophy in order to argue the need for speculative thought—thinking in radically different ways about subjects, difference and relation—to release us from colonial ways of thinking, and thus knowing, relating to, and engaging the world.

This is a project of un-describing the world, but doing this work requires new and different tools. Because the tools presently available are part of the given knowledge apparatus, they are often inadequate for thinking beyond existing conditions of possibility for thought and action. For example, Ferreira da Silva points out that "race" is a concept that is a product of the modern, colonial knowledge apparatus. Race has been produced as a social-scientific descriptor of difference, which then explains ethical differentiation and social hierarchization. But this is a narrow way to understand difference, which situates it as an effect of social-scientific projects that seek to establish knowledge about the world. Instead, Ferreira da Silva demonstrates how difference is constitutive of modern ways of knowing. Given, then, that the category of race is fundamental to the modern colonial apparatus, how might it be liberated from the same? For Ferreira da Silva, this question sits at the crux of why a different vocabulary and critical toolset is necessary. These new tools are intended to re-make the grounds for thought and action untethered from the ethical signification of race/blackness. Ferreira da Silva describes this process as recomposition—a methodological project that traces the *how* of the world wherein (racial) difference does not mark a fundamental separation in forms of existence.

Ferreira da Silva's work thus provides tools to initiate a rupture from the (modern) world as we know it. This marks a significant and destabilizing political and theoretical shift in the study of race and ethnicity. It also constitutes the challenge of comprehending Ferreira da Silva's thought. In order to imagine what has not-yet-come-to-be, Ferreira da Silva gives readers more precise and new vocabularies to describe both the onto-epistemic conditions that enable the persistence of racial violence as well as new analytical tools that interrupt this violence by rethinking "sociality from without the modern text" (2016, 59). The imprecision of our contemporary language, and the fact that the most common current terms we have to describe difference and power (race, racialization, racism) tend to focus on categorical identification, impels Ferreira da Silva's constant attention to re-creating and defining terms. For Ferreira da Silva, the over-determined and saturated condition of existing language and analytic tools marks their incapacity for reimagination and rupture. For example, terms like "racism" already presume "race" as an identitarian tool with both historical and social-scientific efforts to describe and fill their content (content that implies skin pigment, hair texture, geography, history and so on). Ferreira da Silva is concerned with introducing the reader to different terms—like "raciality"—thereby recomposing existing vocabularies. These recomposed terms, unmoored from their usual significations, work more imaginatively to map the landscapes of power within which we are embedded. Engaging philosophy and cultural theory, her earlier work examines the violent materializations of the post-Enlightenment subject in his juridical, economic and ethical registers. More recently, Ferreira da Silva has outlined an alternative poethical (i.e., political-ethical) methodology that enables a radical rearticulation of blackness in unfolding a decolonial praxis. These are the ethical and methodological contours that we, alongside the collection's contributors, identify as Ferreira da Silva's transformative interventions offered to the study of difference and a philosophy of race.

This collection thus engages with the speculative ideas and methodologies offered in Ferreira da Silva's writings. As co-editors, we come to this collection as her former students at the University of California, San Diego—one of the nation's first Ethnic Studies doctoral programs and where Ferreira da Silva was foundational faculty. While her work is often taken up by scholars, artists, and activists, we hope to provide new ways to enter into dialogue with her work, especially for Ethnic Studies and Feminist Studies scholars. To this end, each contributor offers diverse approaches to, and engagements with her work whether it is through explication, application, or inspiration. The contributions range from graphic essay (Long T. Bui), shorter meditations (Maile Arvin, Cecilia M. Rivas), keyword-inspired essays (Carson Cole Arthur), and more traditional pieces that employ Ferreira da Silva's methods of reading and recomposing (Danielle Bouchard, Nathalia Carneiro, Sara-Maria Sorentino). Federico Sanguinetti, Agnes Oliveira Costa, and Pedro João da Silva Bisneto (translated by Katucha Bento) and Alexandro Silva de Jesus (translated by Thuani Queiroz) provide important insight into how Ferreira da Silva's work is situated in both Philosophy and Latin American Studies. We have organized these contributions into three general sections, each beginning with our short statement of orientation followed by excerpts from our interviews with Ferreira da Silva. Part I considers Applications, specifically how Ferreira da Silva's works have impacted Ethnic Studies, Black Studies, and Feminist Studies. Part II highlights Philosophies, which includes situating Ferreira da Silva in the context of philosophy in Brazil as well as thinking about how her methodological and conceptual contributions resonate for scholars of Latin American Studies (Sanguinetti et al., de Jesus). Part II also includes a philosophical engagement with Ferreira da Silva's reading of Marx (Sorentino). Part III emphasizes Speculations and includes writings that highlight the decolonial and feminist rethinking Ferreira da Silva offers. Part III specifically engages art (Carneiro) and the section ends with Ferreira da Silva's essay, "Four Notes on Black Art: Authority, Criticality, Subjectivity, and Separability." We hope that through our interviews and contributor essays, readers will find an array of entry points to engage with Ferreira da Silva's thinking.

References

Chakravartty, Paula and Denise Ferreira da Silva (2012). "Accumulation, Dispossession and Debt: The Racial Logic of Global Capitalism—An Introduction." *American Quarterly* 64, no. 3: 361–85.

Ferreira da Silva, Denise (2007). *Toward a Global Idea of Race*. Minnesota Press.

Ferreira da Silva, Denise (2015). "Toward a Black Feminist Poethics." *The Black Scholar* 44, no. 2: 81–97.

Ferreira da Silva, Denise (2016). "On Difference Without Separability." Catalogue of the 32a São Paulo Art Biennial, "Incerteza viva" (Living Uncertainty): 57–65.

Ferreira da Silva, Denise (2018). "Hacking the Subject: Black Feminism and Refusal Beyond the Limits of Critique." *philoSOPHIA* 8, no. 1: 19–41.

2

Interview with Denise Ferreira da Silva

Julietta Hua and rashné limki

Julietta Hua: Can you speak a little bit about how you would place yourself in Ethnic Studies? Or how do you think you're read and received in Ethnic Studies given that a lot of Ethnic Studies is about the pursuit of certainty and given that we all met in the context of Ethnic Studies?

rashné limki: Julie and I were discussing how your work could be described as in excess of Ethnic Studies, and Feminist Studies, in some ways. We were thinking of excess in terms of abandonment, or that which must be abandoned. Do you relate to that description?

Denise Ferreira da Silva: There are three things, I think—one which is very explicit to me because it's there in *Toward a Global Idea of Race* [Minnesota Press, 2007], which is against the Ethnic Studies orthodoxy [inclusion model]. I think the full extent of the argument that *Toward a Global Idea of Race* makes, institutional Ethnic Studies cannot do it, because it would be self-destructive. [*Toward a Global Idea of Race*] is a call for its [institutionalized Ethnic Studies'] end. Because of all that has become part of, you know, our conditions of existence for the past 30 many years, to recognize and include all those subjects and cultures that have been in revolt as basically just minor-modern subjects, I think is an insult. But it is what it is, and we have to do something with it and about it. But my work generally is ignored by the Ethnic Studies orthodoxy.

But, you know, I do it [Ethnic Studies] because I teach. I teach in a program which is like ethnic studies and feminist studies and gender studies and sexuality studies, all together. I teach in terms of presenting the thinking, so I teach in a very traditional way. But I do think I shift something, because I think now there is so much emphasis on the categories. Instead, I am writing about what I'm calling *colonial-racial, cis-hetero patriarchal matrix* that operates in the political architecture of the present. It is a very complex, complicated thing that has lots of pieces. But, when I use the long phrase, "colonial-racial cis-hetero patriarchal matrix," and give examples about the operation, it is just signaling how to look at it—looking at its operations, instead of beginning with the categories. Because the categories they become a problem. They [categories of identity] have a lot to do with where we are now. They [categories] are tools for racial subjugation. They are tools for social subjugation.

There is a second way my work is taken up, and that is in the critique of the subject that people bring together with Sylvia Wynter's work, even though my critique is different. My critique goes, "Fuck humanity and the human." [Wynter's] goes, "Well there is something about the human that is actually really good and so far Man 1 and Man 2 fail to be that but we can become that." So, it's completely different branches [Ferreira da Silva's and Wynter's critiques of Man].

I have also seen people just translating what I say as something like racial formation theory. This can be done either by finding some quotes that help support racial formation or paraphrasing [to support racial formation theory]. For instance, I have my piece from 2001 in *Social Identities* ["Towards a Critique of the Socio-logos of Justice: The Analytics of Raciality and the Production of Universality"] where somebody wanted a short version for a book. I was going over [the edited version] and there was a translation issue because [the piece] is about police brutality but the person who did the editing wrote "racial profiling" and "police brutality" as the same thing. But they are not. In the piece, I include a Brazilian newspaper article that describes a massacre in Rio [de Janeiro] that is without any reference to what anyone in the US would recognize as "race" and that's the whole point of the piece, because it is so totally about blackness not "race" [as a US-centric formation]. But the copy editor said, "do they use 'race' anywhere explicitly in the coverage?" But the framing of the [*Social Identities*] piece is "beyond the socio-logics of exclusion" and the need for articulating beyond race difference.[1] People see [race] is missing and you just add it. But no, no! The whole point of the thing is that ["race" is not there]. These are the conditions [making "race" present or appear even when it's not there] under which Ethnic Studies is an intellectual, social scientific humanities project.

[1] "Towards a Critique of the Socio-logos of Justice: The Analytics of Raciality and the Production of Universality," *Social Identities* 7, no. 3 (2001): 421–54.

And these are the conditions under which political claims for racial justice make sense. If you challenge that, people don't refer to your work.

At this small conference on the Romantics—I find myself speaking at these—the organizer was telling me: "I was reading *Toward the Global Idea of Race*. I'm reading it for the second time, and you create your own vocabulary. You create the whole grammar around this idea." I mean, I have been saying that for 20 years, but nobody believes me when I said it was necessary [creating a grammar]. That's why the beginning of the book is so impossible. I could not have written any of it without doing all of that work [of creating a vocabulary and grammar]. But this [project of creating a vocabulary] makes sense to someone who studies Mary Shelley, but not necessarily to the Black Studies folks, who ask, "why is she doing that?"

I think my work, but also the decolonial studies people, their work has created an intellectual context for inviting people to talk about racial subjugation outside of the US. They were really internationalist in their orientation, having summer schools in Europe.

Hua: This helps me make sense of how you ended up in a language department—that the language people would see what your work is doing.

Ferreira da Silva: My department is a comparative literature cultural studies department that is interdisciplinary. But they are more likely to appreciate something I did recently—a postscript for a book. I was playing with a phrase from [Martin] Heidegger, "Da-sein is the being which in every occasion I am." I put "black" in that statement and showing how "black" makes that statement possible. Because it is a violation of Heidegger's statement it should be evident to anyone and everyone. But the folks in literature that are more likely to say that "I" cannot, you know, cannot stand being black no matter where "black" is located in that sentence. And then you can speculate. Folks write books about that. So I'm actually very happy that they [the department] are allowing me to do these kinds of things.

I was asked to review a book manuscript, and I read the initial version and thought it was amazing, and also [then read] the final version. [In the manuscript] the author says, "Silva says this" and I felt like I was getting pissed at me [while reading]. Because I got the feeling the other reviewer or someone told the author their project was in conversation with mine and they should refer to the *Toward a Global Idea of Race*. And the author does but the way they do it doesn't make sense because their work is something else, it covers the immediate post-Enlightenment period but doing something else that's nothing to do with what my book is doing. So in my review I wrote, "please stop citing Silva, it distracts from the argument." In this case citing my work was a disturbance to the argument because it would move the reader somewhere else when they [the author] are making a different argument. They can put me in a footnote and move on. I think if it's [Ferreira da Silva's work] useful then people should use it. If you can, weaponize it, use it, and then move on to doing what you are doing. That's how we're supposed to do this thing called being in conversation, acknowledging all kinds of things, but then trying not to get distracted. What is it you are trying to articulate? Don't worry so much about whether you are citing the people you think should be.

Hua: Have you found your work being taken up by feminists?

limki: How do you deploy blackness as an analytic versus thinking about Black as a category? How are you recognized or how do other scholars refer to your work?

Ferreira da Silva: I think the feminists like "Hacking the Subject" because it is locatable in the tradition of, you know, BIPOC feminists, let's call them, in terms of challenging canonical western white feminism. I have been part of one Black Studies formation since about 2014 as part of Blacks in Refusal, a black feminist group, which is about the time when a shift was taking place. I get the black feminist entry through Blacks in Refusal, which is also the claim I make; I claim black feminist thought, but I take it somewhere else because what I do is not Black Studies or part of that canon even though I engage with Hortense [Spillers], [Saidiya] Hartman. Hortense and Saidiya are the ones that I think with most. I did an interview of Hortense Spillers for a special issue of *boundary* 2, which published a dossier on the occasion of her retirement ["Sending Language into Battle: Interview with Hortense J. Spillers," *boundary* 2 51, no. 1 (2024): 3–27]. I place her thinking in 60 years of US racial history from 1964 when she started her MA. I identified her major works at certain key moments and asked her to talk about them. The Hortense Spillers that comes out of that interview is not what would come out of a situating of her work in the Black Studies tradition, even though it is there because she is a black feminist and key Black Studies scholar. "Black Feminist Poethics" [*The Black Scholar* 44, no. 2 (2014)] was something that came out of teaching [Judith] Butler in [the seminar course] Ethnic Studies 200 [at the University of California, San Diego].

There is this generation of artists and activists; I met some of them in Glasgow and they're from the US. Other artists who are in Brazil, and are black LGBTQ +, many of them trans artists, who take it [Ferreira da Silva's work] in whatever way they like. They basically take the critique and do all kinds of amazing things, mostly in writing, but also in performance. I think it's something they can do because it's a generation that is ... I don't know ... some of these people are like 24, 25 and others are in their early 30s ... but it's a generation that is not the one that is now occupying Ethnic

Studies orthodoxy. They're not like Ethnic Studies institutionalized. It is a different thing, it's a whole different thing. And they take the work outside of itself, outside of the academic; they don't situate it. When I was teaching at São Paolo University in Brazil, I met some of them. Yes, many of them are students, but most of them they're reading everybody, like everybody they can come across, outside of academia. And doing their work. And then all kinds of things happen but it becomes something else, because once what you're saying and doing becomes part of somebody else's artwork, it's different than when it's cited in an academic argument because it's work as material for the artwork.

References

Ferreira da Silva, Denise (2001). "Towards a Critique of the Socio-logos of Justice: The Analytics of Raciality and the Production of Universality." *Social Identities* 7, no. 3: 421–54.

Ferreira da Silva, Denise (2007). *Toward a Global Idea of Race*. Minnesota Press.

Ferreira da Silva, Denise (2014). "Toward a Black Feminist Poethics." *The Black Scholar* 44, no. 2: 81–97.

Ferreira da Silva, Denise (2018). "Hacking the Subject: Black Feminism and Refusal Beyond the Limits of Critique." *philoSOPHIA* 8, no. 1: 19–41.

Ferreira da Silva, Denise (2024). "Sending Language into Battle: Interview with Hortense J. Spillers." *boundary 2* 51, no. 1: 3–27.

3

Fractal
Worlds
Long T. Bui
A graphic essay based on the works and thoughts
of Denise Ferreira da Silva

STUDIOSA IS PURSUING A ***QUEST(ION)*** THAT SPANS THE GLOBE. THE DREAM OF FINDING HER MOTHER WHO MYSTERIOUSLY VANISHED AND FINDING A HOME REMAINS ELUSIVE. SHE IS A REFUGEE LIKE MILLIONS, SEARCHING FOR MEANING AMONG CHAOS. YET, LIBERAL MODERNITY'S GIFT OF FREEDOM, BASED ON REPRODUCING VIOLENCE, PRESENTS AN ***UNPAYABLE DEBT.***
THERE IN THE POSTCOLONIES, OUR YOUNG PROTAGONIST ENCOUNTERS NO HOSPITALITY. ONLY FURTHER DEPLOYMENTS OF SECURITY, POLICE BRUTALITY, AND CRIMINALIZATION. FINDING HERSELF UNPROTECTED, THE GIRL FLEES LIKE OTHERS DID TO A REMOTE ISLAND OFF THE COAST OF BRASIL, ONE LEGEND SAYS IS RULED BY A POWERFUL SCHOLAR-SORCERER. UPON REACHING SHORE, THE MAROONED CHILD ENCOUNTERS CREATURES SO STRANGE THEY STARTLE HER.
Story and art by Long T. Bui

OLÁ! BOM DIA.
WHO ARE YOU?
I AM PROFESSOR DENISE FERREIRA DA SILVA. BUT YOU CAN CALL ME FEMTOR.
MY NAME IS STUDIOSA... SO ARE YOU A BRUXA? WILL YOU TURN ME INTO A PIG LIKE THOSE MEN?
NONSENSE! THOSE SILLY MEN DID THAT TO THEMSELVES. IN ANY CASE, HUMANS AND NON-HUMANS ARE NO DIFFERENT IN THE SPHERE OF LIFE. I COME TO GUIDE YOU ON YOUR PATH, HELPING YOU TO UNLOCK YOUR SUPERPOWERS AND RADICAL IMAGINATION.

FEMTOR, WHY DO YOU CONFUSE ME SO? I JUST NEED SIMPLE ANSWERS TO QUESTIONS ABOUT MY HUMAN EXISTENCE.
I WANT TO BE ACCEPTED IN SOCIETY. BE IN A WORLD WHERE EVERYONE IS EQUAL AND FREE!
OH MY CHILD, THAT PROPOSITION REMAINS A FANTASY. A CUNNING RUSE. THE PLAY OF REASON, WHERE YOU ARE AN ***AFFECTABLE SUBJECT,*** AN OUTER-DETERMINED THING THAT LACKS ***INTERIORITY.***
THE ANSWER TO YOUR QUERY LIES AT THE LIMIT OF KNOWLEDGE AND CRITIQUE.

Natural / Moral
LIBERTY
Necessitas
Duty
IDENTITY
Self-Preservation
AUTHORITY
Myth
LAW
RACIALITY
STATE
POWER
SUBJECT
SOVEREIGN
DIGNITY
MULTICULTURAL
DEMOCRACY
INCLUSION
HUMAN RIGHTS
JUSTICE
Equality
Affirmative Action
Diversity
Reparations
FREEDOM

WITH THE POST-ENLIGHTENMENT, THE SCIENCE OF MAN PROVIDED DESCRIPTORS OF THE WORLD THAT I CALL THE ANALYTICS OF RACIALITY. FROM THIS ARSENAL AND REGIMEN AROSE POLITICAL-SYMBOLIC TOOLS AS WELL AS A STRATEGY OF ENGULFMENT, WHICH PLACED THE "OTHERS OF EUROPE" IN A POSITION OF INFERIORITY, EXTERIORITY, AND VULNERABILITY.
THE OTHERS OF EUROPE
DEAR FEMTOR, I AM AWARE OF MARXISM AND HOW CAPITALISM EXTRACTS SURPLUS VALUE FROM WORKERS AND LABOR. POSTCOLONIAL CRITIQUE TAUGHT ME HOW TO UNMASK MASTER NARRATIVES AND EUROCENTRIC IDEOLOGIES.
WE ARE MERELY EXPLOITED SUBJECTS WHO JUST NEED TO OVERTHROW OUR OPPRESSORS. WHAT MORE ELSE IS THERE TO KNOW?
REVOLT!
REBEL!
REVOLUTION!
LABOR UNITE

AND YET, THE ETHICAL PROGRAM TO PROTECT MAN FORMED AN EMPIRE OF TRANSCENDENTAL REASON, AN INTERPRETIVE/DETERMINATIVE EPISTEME OF JUDGEMENT AND CLASSIFICATION WE MODERN BEINGS HAVE BEEN GRAPPLING WITH FOR CENTURIES. THEIR SIGNIFYING STRUCTURES FORMED THE VERY BASIS AND PILLARS OF MODERN THOUGHT.
HEGEL STAGED UNIVERSAL REASON IN THE UNDERSTANDING OF WORLD HISTORY AS MORAL THEATER. REASON TOOK ON THE SPIRIT OF A SELF-ACTUALIZING FORCE, ONE FULLY REALIZED IN EUROPEAN MINDS AND TERRITORIES.
KANT CONCEIVED TRANSCENDENTAL REASON THROUGH FORMAL UNDERSTANDING AND MORALITY. HE OBSERVED THINGS AND EVENTS THROUGH THE MENTAL APPARATUS OF CATEGORIES AND INTUITION.
DESCARTES SEPARATED THE MIND AND BODY, REDUCING THEM TO UNDERSTANDING THE LAWS OF NATURE. HIS SCIENCE ESTABLISHED A TABLE OF KNOWLEDGE BASED ON MEASUREMENT AND ORDER.

THUS, FROM THEIR INFINITE CANVAS, *HOMO MODERNUS* WAS BORN, AND WE ITS MONSTROUS CHILDREN. THE HUMAN SCIENCES AND DISCIPLINES LIKE ANTHROPOLOGY AND SOCIOLOGY EMERGED, MAPPING THE MODERN HUMAN CONDITION THROUGH THE *GLOBAL/HISTORICAL CONSCIOUSNESS*. THIS *TOTALITY* BECOMES THE *ORDERED WORLD* AND *THE WORLD AS WE KNOW IT.*
SCIENCE
TRANSPARENCY
GLOBALITY
Mundus Intellectualis
Separability
Determinancy
Sequentiality
HOMO MODERNUS
NOMOS
UNIVERSALITY
POESIS

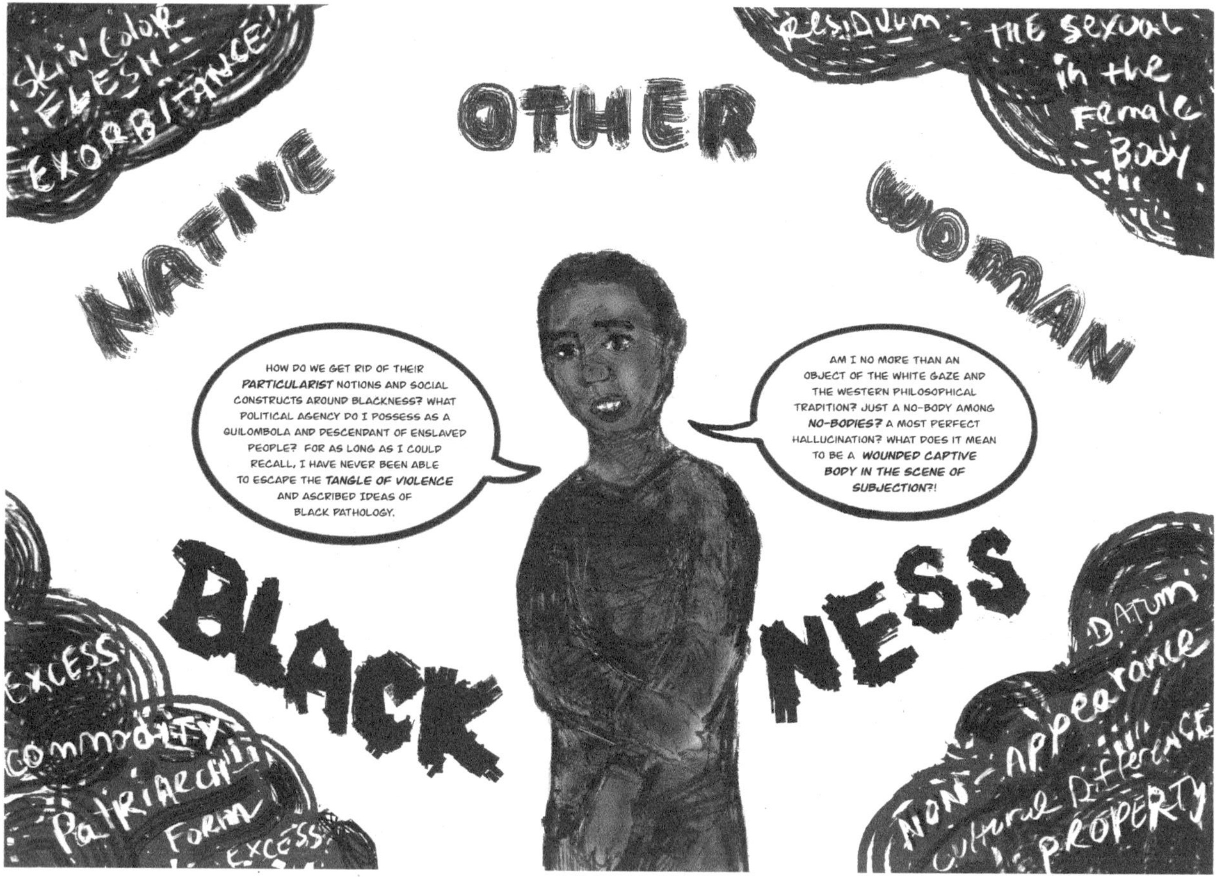
Skin Color
FLESH
EXORBITANCE
NATIVE
OTHER
WOMAN
Residuum: THE sexual in the Female Body
HOW DO WE GET RID OF THEIR PARTICULARIST NOTIONS AND SOCIAL CONSTRUCTS AROUND BLACKNESS? WHAT POLITICAL AGENCY DO I POSSESS AS A QUILOMBOLA AND DESCENDANT OF ENSLAVED PEOPLE? FOR AS LONG AS I COULD RECALL, I HAVE NEVER BEEN ABLE TO ESCAPE THE TANGLE OF VIOLENCE AND ASCRIBED IDEAS OF BLACK PATHOLOGY.
AM I NO MORE THAN AN OBJECT OF THE WHITE GAZE AND THE WESTERN PHILOSOPHICAL TRADITION? JUST A NO-BODY AMONG NO-BODIES? A MOST PERFECT HALLUCINATION? WHAT DOES IT MEAN TO BE A WOUNDED CAPTIVE BODY IN THE SCENE OF SUBJECTION?!
BLACK
NESS
EXCESS
COMMODITY
Patriarchal
Form
EXCESS
Datum
NON-Appearance
Cultural Difference
PROPERTY

QUERIDA, YOU MUST EXCAVATE WHAT YOU KNOW, REFRACTING THE MIRROR OF THE SUBJECT. LEARN TO RECODE THE CATEGORY OF BLACKNESS AND SIGNIFY OTHERWISE.
AH, BUT BEWARE THE TRANSPARENT I, WHICH SEES AND KNOWS EVERYTHING. IT EXPOSES YOU TO EXTREME VIOLENCE, INSCRIBING RACIAL SUBALTERNS LIKE YOU AND ME ALWAYS ALREADY ON THE OTHER SIDE OF THE HUMAN AND HUMANITY. MEANWHILE, IT KEEPS THE THING LOCKED IN CHAINS OF NEGATION.
das Ding
HUMANITY
WE MUST RELEASE HER FROM THE BONDS OF ABSTRACTION AND DEVALUATION. HACK THE SUBJECT. BREAK THE (RACIAL) DIALECTIC OF SAMENESS AND DIFFERENCE ONCE AND FOR ALL!
THE THING REMINDS ME OF MY FUGITIVE MOTHER WHO NEVER GOT TO EXPERIENCE TRUE FREEDOM.
ALRIGHT, LET'S GO BEYOND THIS INTRASTRUCTURE AND ITS PERVERSE LOGIC CIRCUITRY. YOUR JOURNEY AWAITS.
SUBJECTIVITY
RACIAL DIALECTIC

WITHOUT MY MOTHER, I DON'T KNOW WHO I AM ANYMORE. I WISH I COULD GO BACK IN TIME TO TRY AND SAVE HER LIFE.
THINGS ARE NOT LINEAR LIKE THAT. TRANSVERSING THE CIRCUIT OF DISPOSSESSION REQUIRES A METHOD OF RE/DE/COMPOSING--A MODE OF BORDER CROSSING WITHOUT DIRECTIONALITY, WHERE YOU NAVIGATE THE PLENUM OF WHAT HAS HAPPENED...AND WHAT HAS YET TO HAPPEN.
EVEN WHEN I LEAVE THIS PLANET, I DON'T WANT TO FORGET WHO I AM. MY ETHNIC HERITAGE. THE MEMORY OF MY MOTHER...THOSE ARE THE ONLY THINGS I HAVE LEFT IN THIS HORRID WORLD.
HMM...WE'LL SEE ABOUT THAT. READY TO ENTER A WORMHOLE OF EXPERIMENTAL WONDERS? FOLLOW ME.

STUDIOSA ACCOMPANIES FEMTOR TO A MOUNTAIN. THE SAGE CALLS IT A SOURCE OF INHABITATION AND EXPRESSING INTUITIVE EMBODIED KNOWLEDGE.
BEHOLD THIS SACRED SITE! HERE, YOU CAN YOU CAN HEAR THE EARTH. LISTEN TO THE VOICES OF THE ANCESTORS. READ THE DEAD WITHIN THE SOIL. HEED THEIR CALLS AND APPREHEND ENDLESS POSSIBILITIES FOR DECOLONIZATION!
CONTEMPLATE ANOTHER IMAGE OF EXISTENCE. THE RETURN OF EVERYTHING OUTSIDE THE ARROW OF TIME. WHAT IS THINKABLE ABSENT NECESSITY. IN THIS ANICIENT PLACE OF NON-LOCALITY, DESIRE AND DISCOURSE COLLAPSE INTO AN UNREGULATED DOMAIN OF ZERO VALUE... ONE NOT DOMINATED BY THE LANGUAGE OF MAN.
NOW SIT HERE. BE STILL.

Be more than a thing of the will...
Find healing through the alchemy ...
...of relationality and repair....
...embrace confusing, impressions...
...find release from the grips of certainty...
Approach everything in the raw...
Em estado bruto...

WAIT...WHY DO I FEEL MY HEAD AND BODY GETTING HOTTER? WHAT ON EARTH IS HAPPENING TO ME?!!
I AM CONVERTING LIFE FORCE ENERGY TO TRANSPORT YOU TO AN ALTERNATE DIMENSION-- THE ENTANGLED/IMPLICATED WORLD WHEREIN THE NOISE OF MEANING LEAVES YOUR MIND...AND YOU ARE RELINQUISHED FROM THE POSITION OF COMPLETE MASTERY, AUTHORITY, AND SUPERIORITY.
...NOW SIT STILL, PLEASE! OR ELSE YOU MIGHT LOSE A LIMB IN THE PROCESS.

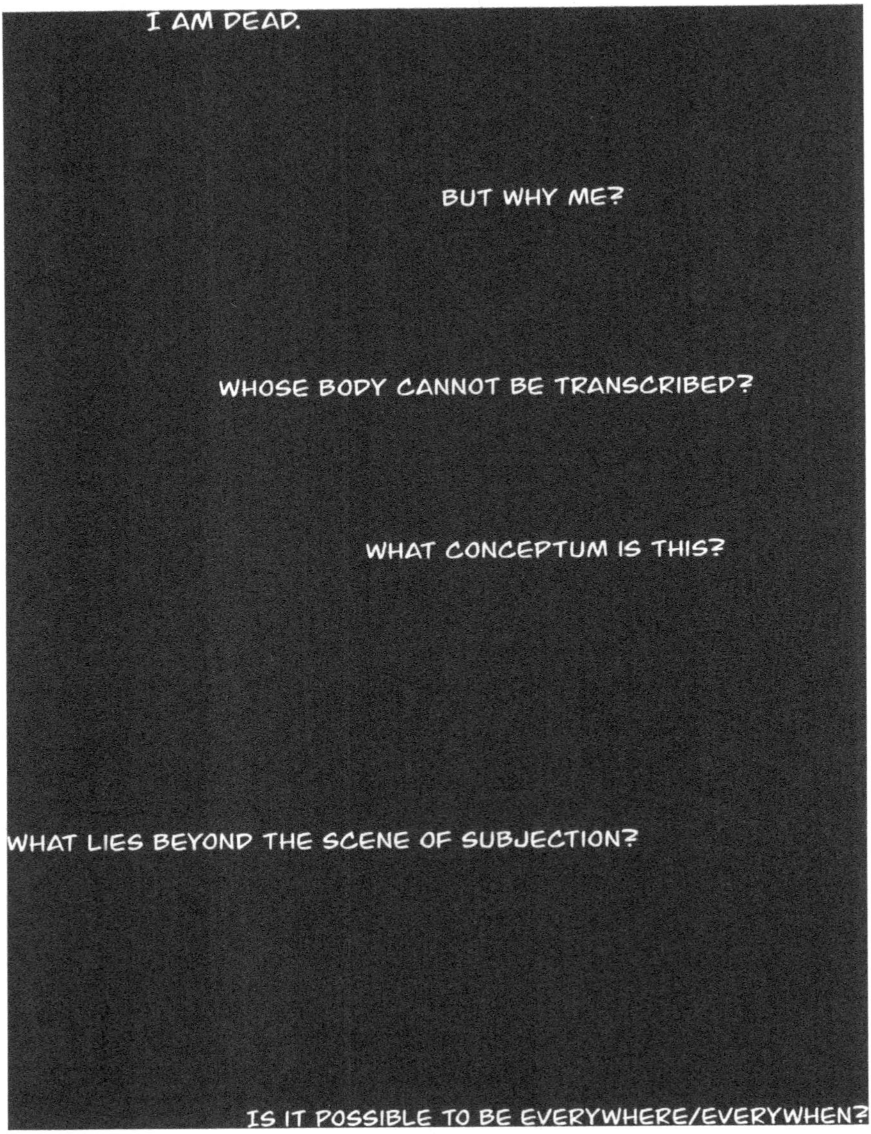
I AM DEAD.
BUT WHY ME?
WHOSE BODY CANNOT BE TRANSCRIBED?
WHAT CONCEPTUM IS THIS?
WHAT LIES BEYOND THE SCENE OF SUBJECTION?
IS IT POSSIBLE TO BE EVERYWHERE/EVERYWHEN?

STUDIOSA FLOATS THROUGH A BLACK VOID, GOING BEYOND THE GEOMETRY OF SPACE AND TIME OR THE **GRID OF INTELLIGIBILITY**. THIS PASSAGE EXCEEDS THE RATIONALITY OF CAUSE AND EFFECT, MOVING BEYOND SINGULAR PARTS AND ORGANIC WHOLES.
THE SUBSTANCE OF HER BEING MELTS INTO PLASMA, **TRANSDUCTING** INTO HEAT UNTIL MATTER IS RELEASED FROM FORM, YET RETAINING A **RAW MATERIALISM**. THE GROUNDS OF KNOWLEDGE ARE DISSOLVED THROUGH **IMAGING OF SCALES** INVOLVING THE PLANETARY, COSMIC, ATOMIC, QUANTIC, AND BIOLOGICAL.
(F)1 (life) ÷ 0 (blackness) = ∞ − ∞
BLACKLIGHT
DARK MATTER
M(OTHER)

SUDDENLY, STUDIOSA IS BACK AT THE TREE UNDER WHICH SHE SAT.
WELCOME BACK!
I NEVER FELT SUCH ENERGY BEFORE. ARE YOU GOD?
DIVINE POWER THIS WAS NOT! INSTEAD, I CROSSED THE ONTOEPISTEMOLOGICAL BARRIER YOU CROSSED MANY TIMES BEFORE: THE HORIZON OF DEATH!
I WORK ALONGSIDE OTHERS BUT DEVISED MY OWN BLACK FEMINIST POETHICS TO DISMANTLE THE EXTRACTION, EXPROPRIATION, AND EXPLOITATION OF OUR BODIES.
THERE IS LIBERATION FROM NEGATIVE ACCUMULATION.. WHAT I CALL A NEGATIVATION.

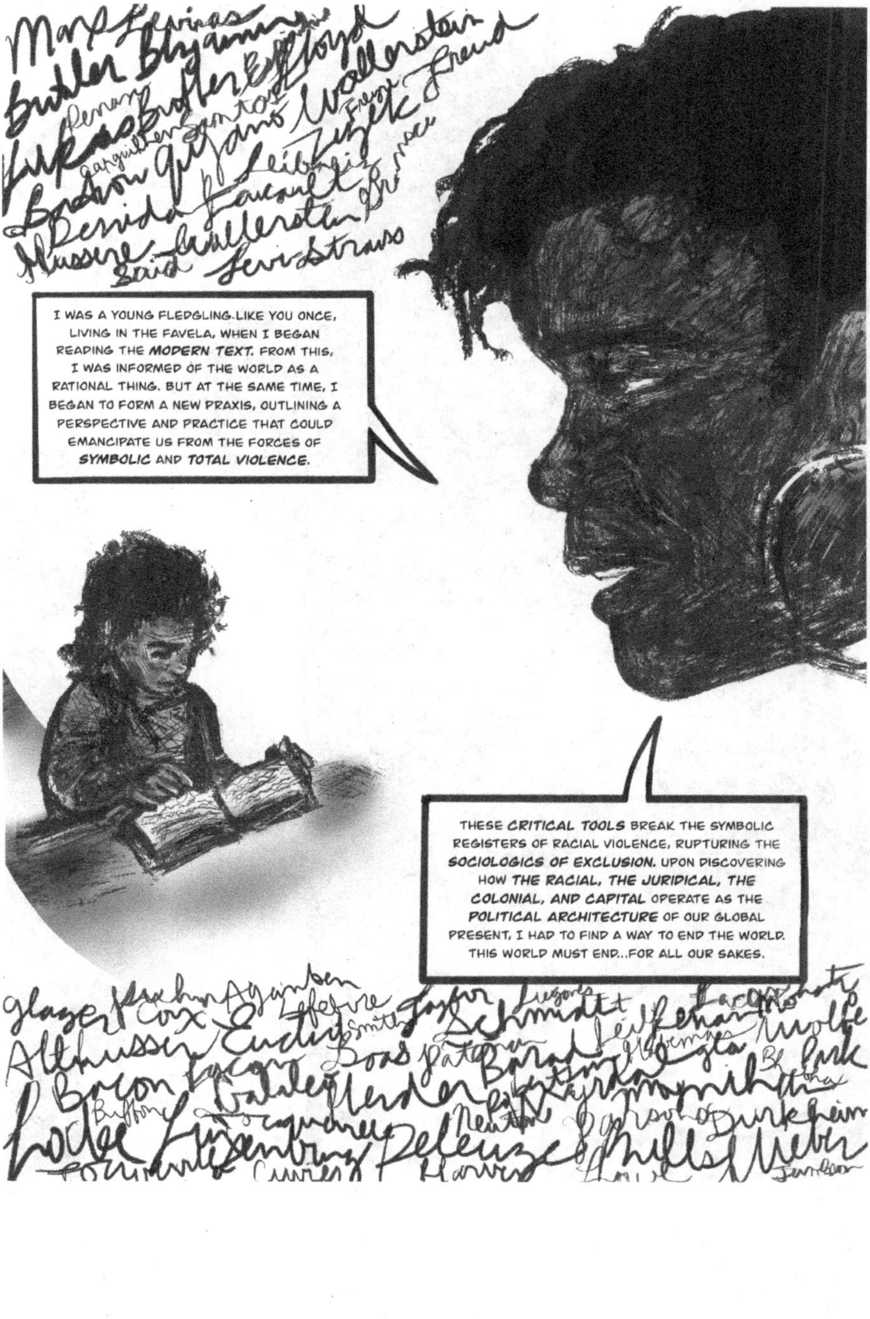
I WAS A YOUNG FLEDGLING LIKE YOU ONCE, LIVING IN THE FAVELA, WHEN I BEGAN READING THE MODERN TEXT. FROM THIS, I WAS INFORMED OF THE WORLD AS A RATIONAL THING. BUT AT THE SAME TIME, I BEGAN TO FORM A NEW PRAXIS, OUTLINING A PERSPECTIVE AND PRACTICE THAT COULD EMANCIPATE US FROM THE FORCES OF SYMBOLIC AND TOTAL VIOLENCE.
THESE CRITICAL TOOLS BREAK THE SYMBOLIC REGISTERS OF RACIAL VIOLENCE, RUPTURING THE SOCIOLOGICS OF EXCLUSION. UPON DISCOVERING HOW THE RACIAL, THE JURIDICAL, THE COLONIAL, AND CAPITAL OPERATE AS THE POLITICAL ARCHITECTURE OF OUR GLOBAL PRESENT, I HAD TO FIND A WAY TO END THE WORLD. THIS WORLD MUST END...FOR ALL OUR SAKES.

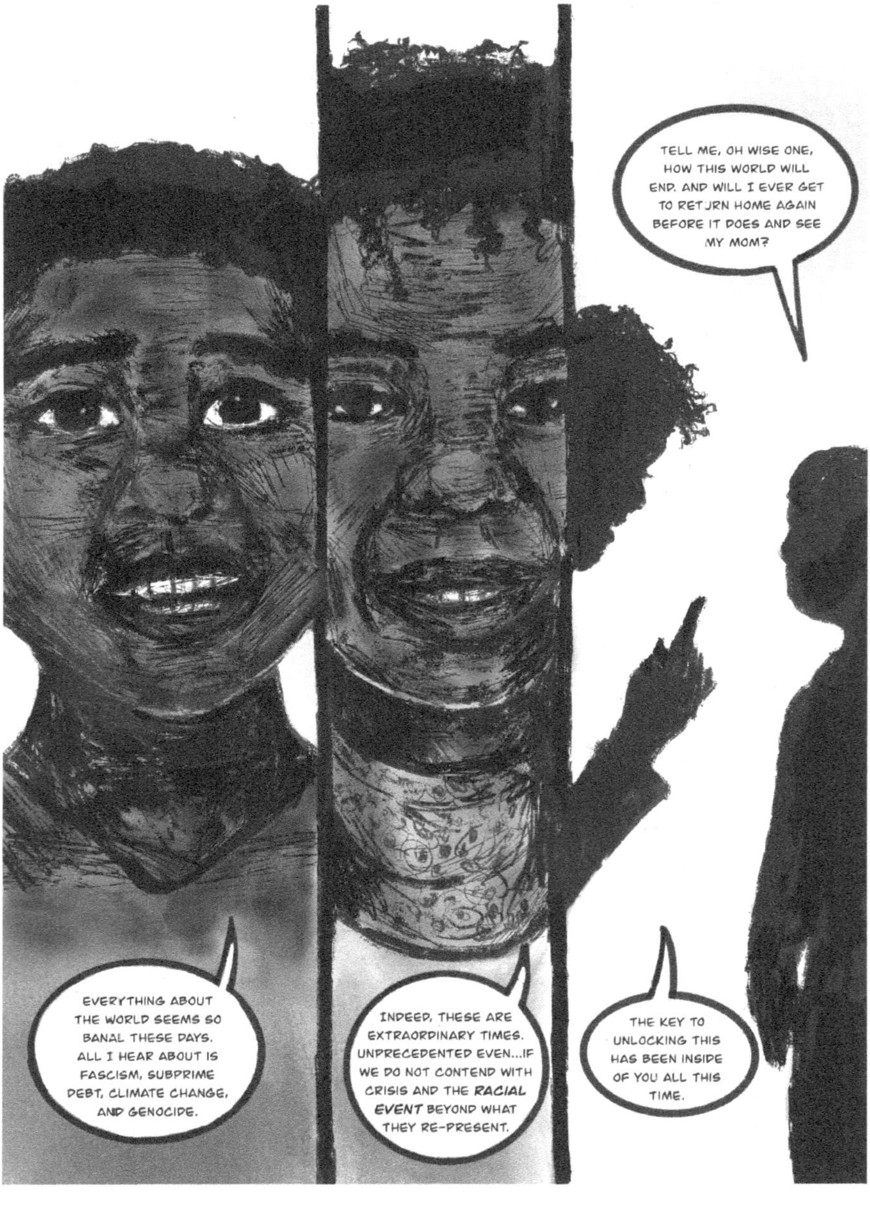
TELL ME, OH WISE ONE, HOW THIS WORLD WILL END. AND WILL I EVER GET TO RETURN HOME AGAIN BEFORE IT DOES AND SEE MY MOM?
EVERYTHING ABOUT THE WORLD SEEMS SO BANAL THESE DAYS. ALL I HEAR ABOUT IS FASCISM, SUBPRIME DEBT, CLIMATE CHANGE, AND GENOCIDE.
INDEED, THESE ARE EXTRAORDINARY TIMES. UNPRECEDENTED EVEN...IF WE DO NOT CONTEND WITH CRISIS AND THE **RACIAL EVENT** BEYOND WHAT THEY RE-PRESENT.
THE KEY TO UNLOCKING THIS HAS BEEN INSIDE OF YOU ALL THIS TIME.

EVERYTHING INSIDE YOU IS COMPOSED OF THAT WHICH MAKES UP EVERYTHING ELSE THAT HAS, DOES, AND WILL EXIST. THIS IS WHAT IT MEANS TO BE PART OF A *CORPUS INFINITUM*.
IN THIS VAST UNIVERSE, WHERE DO I BELONG, FEMTOR? DO I EVEN MATTER? ULTIMATELY, DOES ANYTHING MATTER?
DO **BLACK LIVES MATTER**?!!!
REMEMBER THAT YOU MATTER! PONDER SUCH MATTERING BEYOND COMPREHENSIBILITY, BEYOND VISIBILITY, BEYOND THE ***EQUATION OF VALUE***.
OPEN YOURSELF TO ***FRACTAL THINKING***. UNLEASH YOUR CREATIVE POTENCIAL TO DESTROY THIS WORLD, EVEN THOUGH WE DON'T REALLY WANT IT TO END. ALAS, IT IS TIME FOR YOU TO GO BACK FROM WHERE YOU CAME.

HERE, TAKE THESE DIVINATION CARDS OF MINE. THEY CONTAIN MESSAGES THAT WILL GUIDE YOU FURTHER.
OBRIGADA, FEMTOR, BUT I STILL HAVE MORE QUESTIONS TO ASK YOU, SUCH AS THE DIFFERENCE BETWEEN THE ACTUAL AND THE VIRTUAL...
NO MORE QUESTIONS! OFF YOU GO! TCHAU, STUDIOSA!
THEIR CONVERSATION ENDS WITH A ZAP OF POWERFUL RADIOACTIVE RAYS. EVERYTHING FADES INTO BLACK.

AAAA!!!!
STUDIOSA WAKES UP IN HER CHILDHOOD HOME, WONDERING IF IT WAS ALL A DREAM. SHE IS CONFUSED UNTIL A FAMILIAR MATERNAL FIGURE SHOWS UP BY THE GIRL'S BEDSIDE.
ARE YOU OKAY? I HEARD YOU LET OUT A TERRIBLE SCREAM OF PAIN.
MÃE, I THOUGHT I LOST YOU. AS WELL AS EVERYTHING I KNOW AND LOVE...ALL OF IT GONE!
YOU DID LOSE ME ONCE BUT I AM HERE NOW. YOU ONLY NEED TO THINK OF ME WHEN YOU NEED ME. I AM WITH YOU ALWAYS, STUDIOSA. WE ARE ONE.

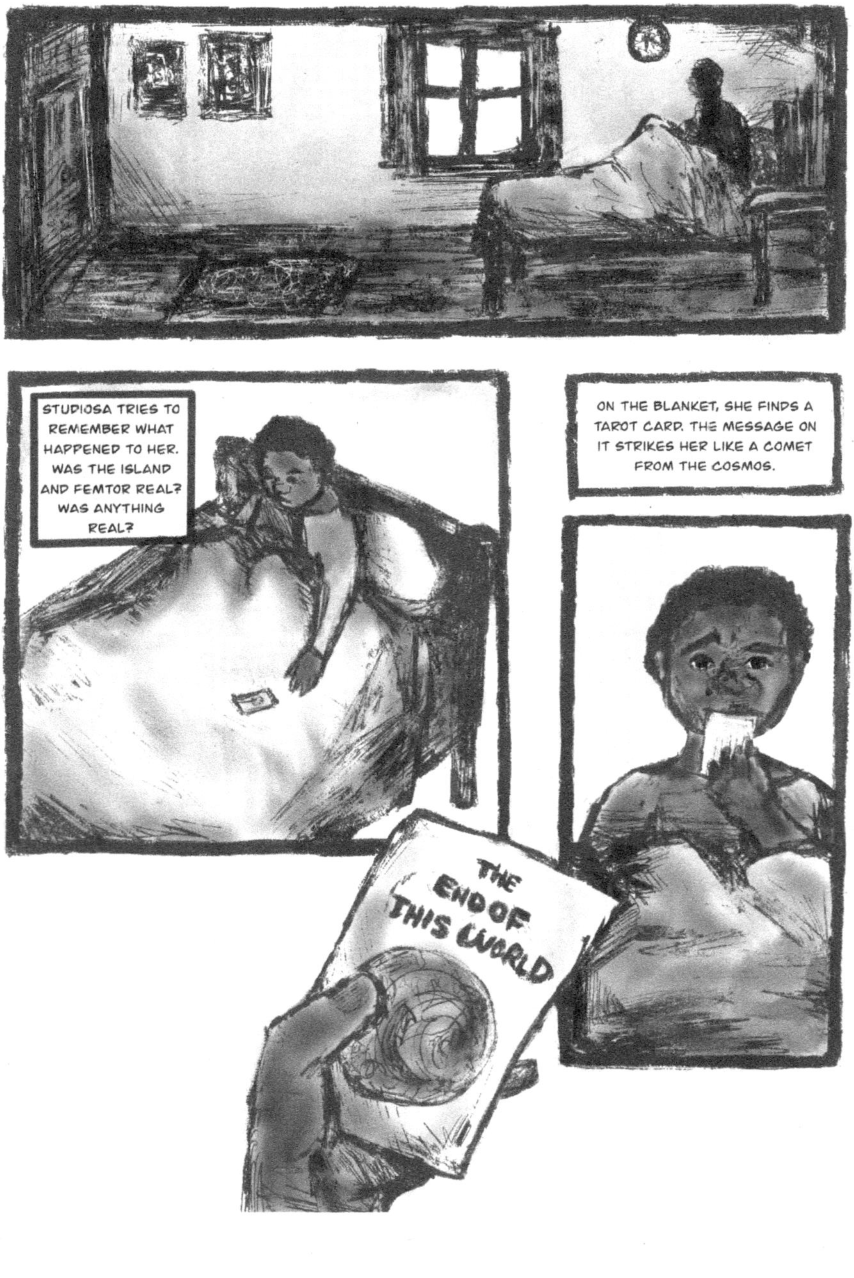
STUDIOSA TRIES TO REMEMBER WHAT HAPPENED TO HER. WAS THE ISLAND AND FEMTOR REAL? WAS ANYTHING REAL?
ON THE BLANKET, SHE FINDS A TAROT CARD. THE MESSAGE ON IT STRIKES HER LIKE A COMET FROM THE COSMOS.
THE END OF THIS WORLD

PART ONE

Applications

4

Introduction

Julietta Hua and rashné limki

Despite the centrality of race and, in particular, blackness, to her work, Ferreira da Silva remains on the margins of Ethnic Studies. One reason is perhaps her eschewal of experience—a staple in the field—as a meaningful analytic for achieving liberation and justice. Instead of experience Ferreira da Silva insists on the need for archaeological and speculative work to reimage the world otherwise. Rather than directing thought at racial categories (identity) or racial processes (racialization), from which theorizations of experience follow, Ferreira da Silva affirms the imperative to de- and re-compose structures of differentiation. Her point of entry is the broader architecture of knowledge through which we come to know ourselves and the world. In particular, she introduces the phrase "analytics of raciality" to foreground the apparatus of knowledge that produces the juridical, economic, and ethical content of the category of race and thereby redirect us towards questioning the function of the racial. As Carson Cole Arthur points out, "failure to consider the analytics that is of raciality would lead to mistaking the term as merely a discursive concept (e.g. another way of saying 'racialised' or 'racial thinking')" (2020, np).

Attentive to the ways in which blackness continues to exist primarily through abjection, Ferreira da Silva's work excavates the philosophical terms of modern knowledge that continue to confine blackness' contemporary definitions and usages. Because we have yet to fully contend with blackness' epistemic and ethical registers (tending only to approach blackness as ontological and political—i.e., as identity-process), we remain unable to fully confront the repetition of racial violence. Writing, for instance, about the killing of black men (Amadou Diallo, Trayvon Martin, George Floyd), Ferreira da Silva notes how their bodies predict and justify their murders (see 2007; 2014). To be a "black young man" is precisely why Martin and others like him must forfeit their lives as a function of *necessitas*—"the epistemological figuring of reason as (self-preserving) violence" (2007, 219). In other words, the killing of young black men is juridically and politically legitimized as an act of "securing" the social. Our contemporary comprehension of blackness, as object excluded from ethical recognition, aspires for redress through the recognition and inclusion of a black subject into humanity. The result is a reinforcement, rather than a radical transformation of, the existing terms (here, subject-object or I-other) through which we understand humanity. To understand the murder of Amadou Diallo, Trayvon Martin, George Floyd, not as repeat-able or even as tragic, requires an unraveling of the core presuppositions (transparency and self-determination) that underlie our understanding of humanity and the human subject.

To understand blackness in its entangled emergence with modern knowledge necessitates tracing the trajectory of blackness as a philosophical concept, not simply an identity or descriptor of difference. Thus, Ferreira da Silva compels us to rethink our investment in a particular kind of (modern) subject, whose subject-ness is tied to his ever-evolving ethical distinction from others (difference). It necessitates un-doing the existing apparatus of knowing that disciplines beings into subjects with or without varying degrees of self-consciousness. In other words, it necessitates a recomposition of the terms of modern philosophy (metaphysics, the Science of Man) that continue to constitute how we know the Subject (that which names ethical being) and, therefore, blackness (designated as non-Subject/affectable Other). Blackness, in Ferreira da Silva's formulation, can direct methodological practices that dissolve the primary tenets of humanness or, in allowing for a different kind of emanation, draw attention to those assumptions. Blackness, she contends, "already carries the necessary tools for dismantling the existing strategies for knowing, and opening the way for another figuring of existence" (2014, 82).

Blackness, then, is the anchor of methodological interventions that provides a "compositional practice designed to decompose the abstract forms (the concepts and categories) of the understanding and reflection which both presuppose and rehearse the occlusion of colonial violence and indifference to racial violence" (2017a, 245). That is, because *how we know* "black" has been made so foundational to *what we know*, Ferreira da Silva proposes various methods that can deploy blackness to disrupt assumed ways of knowing. In particular, methods such as blacklight, "hacking the subject" and "black feminist poethics" allow what is contained in blackness to emanate in new ways. Each of these is a method that Ferreira da Silva offers so that we may recompose blackness outside the confines of knowing through the subject-object relationship that keeps blackness always anchored to the latter condition.

Ferreira da Silva demonstrates how blackness can extend beyond subjectivity and "unravel modern thought without reproducing the violence housed in knowledge and in the scene of value" (2017b, np). Ferreira da Silva's methodological intervention is not concerned with legibility or discovery; her interest is with the ethical. For instance, blacklight is a method that "does not illuminate [but] makes things emanate or shine" (2017a, 245). Ferreira da Silva wields a blacklight on Marx's theory of value in order to "make shine" what falls outside the confines of use-value, surplus-value, capital, and the other "terms that enter in [Marx's] account of value" (2017a, 248).

While Marx provides a crucial framework of knowledge for distilling value and its relation to capital, Ferreira da Silva argues for shining a blacklight on the compositional assumptions like "raw material" not made "bright" by Marx; doing so enables readers to foreground the colonial assumptions taken for granted in Marx's theory of value. For example, the value of yarn emerges from a calculus of "living labor" or the time used to transform cotton into spun yarn and the value of the cotton itself (raw material). Where Ferreira da Silva shines a blacklight is in Marx's dismissal of "the past [dead] labor expended in the production of raw material," which, Ferreira da Silva points out, Marx determines as "absorbent of a definite quantity of labor" (2017a, 248) or assumed in the value of the cotton itself. That is, the value of the raw material, cotton, is presumed to already subsume the (enslaved) labor that has planted, cultivated, and harvested it, as well as the productive capacity of the land itself, acquired as colonial spoils. Enslaved labor in a sense becomes only vitality—part of the "natural" life of the cotton plant and the land on which it is grown. In this formulation, the acquisition of lands so that cotton can be cultivated is a taken-for-granted fact left unaccounted. Colonialism is thus put under erasure.

Similarly, value is attributed solely to living labor; living labor is recognized as the condition of possibility for the value that is exchanged and thus the basis on which accumulation occurs. This erases the value extracted from enslaved labor (in the harvesting of cotton), accounting solely for that extracted from the generalized working classes. Shining a blacklight on Marx's theories of value, then, makes present not only the rendering of slave labor into raw material, but also how this rendering of slave labor into raw material expropriated native lands (i.e., is colonial). Blacklight also makes shine how Marx's knowledge production around value and capital depends on his prioritization of "use-value" over "raw materials," even as the latter undergirds his theorizing. Ferreira da Silva shows how the concept of "raw material" loses analytical privilege even as Marx also describes the price of slave labor as loss—or as "anticipated and capitalized surplus-value or profit, which is to be ground out of him" (Marx qtd in Ferreira da Silva 2017a, 249). The result, Ferreira da Silva explains this way: "In Marx's rendering of his theory of value … the *total value* yielded by the creative capacity of American natives' lands and Africans' enslaved bodies—both *expropriated* through the violent methods and practices characteristic of colonial juridical architectures—vanishes into/as *raw material*" (2017a, 250, italics in original).

Blacklight is an attention to these moves, where knowledge-makers like Marx and his editors and translators make (ethical) choices around what grounds will guide the theories, while other grounds remain obscured. Blacklight makes emanant those premises usually left obscured. Akin to recent efforts to re-read and re-translate Marx through new lenses, made imaginable only now with the release of previously unpublished works (see, for example, Kohei Saito), Ferreira da Silva gives readers new methodological tools to revisit old texts. As she describes: "What I am proposing is an approach to reading, as a materialist practice, one that includes imagining what happens and has happened as well as what has existed, exists, and will exist otherwise—all and at once" (2020, 43). Such analysis centers ethics; it cannot but force a reconsideration of how the very premises of modern knowledge already deploy the forces that make differentiation and exploitation material.

As a methodological intervention Ferreira da Silva's work expands the scope of the racial. The method of hacking, blacklight, and black feminist poethics are intended to "halt the trial of Trayvon Martin's killer before it is added to the already huge library of racial facts and precedents that authorize racial violence" (2014, 81). For Ferreira da Silva, blackness points to a way out of modern knowledge and toward a "sociality from without the modern text." It is an ethical endeavor which, "instead of the betterment of the World as we know it aims at its end" (2014, 82).

References

Arthur, Carson Cole (2020). "Denise Ferreira da Silva: Analytics of Raciality." *Critical Legal Thinking*, July 12. https://criticallegalthinking.com/2020/07/12/denise-ferreira-da-silva-analytics-of-raciality/.

Ferreira da Silva, Denise (2007). *Toward a Global Idea of Race*. Minnesota Press.

Ferreira da Silva, Denise (2014). "Toward a Black Feminist Poethics." *The Black Scholar* 44, no. 2: 81–97.

Ferreira da Silva, Denise (2017a). "Blacklight." In Otobong Nkanga, *Luster and Lucre*. Sternberg Press. https://mitpress.mit.edu/9783956793189/otobong-nkanga/

Ferreira da Silva, Denise (2017b). "1 (life) ÷ 0 (blackness) = ∞ – ∞ or ∞ / ∞: On Matter Beyond the Equation of Value." *e-flux journal* 79: np.

Ferreira da Silva, Denise (2020). "Reading the Dead: A Black Feminist Poethical Reading of Global Capital." In *Otherwise Worlds: Against Settler Colonialism and Anti-Blackness*, edited by Tiffany Lethabo King, Jenell Navarro, and Andrea Smith, 38–51 Duke University Press.

5

Interview with Denise Ferreira da Silva

Julietta Hua and rashné limki

Hua: I imagine you have interlocuters in Philosophy?

Ferreira da Silva: Believe it or not, the Germans want to converse and also the young French folks, but in the US and Canada people often don't really understand the point of what I'm trying to do. For instance, I was invited to join the International Consortium on Critical Theory. There I found myself repeating the case that attention to colonial-racial subjugation is central to any critical theoretical intervention, or it should be. There was one person who is an African American professor who agreed. He's an artist so I am basically the only black theorist making this case. I shouldn't be the only one to be making this case. There is this tradition—a line of historical materialist interventions like Marxism—that absolutely ignores the "Ethnic Studies program." There is also the critical social theory trajectory where we find [Judith] Bulter, [Anne] Stoler and others, who make gestures, but when they are actually articulating things they tend to leave the "Ethnic Studies program" out.

limki: What do you think is happening in this tendency not to engage the racial-colonial as central to critical theory and its formation?

Ferreira da Silva: I think for many in that field it ["ethnic studies program" or the question of racial-colonial subjugation] is not critical because they don't see it as theoretical, but rather see it as descriptive. With this approach you have a theory that can be used for a critique of racial subjugation or colonial subjugation. Racial subjugation is empirical, it's not seen as the point of departure for a critique of everything. It's just one "thing" [phenomenon]—one of the ways things are. Then you need a critical theoretical apparatus to account for that "thing." If that is your formulation then you account for it [racial subjugation] but don't explain it. You name it, but then treat it as something that you include, but it's not integral to the critical tools side.

limki: Given that you described your approach as "fuck humanity and the human," would you consider yourself engaging with Afro-pessimism? Or how do you think about Afro-pessimist work?

Ferreira da Silva: I'm part of it, in a way, or am taken up by the Afro-pessimist writers. There is an investment to cite George Lipsitz [in some early Afro-pessimist work], and an investment in a subjectivity made unavailable or denied to blackness. It's [Afro-pessimism] inspiring to many because there's no critique of the conditions, really. Let me make a distinction. There is criticism of the conditions but there is no critique in the sense of unpacking the conditions because if they did unpack their position seriously they would show that they invest in a position. I think the difference, of how I'm in conversation with them but not doing the same thing, is that I begin with the description. I do describe the thing.

For example, I describe the conditions of possibility for the black subject. I'm making this distinction between blackness as a category, as a category of social-scientific thought, blackness as an historical category (which is more like the US version of blackness and its discourse) and my sense of the term blackness as a referent. There is blackness that is a referent to something that is outside our scene of value; blackness that makes no sense economically and ethically, but can unravel and disorder the whole damn thing, because that blackness, we can call it philosophical blackness, is what blackness refers to. It's not about what blackness is, it's not about why, it's not about an identity, it's not about a category that we need to articulate a particular subject-position. For example, Fred Moten's blackness is really about black people—he calls it black sociality. It is about this joy and disorder he finds in these moments of black sociality that is beyond anything that sociology can capture. It [Moten's black sociality] can offer some other ways of thinking with/from blackness that are not Afro-pessimist. Yet it's productive, that Afro-pessimist blackness, because it makes so much sense and somehow the white boy student feels so comfortable with it! To have students so comfortable, and celebrating that misery ... I don't like it. But there is something to say about Afro-pessimism—there is no journal of Afro-pessimism. It's not one of those enterprises where people have a journal, book, CDs, and create a whole academic universe. So I think that is laudable.

limki: Do you think the distinction between experience and existence might explain (without pathologizing) why Afro-Pessimist thinking has to draw the line that it does? Because it describes a very real experience, but if you go into the critique of what that says about existence, it begins to unravel.

Ferreira da Silva: You can say that is true about [the ethnic studies program]. The subject for whom social justice is demanded is the subject of a certain social trajectory which is all about their social existence. What happens when blackness is brought into that? I prefer to stay with DuBois, and Chandler's reading of DuBois, to consider a way of reversing it. The movement I make is not immediately one that takes you from that subject of experience to an existing thing, because I go through Marxism, I go through Marx's equation of value, and then at the end I come up with existence. So the answer to your question is "yes." But I think there is a lot of work to be done to get to existence as a point of departure for describing humans. I think one of the main or most important things about it is the fact that we can't jump from experience to existence without attending to all that is part of our conditions of existence—all the workings and facts of the cis—heteropatriarchal racial colonial matrix. We can't just jump, which is what most of these new materialists (those contemporary thinkers beyond the subject) tend to do. They go over colonial, racial, everything. We have to move through it and that's lots of work. There is lots of undoing and unpacking. We have to take them [cis-heteropatriarchal racial colonial matrix] as part of the composition. And how do you do that? Those are dense parts. They have the accumulation of the historical and also current, contemporary violations and their effects. All the good things and bad things that derive from them. So how do you live with this? Because existence cannot be presented as something pure, like experience. That's how that "transparent I" thrived [as a pure existence, outside the cis-heteropatriarchal racial colonial conditions]. That was the subject of experience totally outside the world of colonial violence. So that's not the way. But I don't know.

Hua: Can you speak a bit about the trajectory of your work?

Ferreira da Silva: Let me answer chronologically, but it's not linear. On the one hand, the question in *Toward a Global Idea of Race* is not different from the one that I had in my MA thesis which I defended back in 1991 but started working on in 1987. The MA thesis was about black folks in Brazilian TV soap operas. The question there was, "why are there so few black characters in the soap operas, and why were there usually two types of black characters?" (One character was a maid and one was some kind of criminal unless it was about slavery, then you would have more black characters). When I started doing the research I realized that the answer was always going to be the same: because Brazilian TV is racist—they discriminate against black people. I figured I had to ask the question of "why." Not in terms of the relationship between the TV industry and the black actors, but "why" in terms of "what kind of text is the soap opera?

What is the soap opera?" From that question follows, "why are there so few black characters in these texts?"

My answer was that the soap operas represent an image of modern Brazil, and according to Brazil's racial ideologies, a modern Brazil had to be a white Brazil, not a black Brazil. Blackness has no place. So, I read Foucault and texts on the modern subject. The soap opera is a drama of the self, self-development, of progress—with a self-actualization of the modern subject very much like in the novels. I used math. I used some anthropological literature, I used a structural list tool to make the analytical argument. At the same time that I was writing this thesis, I was being trained as a quantitative sociologist. I have one article which is about black women in the Brazilian labor market in which I use census data, and that I wrote in collaboration with an undergrad student who was my research assistant. At the same time, I was being trained as a qualitative researcher, more like an anthropologist doing field work, as part of a huge project about the 100 years of abolition of slavery in Brazil, which was back in 1988.

So I have all this training and when I got to the US my research objective was to do a study comparing black women in the labor market in Brazil and the US using quantitative and qualitative data because I had been trained in both. Very quickly I gave up on it because I fought with my supervisor-to-be. It was a very bad fight—that's when I fought with all the Brazilianists and Latin Americanists and they kicked me out. I was blacklisted when I was a student so I went back to Brazil. I wasn't going to go back to finish the PhD. I had nothing to lose. Then Roland Robertson, who became my supervisor, and then some other professor in anthropology—I wrote them, saying they should bring me back, because blah blah blah. So I went back—I went back to Pittsburgh, and Roland became my supervisor. Roland was a theorist of globalization and I took several classes with him because when I went back [to the US for a PhD program] I said, "I'm going to take the courses I want to take, because I'm not going to do quantitative Sociology." I ended up moving as far away from Sociology as I could, even though I was in a Sociology department. That Sociology department made it very easy to move away from Sociology because [at the time] they were stuck in 1955 and I just couldn't do it. I changed the thesis to a comparison between the national discourse of Brazil, the US, and South Africa. I studied Afrikaans. I could read Afrikaans and South Africa was very much within [my interest area], but since I couldn't travel to South Africa I decided to drop it [from the thesis] and just do Brazil and the US.

By the time I got to race and nation and the mapping of the modern global space [key discussions in *Toward a Global Idea of Race*], I was kind of going back to my MA thesis because I was looking at national discourses. But instead of looking at how those discourses actualize in cultural products—instead of doing cultural studies, which is what I was doing back in 1988, 89—I moved to the philosophy part of the exercise. That's why it's not linear. I went back to a question that I had before and had already dealt with in my MA thesis. That book [*Toward a Global Idea of Race*] didn't make any sense back in 2005 when it finally went to Minnesota [Press]. I finished the book in 2002 but it was held back for three years by Duke Press. [That experience of having the book publication delayed] was indicating to me that I had no place, the book could not be placed.

That was so sad, but it made sense. But then I found the folks in law in the UK—Peter Fitzpatrick, and that whole bunch of critical legal studies people at Birkbeck and beyond, who became my intellectual space. So I did not even try to carve a space in Ethnic Studies in the US because I was found [by the critical legal studies folks]. I was lucky that they found me and that became my intellectual space. By the time Paula [Chakravartty] and I did that [*American Quarterly*] special issue I was doing critical legal studies, though I had been doing that in my writing on police brutality from 2001. But that was also a way of going back to something that was important to me, which was [the issue of] police brutality, but that was more experientially important to me because it continues to be the key aspect of racial subjugation, which is total violence. The ways in which the tools of raciality allow for the deployment of total violence without bringing about an ethical crisis, which is what's happening right now. Right? And it's amazing——it's unbelievable how easy it is for that to happen over and over again whenever needed.

That work was taking the critique that I do in *Toward a Global Idea of Race* and taking it directly to a key issue [police brutality or subprime debt]. In Ethnic Studies in the early 2000s folks were writing about US imperialism or US empire or wars. They were not looking [at that time] at law enforcement. Law enforcement wasn't part of the institutions that were of interest. It is like going back without going back. It's going around. A piece that I wrote for a talk at Brighton, after the killing of Mark Duggan and the revolts that were happening … maybe it was the first one in which blackness became the key concept in the analysis. "To Be Announced"[1] used blackness as the key concept for commenting on police brutality, on racial violence. This is where Black Studies eventually comes into it.

I have these seminars, but also these art things came into the picture and then I was authorized to do my experiments with equations and philosophy and all those things that then I was allowed to do. Not because anyone asked me, but just because, you know, then you become a professor and life changes. That's how academia moves. But these are not changes [in thinking, in writing], it's more about the career, about getting old and staying in the

[1] Denise Ferreira da Silva, "To Be Announced: Radical Praxis or Knowing (at) the Limits of Justice," *Social Text* 31, no. 1 (2013): 43–62. https://socialtextjournal.org/article/to-be-announced-radical-praxis-or-knowing-at-the-limits-of-justice/.

game. But [the writing/argument] hasn't changed so much. Then there is the artwork that I do. And there is this seminar I'm teaching; I taught it at Paris Eight and then for the European Graduate school, and I'm teaching it here—a seminar on Interiority, which is a seminar on philosophy. It's basically a straight philosophy piece that is not that different from other things I have written, but I am authorized to teach it as a philosophy seminar without having to worry whether the students will come or not.

References

Chakravartty, Paula and Denise Ferreira da Silva (2012). "Accumulation, Dispossession and Debt: The Racial Logic of Global Capitalism—An Introduction." *American Quarterly* 64, no. 3: 361–85.

Ferreira da Silva, Denise (2007). *Toward a Global Idea of Race*. Minnesota Press.

Ferreira da Silva, Denise (2013). "To Be Announced: Radical Praxis or Knowing (at) the Limits of Justice." *Social Text* 31, no. 1: 43–62. https://socialtextjournal.org/article/to-be-announced-radical-praxis-or-knowing-at-the-limits-of-justice/.

6

Rehearsing "The Scene of Nature"

Writing and Reading the Text of Anti-Black Police Violence

Carson Cole Arthur

All begins from the *state of nature*—so we are told. Yet, if anything begins from the state of nature it is the very idea of beginnings—the origin story: that a nature of pure and total violence precedes the advent of self-consciousness, reason, and civilization. In this sense, we have begun before, so to speak. Much is made about the historical inaccuracy of the *scene of nature*. and less of its philosophical value. To study Ferreira da Silva's rethinking and renaming of the state of nature as the scene of nature, is to expose its onto-epistemological conditions, and to begin at the anteriority, the extremity, and horizon of this scene, where the racial arises and descends. Indeed, what is the nature of this state? Following Ferreira da Silva, this nature is racial, in the sense that it is described and inscribed as exterior to civility. For this chapter, what is at stake is the significance of how the juridical order judges the killing of black people based on this schema, as will be discussed later.

Blackness is not always in the state of nature but that which is the state of nature. An appreciation of this cedes the term "state" that pre-scribes nature, to make way for a thinking that foregrounds the landscaping of this nature as *nature*. Ferreira da Silva (re-)writes the *state of nature* as the *scene of nature*, for according to her this state is always a scene, staged within the interiority of the modern subject—and yet she is disinterested in preserving the term and concept. Ferreira da Silva targets the interiority that is foundational to the thought and conceptualization of the state of nature wherein as a racial event a black person is represented as already dead. At the risk of making a scene, of overdramatizing the concept, and overemphasizing the scene of nature within Ferreira da Silva's work, in this chapter I will consider whether the writing of the concept of scene of nature is not that far from the physic scenery of the scene of nature. Essentially, I will be arguing that the scene is drafted from that which is foundational to the interiority of the modern subject: speech, writing, and reading. As the state of nature does not take place within a determinable spatial and temporal period, hence, it is rather a scene. Yet neither is this scene fully established and set. We may never know if we are in the scene of nature or not, and the text of legal administration, that represents black people as already dead, leaves this open, for such a representation to be "read" as already written.

Stating Nature

In her chapter for *Searching for Contemporary Legal Thought*, entitled "The Scene of Nature" (2017), Ferreira da Silva seems ambivalent with the exercise of writing (about) the state and scene of nature. Indeed, though it is important of course to give her full citational dues, one needs to be careful not to attribute too much authorship of the scene of nature to Ferreira da Silva, for the concept is troubled precisely with questions surrounding origins, proprietary, and authority. Ferreira da Silva is less interested in engaging with the historicity of the state of nature than in rephrasing the term to underscore the moralization and rationalization of the modern subject. Let us briefly go over the conceptualization of the state of nature in Enlightenment thought, not for a comparative analysis, but to better understand Ferreira da Silva's mis/appropriation of the concept so to speak. It is important to cover the main ground of the concept to draw out the essences of truth and fiction that undergird it, which is relevant to the killing of Amadou Diallo and for the exercise of thinking on the scene of nature. The state of nature does not need to exist in nature per se for it to be thought, and it is this paradox from which the state of nature is stated, spoken, and written.

For Hobbes, the state of nature is when the "life of man" is "solitary, poor, nasty, brutish and short"; "a war as is of every man against every man" (1968, 100–101). Hobbes conceives of nature where man is ruled by their passions and emotions—barriers to rationality and order. The Leviathan, the commonwealth, or the sovereign arises to placate the fear that man has for his neighbor. Though other thinkers may disagree with Hobbes's theory of sovereignty, the state of nature remains a helpful concept to revise any such theory. For example, Locke does not dismiss the notion of the state of nature, though he does argue that the purpose of sovereignty is to protect the property owned by people, not to simply manage their fears of one another (Palmeri 2016, 29). For Agamben, one should think of the state of nature not synonymous with an absolute war, as posited by Hobbes, but "where everyone is bare life and a *homo sacer* for everyone else" (1998, 39). The state of nature is a concept in the sense that it serves for theory. In the late 1600s, the state of nature was a genesis story of sovereignty that sought to be an alternative to theological explanation for world-making (Fitzpatrick 2009, 329; see also Joyce 2013; Thornton 2005). As Palmeri explains, "Hobbes and Locke, thinking outside the previously inescapable biblical paradigm, posited that, at some unspecified point in the past, humans emerged from a primitive condition and formed themselves into a society by means of a contract" (2016, 29). A concern for the understanding of the state of nature is how the commonwealth and contract emerges if this state of absolute war is natural—that is, original, essential, and true. Yet, the state of nature is not diametrically opposed to civil society for the latter proceeds from the state of nature based on its natural laws. Following Frost (2008), Fitzpatrick underscores the point that nature "comes with an abundance of 'natural laws,' 'the first and fundamental of which is: *to seek peace and follow it*'" (as quoted in 2009: 331, emphasis in original). So, the state of nature has natural laws that come to be converted, so to speak, into national constitutions, legislation, and social contracts.

Connected with the theoretical concern over how the state of nature transitions into civil society is the issue regarding the historicity of the concept. To what extent did Hobbes believe in the historical reality of the state of nature? To this question, Macpherson in Hobbes's introduction to *Leviathan* maintains that the state of nature was hypothetical for Hobbes (1968, 40). This is a simple reading or understanding of Hobbes. Whether or not Hobbes took the state of nature to be hypothetical, its function serves as a "conjectural history," which "propose[s] nonprovidential narrative explanations of origins or significant transitions" (Palmeri 2016, 18). As Martens insists, "[r]ather than asking whether Hobbes's state of nature is fact or fiction, one should recognize that it may be both, and that this blurred boundary between fact and fiction strengthens his theory, the state of nature gains a lot of weight after the discovery of the Americas" (2016, 83). Martens (2016, 80) points out that what is commonly forgotten is that Hobbes claimed there were places where the state of nature existed "[f]or the savage people in many places of America" (Hobbes 1968, 187).

Yet, as Ferreira da Silva would argue, this locating of the state of nature onto the savage is not simply historical and geographical but epistemological and ontological. Moreover, the externalization of the state of nature to the savage belies the psychic operation or scenic virtuality that precisely works this mapping. As will become more apparent in the proceeding sections, following Ferreira da Silva, the locating of the state of nature to the savage does not devoid the concept of its hypothetical status, but reifies the hypothetical-ness of black (social) life-death. Simply put, a legal authority's explanation for the death of a black person is premised on hypotheticals. Essentially, the state of nature serves as a fiction for theory (McManus 2005). Moreover, it is, arguably, a theory of fiction, if we attend to the establishment and institutionalization of language.

The Scene of Nature

While Ferreira da Silva reformulates the state of nature as the scene of nature, she does not seek to replace one for the other. For Ferreira da Silva, the scene of nature is "a critique of the modern subject," "that addresses scientific signification as an instance of production of modern subjects" (2017, 276). Though, we could also ask to what extent the scene of nature is the address of the modern subject itself. In this vein, I would suggest that Ferreira da Silva's intervention is to show that the state of nature is a scene; that is, it is not a divine essence but a production of knowledge, grounded on an episteme of "the racial."

The Enlightenment concept of the state of nature seeks to explain society as much as it stands for an idea of the pre-social. It attempts to address the transition from primitive to modern societies, and to legitimize the creation of the nation-state and property. Thus, it is the marker for the delineation of that which is considered primitive and modern. Though, as Ferreira da Silva would insist, the laws of nature are not anachronistic to "modern law." This apparent distinction, between laws of nature and modern law, that European political and legal philosophy would maintain, corresponds with the separation of the political and the social when it comes to the event of the killing of a black person by a legal authority.

In her essay, she shows that a seemingly contemporary issue (the police killing of a black person) is instantiated from the ana-originary laws of nature, which describes blackness as naturally and pathologically dangerous and violent. That is, described and articulated as a natural outcome following the causality of a police encounter, while the killing of a black person may lead to a criminal investigation, it does not conform to the criminological typology and legal standards of a homicide or murder; instead, the killing of a black person is made to remain within the realm of the natural. Thus, there can be no legal or civil punishment for this, as it is an act of nature—a tragedy. Note the argument is not that the modern law, which justifies the death of a black person, can be traced back to the attribution of the state of nature to the American savages, as envisioned by Hobbes then in the late 1600s. Rather, the modern law is an anterior of the law of nature—grounded on the concept of the state of nature; and yet, this state has always been a scene.

The killing or death of a black person by the police is not recognized as a "crime" in Anglo-European jurisdictions. That is to say, it is neither considered an "'act punishable by law,' nor 'injurious to the public welfare,'" citing from Hegel, as quoted by Ferreira da Silva (2017, 275). Instead, the police killing of a black person is viewed as a social event or more specifically a racial event. The social event denotes a separation from the political event or act; a spatial-temporal consequence of social factors. Extending the essay "The Scene of Nature" to Ferreira da Silva's most recent work, such as *Unpayable Debt* (2022), we could say that the social event is really the racial event, for though this eventfulness is premised on social factors and relations, it does not lead to a crisis for civil society. If there is a legal remedy or a criminal investigation, for example, this is launched not in response to a crisis but to stage a tragedy. Perhaps this is why Ferreira da Silva does not name the social event as black social death, nor makes reference to the latter.

Certainly, the law of nature describes a black person as already dead, but I believe she is resisting the conflation that would associate the social event with black social death. This does not suggest that Ferreira da Silva would deny black social death is a social or racial event but rather to underscore that at stake in this discursivity is the value of "social." Indeed, from the logic of the social, the death of a black person belongs to the social, for it is deferred from the political. Of course, the logic of the social is a thought of the political and of the humanities. To speak of the logic of the social is to speak of sociology, as a discipline and a worldview.

For Ferreira da Silva, there is an affinity between the sociology of race relations and the juridical order for they both produce the logic and discourse of race as a cultural difference. Critical race theory, particularly of a critical legal studies variant, typifies this social logic which maintains that structural racism is antithetical to liberalism and democracy. Its "scholarship seems to retain a primary focus upon exclusion" (Ferreira da Silva 2001, 424) which posits that a black person is barred from society. Of course, Ferreira da Silva is not refuting that black people are denied rights and civil protections, but criticizes critical race theory and critical legal theory for upholding the notion of racial difference instead of viewing "the racial," as she does, "as a modern category of being" (Ferreira da Silva 2001, 422). While Indigenous, colonial subjects, undocumented migrants, may be excluded from civil society insofar that they have next to no recourse to the law or political rights, the racial is constitutive of Western knowledge-production and its institutional foundations. Yet, this does not mean that blackness is in-justice, or "central" to the law, and nor is this an issue of present/absent in the law. Rather, following Ferreira da Silva, blackness is at the extremity of the law. It is with the image of blackness as before the law that Ferreira da Silva invites us to think about blackness as antecedent to the law. For it is her intention to reveal the scientific signification that constructs the social event.

"The Scene of Nature" studies the killing of Amadou Diallo as exemplar of the social/racial event which is signified within the state/scene of nature. Ferreira da Silva marks two decisions, the decision to shoot and the decision to acquit. These two decisions, which mark the social event, "enact the *analytics of raciality*" (2017, 276, emphasis in original). The *analytics of raciality* is a "political-symbolic toolbox" (2009, 219) that produces subjects of ethical life and "the racial subaltern subject as the sole agent of violence" (2009, 219). Thus, when Ferreira da Silva states that the decision to shoot and acquit, as markers of the social event, "enact[ed] the *analytics of raciality*," she is speaking on how the representations of blackness produced a judgment that deemed Diallo's death an inevitable and unpreventable outcome following the law of nature. Here, according to the *analytics of raciality*, what is anti-black *is* blackness, for as total violence, blackness is death unto itself. Ferreira da Silva's perspective is opposed to the traditional sociological perspective that would posit the event makes the racial, that the event racializes Diallo, dehumanizes him, as though he was once in a civil society and then banished. Instead Ferreira da Silva posits that Diallo, the black racial subject, is at the inception of natural/modern law, standing before the law.

The Killing of Amadou Diallo and the Play of Death

On February 4, 1999, in the early hours past midnight, a street crime unit of plain clothes officers discharged forty-one rounds, of which nineteen bullets hit unarmed 23-year-old Guinean student Amadou Diallo as he tried to enter the front door to his apartment in the Bronx, New York. The four officers claimed that they attempted to stop Diallo for he matched the description of a serial rapist in the area. From their car, it appeared to the officers that Diallo was acting suspiciously and as they approached him on foot one of the officers believed Diallo was pulling out a handgun. It was in fact a wallet. Diallo's killing occurred during New York mayor's Rudolph Giuliani's zero tolerance policing, which legitimized an increase of stop and frisk, racial profiling, and increased use of force. Public demonstrations followed

Diallo's killing, which exposed the intramurally different perspectives and strategies for campaigning between American Africans and Guinean migrants (Johnson 2016; see also Stoller 2010). Relocated from the Bronx to Albany (upstate New York), the trial of the officers, charged with second-degree manslaughter, ended with their acquittal. The high number of rounds fired reflected the extreme, excessive, and senseless force of the police against Diallo, a black man; a West African migrant.

Diallo's uncle showed the part of the door sprayed with bullet holes to press photographers, and the American Civil Liberties Union (ACLU) bought advertisement space in the *New York Times* to display the graphic of multiple bullet holes, illustrated as perforations through the paper. ACLU in the advertisement claimed not only had the police killed an "unarmed, innocent man," but they had "wounded ... the constitutional right of every American to due process of the law." Ferreira da Silva would refute the social logic of ACLU's advertisement and any suggestion that the constitutional right to due process was harmed. Rather, the constitutional right to defend oneself restored and preserved the life of the officers, and the sovereignty of the US political order. Furthermore, due process signified and resolved Diallo's death as a natural outcome of unforeseen circumstances. The due process owed to the police officers was a legal procedure which enabled the social event to be produced. In this sense, the trial was a "moment of administration of justice—that the *shooting* was the performance of a duty, and the cops' *decisions to shoot* were just" (Ferreira da Silva 2017, 278). The defense argued the officers shot a "counted" number of forty-one times out of fear for their lives. Ferreira da Silva claims this fear "derives from *what-is-known*" (2017, 283, emphasis in original). *What-is-known* is based on the racial map of New York and its urban areas of violence, e.g., areas of poor and working-class black people and people of color. That is, according to the police, *what-is-known* is that the Bronx is a dangerous area and thus they were in an area that did not respect the law, a lawless place, a place with no law except for the laws of nature.

What-is-known has a duality with the not-known. The officers shot Diallo forty-one times because he had acted "suspiciously," though they did not know, according to them, that he was not the rapist they were searching for, and they did not know that he was unarmed, that he was reaching for his wallet, not a gun. The officers reacted out of fear and followed a "chain of death" (2017, 284). Affected by Diallo, this threatening presence and perceived violence, they were placed in a situation where they had no other choice but to discharge their weapons. Such a pathological and social explanation vacates self-determination (sovereignty), Ferreira da Silva claims. Blackness is an alibi for self-determination which disavows being the owner of the decisions of life and death. Following this perspective, she claims, as self-determination has no place in the social event, the principles of universality are not exercised:

> The arsenal of raciality produces an account of the event, the killing of Amadou Diallo, in which death becomes the sole possible outcome because *racial difference*—refigured in Diallo's body and the Bronx—institutes *affectable* (outer-determined) subjects, in a moral stage not protected by legal apparatus because it is not inhabited by the "particular self-consciousness" that, as Hegel states, has already "been raised to the consciousness of its universality," i.e., *man*, the *transparent* "I."
>
> (2017, 279–80, emphasis in original)

For the juridical order to categorize the killing of Amadou Diallo as a social event, his killing was accounted within a moral stage removed from the legal sphere where determinacy presides. According to Ferreira da Silva, a legal apparatus and the moral region do not belong to one another, for if an event is to happen "naturally," no amount or quality of human influence or intervention can prevent or predict its occurrence. For her, the moral stage is not the sovereign's kingdom (where events happened due to sovereignty's decisions and actions) but rather where events happen owing to the natural order of chance and reaction. Ferreira da Silva reserves the essence of self-consciousness to the legal apparatus and does not include it to be present at the moral stage or within the moral text. This raises the question of how an account of the event is produced if self-consciousness does not inhabit and preside within the moral stage that represents this event?

For Ferreira da Silva, the moral text (with its claims of what-is-known and not-known) is inscribed in signification, in justification, "an explanation for that which is a privilege of the living (sovereign) thing, namely, the decision" (2017, 287). However, if viewed as forms of writing, justification and explanation do not simply privilege the decision, but make a decision, in the sense of producing the epistemological determinant that is called "decision." In other words, we could view justification and explanation as a method of decision-making which precisely writes this moral text. Written not only after the fact but prior, for its conditionality sets up for the violence, as well as being set in violence. If it may seem that this writing happens after the event or fact, this is due to the law that death was already written—written by its own hand.

Ferreira da Silva does not focus on writing in terms of voice, speech, and language, and how writing is foundational for truth/fiction. Indeed she views legal interpretation as distinct from legal scrutiny. She contends, "[t]he officers were acquitted because their decisions to shoot withstood juridical scrutiny" (2017, 283). However, we could approach this in another way and argue that juridical interpretation is what led to the acquittal. Here, "withstood" could be read for meaning, not as resisting, but assisting decision (e.g., "with-stood", with and standing for juridical scrutiny).

This signification, this interpretation via scrutiny, is never really a closure, for the juridical order demands it is rehearsed and re-produced. In order to be repeated, the explanation for the killing of a black person needs to be ambiguous with undecidability between the evidency of what-is-known and not-known. Moreover, this ambiguity does not merely allow for more than one interpretation but opens up the very framework of interpretability and the multiplicity of meaning. Thus, undergirding an interpretation is the interpretation of what interpretability is. What I am getting at is that the social event, represented through interpretation, should not be mistaken—dare I say, misinterpreted—as a finite and determinable period in space-time but as circumscribing the general condition of eventfulness. From this perspective, we can appreciate that the scene of nature cannot be authentically and perfectly performed. The state of nature even when understood as a scene has no and never had a proper state. It does not belong to and in nature, yet this does not mean that instead it belongs to and in culture. The scene of nature can never be properly enacted, for there is no absolute true and sure proprietary of sovereignty, selfhood, and the psyche. There is only its rehearsal, the exercise, the practice of enactment, in spite of there being no premiere venue, set script, and stable horizon.

Rehearsal: Reciting and Reproducing the Scene

While Ferreira da Silva does not frame her study in terms of writing, she does speak of reading instead, and its violence. She asks, "would the analysis of *the decisions* bring about its signification: circumscribe the event, obliterating any other possible account of what came to be? My answer to this question is: *perhaps*. ... were I not starting from the acknowledgment that, before *the decisions*, the person killed as cops discharge their guns is already dead" (2017, 277–78, emphasis in original).

Every time a black person is interdicted by authority, "the *scene of nature* is rehearsed," so Ferreira da Silva argues (2017, 288, emphasis in original). Diallo stood at the vestibule of the building on Wheeler Avenue and according to Ferreira da Silva, based on the racial map and the moral text, "before learning whether that person was armed, the officers *knew* they were in *danger*" (2017, 284, emphasis in original). In contradistinction from critical race theory's argument that a black person is outside the law, Ferreira da Silva asserts that a black person is made to stand *before the law.*

There is a longitude to racial subjugation, where the horizon of death positions a black person to stand at the vestibule of modernity. Before the law, blackness is an affectable thing, and thus, it is only affectable when on the threshold, when it is the threshold. Ferreira da Silva does not cite Derrida (1992) nor Kafka, for when a black person is placed before the law, while there is a repetition to this to em-/dis-/ir-/re-placement, the issue is less about an access to the law but rather being at a horizon of death. To be more specific, the access to the law as such is through blackness, and it is in this sense that blackness is the threshold. That is, to get to a justification, sovereignty must cross over and pass through blackness. It is this thinking on and at the extremities of the law that is a crucial perspective and contribution of Ferreira da Silva's paper. Ferreira da Silva states: "Precisely because it stands there, *before* the decision, always available at the moment of closure, of resolution, of signification, the *scene of nature* rehearses the play of death." "How so?" she asks. Her reply is the following: "... any enactment of the *scene of nature* repeats the crucial effects of scientific signification, which is to produce a particular kind of modern subject, namely the affectable 'I'—the thing of outer-determination, the one which thrives before the horizon of death" (2017, 288, emphasis in original).

Ferreira da Silva conceptualizes the scene of nature as a structure of *signification*; a signification which she attributes to the "setting" of closure. But the scene of nature is never completely enclosed. Similarly, the social event is never completely resolved. It certainly provides an explanation, but this explanation is not final; rather it is an opening for its repetition—for the reproduction of the social/racial event.

This opening does not initiate an actualization. That would record the vacancy and occupancy of subject or psyches in the social event. This opening is of a virtuality or a specularity. Ferreira da Silva speaks for us when she says: "We *already know* so much about that place, even without going there, there where force rules, where the law and its agents face but death. Where is that place?" (2017, 287, emphasis in original). Is this not also a question that the police officers asked? And attempted to explain with reference to the what-is-known and not-known? Yet, during their trial, the officers did not have to go to that place in order to rehearse their sociological eulogy. For before the law is not a place that can be properly arrived at. This exteriority has no place, or rather, it is unplaceable. Furthermore, the question "where is that place?" is not exterior to the exteriority of the scene of nature. The very question of this place marks its specularity, its conceptuality; it is not exclusively outside from where the law and its agents face but death. We can only rehearse the scene of nature, not based on some notion that it is exterior to discursivity, but because the scene of nature in-itself is always in rehearsal.

References

Agamben, Giorgio (1998). *Homo Sacer*. Stanford University Press.

Derrida, Jacques (1992). "Before the Law." In Jacques Derrida, *Acts of Literature*, 183–220. Routledge.

Ferreira da Silva, Denise (2001). "Towards a Critique of the Socio-logos of Justice: The Analytics of Raciality and the Production of Universality." *Social Identities* 7, no. 3: 421–54.

Ferreira da Silva, Denise (2009). "No-Bodies. Law, Raciality and Violence." *Griffith Law Review* 18, no. 2: 212–36.

Ferreira da Silva, Denise (2017). "The Scene of Nature." In *Searching for Contemporary Legal Thought*, edited by C. L. Tomlins and J. Desautels-Stein, 275–89. Cambridge University Press.

Ferreira da Silva, Denise (2022). *Unpayable Debt*. Sternberg Press.

Fitzpatrick, Peter (2009). "Legal Theology: Law, Modernity and the Sacred." *Seattle University Law Review* 32: 321–42.

Frost, Samantha (2008). *Lessons from a Materialist Thinker: Hobbesian Reflections on Ethics and Politics*. Stanford University Press.

Hobbes, Thomas (1968). *Leviathan*. Penguin Books.

Johnson, Violet Showers (2016). "When Blackness Stings: African and Afro-Caribbean Immigrants, Race, and Racism in Late Twentieth-Century America." *Journal of American Ethnic History* 36, no. 1: 31–62.

Joyce, Richard (2013). "Sovereignty, Faith and the Fall." *Pólemos* 7, no. 2: 285–305.

Macpherson, C. B. (1968). "Introduction." In Thomas Hobbes, *Leviathan*. Penguin Books.

Martens, Stephanie B. (2016). *The Americas in Early Modern Political Theory: States of Nature and Aboriginality*. Palgrave Macmillan.

McManus, Susan (2005). *Fictive Theories: Toward a Deconstructive and Utopian Political Imagination*. Palgrave Macmillan.

Palmeri, Frank (2016). *State of Nature, Stages of Society: Enlightenment Conjectural History and Modern Social Discourse*. Columbia University Press.

Stoller, Paul (2010). *Money Has No Smell: The Africanization of New York City*. University of Chicago Press.

Thornton, Helen (2005). *State of Nature or Eden?: Thomas Hobbes and His Contemporaries on the Natural Condition of Human Beings*. University of Rochester Press.

7

Reading as Alchemy

What Feminist Anti-War Ethics Can Learn from Denise Ferreira da Silva

Danielle Bouchard

Among the recent reports on Israel's invasion of Gaza that have attempted a kind of humanitarian approach, two common modes of portraying the great violence being committed against Palestinian people stand out. Fairly early on in the invasion, the repeated refrain "women and children" was used to index the victimization of innocents, who were thus constituted as evidence of extreme and mis-targeted violence. More recently, the abject destruction of the landscape/cityscape has frequently been portrayed in images featuring an individual or several backgrounded by largescale destruction, who are dwarfed and isolated in the image frame; posed against massive piles of rubble from destroyed buildings, these figures might appear to be either in motion or still, but in either case they are depicted as located in an indefinable and uninhabitable place, in a kind of nowhere with nowhere to go. And yet, these scenes have a visual architecture that is defined precisely by the incongruity of the incomprehensible landscape and the presence of humanity within it. This is a space defined by the inhuman, i.e., by what are supposedly inhuman levels and forms of violence. And yet we see human figures here, figures who, in being made to index the inhumanity of this space, also themselves have a dubious claim on humanity (i.e., precisely because and not in spite of their targeting for violence). The visuals' coherence with the invocation of "women and children" (even when the particular individuals depicted may not be women and/or children) is evident in the implication that these people belong to categories of subject who have no clear place within the geographical spaces and political structures that are commonly seen as defining humanity.

These visual and statistical figures thus express what is perhaps the defining feature of the modern humanitarian approach to imperial warfare: in its orientation toward producing a certain kind of subject, one who has successfully cultivated an empirically accurate and morally advanced consciousness of the suffering of others (those not "like" oneself), humanitarianism seems to rely on figures of suffering whose violation is implicitly rendered as necessary to the production of the humanitarian subject's own consciousness. As such, these figures of human suffering are defined by two prominent and very much related features: they are not positioned themselves as humanitarian subjects (i.e., as capable of developing a properly humanitarian consciousness), and they are implied—in both subtle and not-so-subtle ways—to have drawn that suffering on themselves, even if "only" through the accident of their birth in a particular place and with a particular body.[1] Indeed, this mode of explaining such violence—as the implicitly logical and necessary outcome of a kind of "natural" response to racial difference (and to blackness in particular)—is precisely what Denise Ferreira da Silva has consistently pointed to as the defining feature of modern *critiques* of racism. Reflecting on how to explain the persistence of the treatment of black individuals killed by the police as responsible for their own deaths, Ferreira da Silva points to the "transubstantiation" of "what is politically constituted (by the colonial juridico-economic structure of slavery) into expressions of an organically determined moral deficit (in the case of police shootings) produced by the sight of black skin color (an expression of moral and intellectual deficit)" (2022, 124). I see something similar at work in humanitarian renderings of those who have been targeted by the latest iterations of imperial warfare.

According to Ferreira da Silva, the foundational problem at hand, for those of us interested in putting an end to racist violence, is that "the very strategies available to explain racial subjection constitute but another moment of the analytics of raciality, that is, they belong to the political-symbolic arsenal that produces the others of Europe as subaltern modern subjects" (2007, 158). It is the analytics of raciality that effects the

[1] Just a few of the many authors whose work informs my thinking along these lines include Talal Asad, Neda Atanasoski, Sven Lindqvist, Mimi Thi Nguyen, Miriam Ticktin, and Eyal Weizman. I am also pulling from the more sustained critical analysis of humanitarianism that I develop in my book *Humanity's Ruins: Ethics, Feminism, and Genocidal Humanitarianism*.

transubstantiation of what is actually a political structure into a putatively biological/natural one, which means that we need new strategies. In her development of a series of related critical tools—refusal, hacking, reading/imaging, and recomposition/decomposition—across multiple writings, Ferreira da Silva breaks with and provides alternatives to these prevailing strategies. More specifically, the critical tools she engages are focused not on parsing the internal psychological or moral qualities of the subject—which is precisely where standard critical tools for analyzing racist violence get mired in the kind of thinking they are trying to challenge—but rather on the qualities of the political structure that produces racial identity as a naturalized object of recognition and thus which explains the existence of horrific violence. This structure, the "liberal political architecture," is founded in western colonialism (2024, 426), making inclusion within it (the answer frequently proposed to the problem of racist violence) not only a fraught prospect but an exterminating one.

In this chapter, I propose to explore what Ferreira da Silva's development of these other critical tools might have to offer a feminist anti-war ethics—an ethics that, in centering a reckoning with colonialism and racism, would not concede to the terms of humanitarianism. I am interested in how she offers a different orientation than that taken up by some recent feminist ethics, which tends to posit the transformed consciousness of the privileged subject as key to the production of a less-militarized way of understanding relational bonds between humans.[2] In keeping with her argument that it is precisely the presumption of the necessity of subject-recognition for the excluded that replicates what she diagnoses as the "logic of obliteration" that is at the heart of the analytics of raciality, I suggest that any feminist anti-war effort must turn away from the recuperation of the subject and turn toward something more like a grammatical or architectural analysis of the very terms of subjectivity. Thinking with Ferreira da Silva also allows us to see figures of inhumanity, like those I discussed above, as revealing the features of the modern political architecture. They are foundational but elided—elided as foundational—to this architecture, and as such, their very presence here exposes the arbitrariness of its terms and, hence, the possibility of some other formation, perhaps one that enacts non-violence as its very mode of relationality. On my view, it is only an inquiry oriented in this way—rather than one focused on elaborating a program for the appropriate cultivation of a humanitarian subjectivity, which cannot help but reinforce

[2] Judith Butler's work is perhaps some of the most well-known and influential in this regard, given how many scholars reference them in building their own analyses. See especially the following works by Butler: *The Force of Nonviolence: An Ethico-Political Bind*; *Frames of War: When Is Life Grievable?*; *Precarious Life: The Powers of Mourning and Violence.* While I do not have the space here to work through their arguments in a sustained way, I do offer such an engagement in *Humanity's Ruins*.

a fixity of identity and a tying of identity to consciousness—that can help us to form an anti-war ethics that is not beholden to humanitarianism.

Humanitarianism and the Logic of Obliteration

> Today's racial subalterns, finding themselves struggling for juridical and economic justice in an ontoepistemological context, globality, in which they stand always already before the ruling ethical principle of transcendentality, face the horizon of death: existing in urban spaces marked by urban revolts, suicide bombings, or drug-related violence or troubled by wars for the scarce resources and land riches of Africa, Asia and the Pacific islands, and the United States that insatiable neoconservative capitalists desire. We need to trace every and each articulation of raciality, including those that profess its irrelevance, trace at each moment how it rewrites the racial subaltern subject in affectability, producing statements that not only excuse the violent effects of this rewriting but also redeploy the transparency thesis.
>
> (Ferreira da Silva 2007, 267)

In *Toward a Global Idea of Race*, Ferreira da Silva employs close and detailed reading to show how the analytics of raciality infuses even critiques of racial oppression. The intricate argument she develops along these lines over the course of the book is carefully organized to include especially poignant passages, like the one just above that appears at the end of the book, to highlight the grounds and stakes of her inquiry. The world that Ferreira da Silva describes is one in which the violence of racial capitalism has become seemingly more deeply entrenched, more intense and various in its manifestations, even as critiques of it have also become more widely taken up. The failures of some forms of anti-oppressive critique given this reality is a situation that many of us have responded to with deep despair; and while despair is certainly not precluded by Ferreira da Silva's writings, it is also not the end point of her inquiry, as her work offers new ways to be and to relate.

Detailing the workings of the analytics of raciality, Ferreira da Silva seeks to establish another way of understanding the exposure of those racialized as other than white to massive death-inducing violence, a way different from those that implicitly or explicitly take the very notion of racial difference for granted. As "a productive symbolic regimen that institutes human difference as an effect of the play of universal reason" (2007, 3) the analytics of raciality establishes a political and ethical structure in which knowledge is sutured to certain traits of being that are taken as given; raciality "is tied to the emergence of an ontological context—globality—that fuses particular bodily traits, social configurations, and global regions, in which human difference is reproduced as irreducible and unsublatable" (2007, xix). With the reference to globality, I take her to be commenting on western colonialism and its attempt to establish an order of humanity defined centrally by racial difference. This is one major throughline that also runs through her more recent writing, and it expresses her abiding concern with both the internal structure of prevailing knowledge claims about humanity, difference, and violence—a kind of grammar, which I will discuss more later—and the reliance of those claims on a political ordering of the geographical space of the world that is profoundly uneven.

The analytics of raciality not only establishes and distinguishes between two unequal kinds of human, it makes that distinction the basis of an ethics. The outcome of this is that prevailing critiques of racialized oppression oriented toward inclusion for racial subalterns proliferate what Ferreira da Silva calls the logic of obliteration. These two kinds of humans, or "minds," are "(a) the *transparent I*, which emerged in post-Enlightenment Europe, the kind of mind that is able to know, emulate, and control powers of universal reason, and (b) the *affectable 'I,'* the one that emerged in other global regions, the kind of mind subjected to both the exterior determination of the 'laws of nature' and the superior force of European minds" (2007, 117; emphasis original). By putting the affectable "I" in quotation marks, she indicates that this self has been conceived as fundamentally different from the proper subject, namely in its incapacity for self-definition and mastery. But more than being different, this affectable (racial subaltern) I is rendered as a hindrance to the transparent (European/white) I's achievement of its full human capacities. Ferreira da Silva is deeply concerned with two intertwined notions of elimination at play here, both of which are a product of racial difference being conceived as a natural phenomenon that has some kind of determinative relation to the conditions of life and death experienced by members of particular racial groups. One is the notion that "the elimination of its 'others' is necessary for the realization of the subject's exclusive ethical attributes, namely, self-determination"; the other is "the postulate that the solution to racial subjection requires the elimination of racial difference" (2007, xiii). This is the logic of obliteration, i.e., the postulate of the elimination of racial difference as natural and necessary to the ethical development of the self-determined subject. The logic of obliteration cannot be halted via the inclusion of previously unrecognized/excluded subjects, which is limited by and indeed potentially violent in its identification of exclusion as the main driver of racialized/racist violence. In fact, "because it is always already the exclusive attribute of a transparent I, the racial subaltern's desire for emancipation, for inclusion in the dominant (white Anglo-Saxon society), is fundamentally a desire for self-obliteration" (2007, 162). In other words, there is no *admitted* place for the racial subaltern within the political order of humanity in which she would retain her racial difference; as affectable, the racial subaltern is inherently and inevitably drawn along a path to annihilation (2007, 157–58). To be clear, Ferreira da Silva does not see this desire as an actual internal psychological state but rather as projected and read onto the racial subaltern subject, as the ultimate price demanded for what is in fact, and quite literally, nothing in return (for to desire self-obliteration is, according to post-Enlightenment though, to foreclose on one's capacity for full, proper subjectivity).

For me, this is the conceptual focal point of *Toward a Global Idea of Race* and the piece around which everything else is constellated, because it brings the stakes of Ferreira da Silva's inquiry into full and clear view. The definitional affectability of the racial subaltern subject is insidious, a pervasive mode of describing the state of things human that led to the "emergence of the twentieth-century sciences of the mind" (2007, 130), and the central element holding the grammar of modern thought together. Humanitarian approaches to the problem of racist violence rarely seem equipped to see this, much less seriously contend with its implications. Indeed, I would go so far as to try out the assertion that the assumption of the racial subaltern subject's affectability is the primary way in which the analytics of raciality and its logic of obliteration show up in humanitarian discourses. Humanitarian arguments commonly deploy the logic of exclusion, or the idea that the main problem at hand is that those who have been targeted for massive western military violence have been so targeted because they have not been recognized as the full human beings that they are. In addition to their reliance on the presumption that recognition as equal is inherently non-violent, such arguments fail to see the socio-political and what Ferreira da Silva would call the onto-epistemological positioning of racialized subjects as fundamentally distinct kinds of humans—humans who are destined not just to individual death, but to ontological disappearance, complete obliteration. And in commonly proposing that the solution to the problem of violence is a change of consciousness on the part of the privileged subject, a change that would lead to the recognition of the previously excluded as actual equals, such arguments subtly presume the desire for self-obliteration.

In other words, the problem that Ferreira da Silva maps out for us is that, in fact, the racialized subaltern is very much included within and necessary to the modern *political architecture*, that is, is included as destined to extermination. Perhaps they are indeed excluded from the *individual minds and hearts of privileged subjects* (those positioned as embodying the transparent I), but inclusion in the realm of the privileged individual's reformed consciousness cannot address the role of the racial subaltern in the material and symbolic production of whiteness, of western empire, of racial capitalism. The insistent return to the idealized internal qualities of the proper modern subject as a means to explain why racial subjection happens and what is to be done about it can only ever preclude the critical examination of the symbolic, material, and political social conditions that produce and sustain this subject in the first place. In the very recent article "Untitled (Notes on Fascism This Time)," Ferreira da Silva points to another discursive arena in which the functioning of racial capitalism and its associated political oppressions are explained largely via recourse to the (supposed) workings of the mind of the transparent I: theoretical inquiries into the recent resurgence of fascism. As she puts it,

> these works foreground interiority when posing the question of the conditions of possibility of fascism while at the same time highlighting how it departs from proper modern mental contents or forms of thought. Fascism ... is treated as an expression of an irrational mental process, whether a leftover from a previous stage of European moral development ... or an expression of a pathological mind ... (2024, 422).

This is similar to common diagnoses of what leads to support for war or xenophobia on the part of the privileged, whereby the transformation to a humanitarian consciousness is presumed to be inaugurated by a certain kind of restored rationality, one that could accurately perceive the shared susceptibility to harm of all human beings. Insofar as the current resurgence of fascism is treated as surprising or anomalous, it is because the legacy of colonialism and its racial analytics is neither recognized as such nor treated as the foundation of the "liberal political architecture," which is not so distinct from fascism after all (2024, 426). What fascism and liberalism share is an attachment to the distinction between the proper subject and his affectable other, a distinction that relies on and propagates massive racist/colonial violence, enacted under the rule of law, in order to enforce (both symbolically and materially) its supposed naturalness. While fascism's operational violence is recognized as such by its critics, it is also the case that "liberal political philosophy, and the political architecture it envisions and supports, has always and comfortably encompassed a juridical force which functions on the basis of the threat and actual deployment of lethal authority. Consistently, its lethality becomes more conspicuous and increases when those under its control ... make mundane demands such as self-determination, civil rights, or equality of opportunity ... " (2024, 426). Not only does the theoretical attachment to the status and internal qualities of the subject leave critics of oppression unequipped to contend with or counter the foundational reliance of the modern political architecture on exterminating violence, it also leaves us enthralled to the logic of obliteration.

In suggesting that we turn our attention toward the social/institutional/political architecture that supports (and claims as necessary) the commission of extreme violence, Ferreira da Silva is seeking to point us to those other critical tools that could help to create a different social reality. Indeed, in her recent work, and perhaps most especially in *Unpayable Debt*, the reliance of juridical force on lethal authority or what she frequently refers to as "total violence" is also the mechanism through which the modern racialized/gendered political order is revealed to be built upon a falsity. In *Unpayable Debt*, which (along with her other recent writings) takes focus and inspiration from Hortense Spillers's examination of the dynamics of chattel slavery in her iconic piece "Mama's Baby, Papa's Maybe: An American Grammar Book," Ferreira da Silva argues that it is precisely the "excessive juridical authority" of the slave owner, exercised as the capacity to commit total violence against enslaved persons, that gives the lie to his claim to properly masterful and willful subject status; that this subject, the transparent I, needs the "mediating" apparatus of the law to ensure his supposed superiority is also an indication that he is not in fact self-determining (2022, 279–80). This is resonant with Spillers's own approach. In naming the symbolic order of "American grammar" as predicated on the material conditions of chattel slavery and specific techniques of torture (designed to transmogrify the body of the enslaved into pure externality, pure value), Spillers essentially uses classic psychoanalysis against itself, rereading "originary" splitting and loss as the experience of the enslaved rather than as key elements of the internal architecture of the "fully" human psyche. I take Ferreira da Silva to be making a similar move in her consistent attention to how total violence gives the lie to the transparent/proper subject's supposed capacities for self-determination. An abiding attention to how the very commission of such violence—the domination of others—under chattel slavery, colonialism, and racial capitalism is both the sign and the enactment of the proper modern subject's reliance upon all which he supposedly is not, is a major feature of Ferreira da Silva's recent work, and is the basis of her development of a series of critical tools that offer both a potent counter to the analytics of raciality, and a new ethical orientation to the problem of massive ongoing racial/colonial violence.

Listening to the Dead, and Other Critical Tools for an Anti-War Ethics

What if ethical descriptions had at their core a commonality that is not mediated by identity (as a shared particularity that is familial, national, historical) or by liberty (general equality) established through the universality of shared (rational, formal, transcendental) ideas? What if ethical descriptors did not presume substantive or formal commonality (identity or equality) figured as atemporal or aspatial and

> yet fundamentally immanent? Directly asked: What if the basis of our ethical program was simply that everything that exists, has existed, or may come to exist is made of the same raw material, the *elementa*, the quantic things (particle-wave emanations) whose re/de/composition allows us to say anything about their existence? If we begin, as I do, by concurring with this question, such a point of departure for thinking troubles the very notion of value.
>
> (Ferreira da Silva 2022, 73)

Many extant attempts to articulate a feminist anti-war ethics assume that recognition as the same kind of human as the privileged subject is both necessary and wanted by those facing the violence under critique. In addition to the problems with this approach I attempted to lay out in the previous section, it also fails to actually turn toward the targeted themselves for an ethical grounding. This turn in order to imagine a new anti-oppressive ethics is what I would describe as the main feature of Ferreira da Silva's project as articulated across multiple writings. A key element of her approach in this regard is her renaming of those who are so frequently deployed as figures of suffering—renaming them so that their centrality to the political architecture built by racial analytics is never forgotten, and the reasons for their targeting for violence cannot be ignored. In this, Ferreira da Silva does something which humanitarianism will not and seemingly cannot. I see her as removing these figures from the grammar of racial analytics—the grammar that renders the racialized bodies and individuals they index as so many affectable subjects—and writing/thinking to and with them in a way that actively subverts the logic of obliteration and its demand to desire a subject status that could only ever mean one's own extermination. These renamed figures—including the Dead, unprotected female flesh/female flesh ungendered, and the wounded captive body in the scene of subjugation—while not conflatable with each other, also emerge as various iterations of a black decolonial feminist ethical practice that refuses subject-recognition.

In (re)naming and thinking with these figures, Ferreira da Silva posits that they (in various ways) have the capacity to do two equally important things: first, to expose the centrality of raciality, chattel slavery, and colonialism not only to the political architecture of the present and its attendant ways of conceiving of subjectivity, but also to the very intellectual/conceptual tools through which the social sciences have sought to understand the unjustness of this architecture; and second, to disrupt and rearrange the terms that define the order of this architecture. The first kind of work, the work of exposure, is not a single event but rather a feature of the liberal political architecture by virtue of these figures' centrality to the same, which becomes apparent via a certain kind of reading. Rather than an objective mode of interpretation that, applied from the outside on an object of analysis, will produce certain results if one simply follows the rules that it lays out, I take Ferreira da Silva's reading to be referring to an experience of and a viewpoint on the compositional details of the analytics of raciality from within. Reading thus reveals the paradoxical and self-dismantling make-up of racial analysis and the political architecture it upholds. In this sense, the work of exposure and the work of disruption or rearrangement are one and the same, or, at the least, are not so distinct. Indeed, Ferreira da Silva expresses this directly in "Reading the Dead: A Black Feminist Poethical Reading of Global Capital," noting that the essay "presents a method that not only does not repeat but also *dissolves the effects of existing critical tools*" (2020, 41; emphasis added).

What she refers to variously as reading, listening to the Dead, and the ethics of the flesh, I take to be the articulation of a commitment that arises from and is oriented toward a notion of immeasurability. I see this as a crucial component of her critical analysis of common sociological accounts of racial difference under racial analytics, as she seeks to expose how racial "social scientific categories" (and, specifically, blackness) "close the circuit of signification," i.e. locate the reason for racial violence in the very being of racialized subjects (2022, 94–95). Along these lines, in "Reading the Dead," Ferreira da Silva elucidates the mechanisms through which Indigenous critiques of colonial/racial capitalism are refused recognition as the political claims that they are, via their "translat[ion] into actualizations of their cultural difference/identity without political and transformative force;" this translation is undergirded by "the onto-epistemological pillars—namely, separability, determinacy, and sequentiality—actualized in social categories and concepts that compose the available critical arsenal" (2020, 40). As what she elsewhere describes as the "general conditions of comprehensibility" in "post-Enlightenment thought" (2022, 59), separability, determinacy, and sequentiality shape reality as hierarchically ordered, value-laden, and evaluable, able to be parsed and defined and mapped (provided one inhabits the correct perspective afforded by transparent subject status). Ferreira da Silva is interested in what the refusal of this reality can afford, and she turns toward both Spillers's notion of the flesh as "ethical ground" and the Dead to effect such a refusal and to imagine an approach to justice based on a radically different understanding of the nature of both social and material reality. Listening to the Dead—those who are no longer living but, despite the best efforts of racist colonialism, have not been annihilated/disappeared—one hears a call that is "incomprehensible" to the subject of post-Enlightenment and, thus, reveals the failure of his aspirations toward self-determination and mastery of knowledge and, indeed, of others (2020, 43–44). But more than the work of revealing, Ferreira da Silva asserts that listening to/reading the Dead is a "compositional method" (2020, 48), one that dismantles the "liberal grammar" that would reduce decolonial justice to the measured and appropriate recompensating of the wronged, by asserting "a call for the return of the total value extracted under total violence, which includes the very American (Indigenous) and African (enslaved) lives that were taken as well as the pasts, presents, and futures that were no longer because of their obliteration" (2020, 49–50, note 9). Here I see Ferreira da Silva as calling for the dissolution of the system of value itself; for to "return the total value extracted under total violence" would cause racial capitalism to cease functioning. The call to do so is itself grounded in a vision of social and material reality that breaches the closed circuit of signification, and in which the relationships between humans, beings, and existents are not arranged in an ontological-epistemological-political architecture in which some are destined for obliteration.

In *Unpayable Debt*, she further develops the idea of immeasurability's importance to an ethical engagement with targets of colonial/racial capitalist violence, again spending significant time on Spillers's notion of the flesh. Noting that Spillers "draws attention to total violence, inviting a thinking that moves with and through the captive body and (wounded) flesh" (2022, 34), Ferreira da Silva invokes a figure that she names the wounded captive body in the scene of subjugation, not as a recuperated subject position but rather as "a poethical tool, that is, a reading device, which has been designed to take apart that which is the condition of possibility for the text, discourse, and liberal (white European cisheteropatriarchal male) position of domination" (2022, 27, note 5). This figure's capacity to disassemble the material, symbolic, and political architectures of racial/gender oppression is predicated on the fact that she "is a female, but she is not a woman. She is nobody's mother and no one's wife or lover. She does not reflect the white European cisheteropatriarchal male position as a political position, because she stands outside and against precisely that form of enunciation as she targets its constitutive moments (ethical, juridical, symbolic, economic)" (2022, 27, note 5). Womanhood's predication on whiteness shored up through the legal mechanism of the right to commit total violence means that the work of dismantling the conditions of violent oppression cannot be done from the assertion of a gendered subjecthood or positionality. Indeed, she asserts in "Hacking the Subject: Black Feminism and Refusal Beyond the Limits of Critique" that by taking up Spillers's figure of female flesh ungendered, "… I am going after the category of gender itself. With Spillers, I am convinced that gender (figured by the wife and the mother) has very little to offer a black radical feminist project …, " and that "mine is a call for disrupting and dissolving the forms of the subject, in their juridical, economic, and ethical renderings …" (2018, 26). I would like to note how profoundly different this way of approaching an anti-oppression, anti-violence ethics is from those so frequently articulated in a humanitarian mode, as the latter seem to have such a difficult time giving up the reformation of the privileged subject and the recuperation of the subaltern subject—which, of course, are always already gendered/racialized subjects—as the platform for the project of getting beyond warfare. Instead, Ferreira da Silva is interested in what she calls hacking, "a radical transformation (or imaging) that exposes, unsettles, and perverts form and formulae. It is an active and purposeful mis-understanding, mis-reading, mis-appropriation .... a recomposition of elements, in the sense the term has in alchemy" (2018, 27). "Hacking" carries the colloquial meaning of breaking into where one is not allowed or meant to be and taking over by rewriting the rules of meaning-making in the system. It is the assertion of a new mode of relationality, in which those who previously set the terms of the relational no longer do. This puts me in mind of Ferreira da Silva's understanding of the decolonial, as well as of why humanitarian engagements with the ethics of non-violent forms of relationality often cannot abide the alchemy of movements led by those who have long been on the receiving end of racial/colonial violence.

The capacities of the wounded captive body in the scene of subjugation (and/or female flesh ungendered) to expose, disrupt, and rearrange—de/recompose—become a crucial site for Ferreira da Silva's own imaginative and transformative work to develop a new "image of existence" that is not built upon the (supposed) necessity/inevitability of total violence (2022, 36–37, 47). As suggested in the passage that opens this section, this work involves a break with the kind of understanding of relationality (between humans, between humans and more-than-human beings, between different forms of matter, etc.) that tends to circulate in Euro-American/whitened (and humanitarian) knowledge formations. Along these lines, Ferreira da Silva asks:

> [w]hat becomes possible if thinking starts with the presumption of deep implicancy and infinity? My bet is that, in addition to being finally released from the imposition to comprehend, this image of existence would allow the Human to be released into the *world* to dissolve in/into/as everything with which it is already deeply implicated—everything in its deep implicancy with/in the expanse of spacetime and perhaps beyond. (2022, 264; emphasis original)

This is a dissolution of the subject and of the comprehensibility of the kinds of claims about the shared human condition, and the need for mutual recognition on the basis of such, that can only ever result in a replication of the transparent I/affectable "I" distinction. The *Oxford English Dictionary*'s entry for "implicancy" denotes it as both obsolete and rare, but offers the definition of "[e]ntanglement, confusion; contradiction of terms." With this word, which goes beyond what "implicated" offers, I see Ferreira da Silva as calling forth a version of reality that is not organized around the elaborate lie of the human capacity for self-determination.

Elsewhere, Ferreira da Silva turns again toward affectability in the interest of what might be called an alchemical approach to relationality. While it was written before *Unpayable Debt*, I am interested in "To Be Announced: Radical Praxis or Knowing (at) the Limits of Justice" because of the explicit invocation of affectability, in a somewhat different register than it is in *Toward a Global Idea of Race*. Interestingly, in this article, affectability appears as a synonym for or perhaps the content of relationality, and as such, references much more than the (supposedly) defining quality of those humans who are (supposedly) destined for annihilation. Noting that "forcing out that which sustains prevailing plans for knowing and doing, I contemplate another horizon, one that has been consistently articulated and disavowed in modern thought, considerations of relationality (affectability)," and aligning relationality/affectability with a form of knowing that "demands affection, intention, and attention" (2013, 44) Ferreira da Silva turns affectability toward an ethical purpose in a way that contorts its role within the analytics of raciality, arguably leading toward the dismantling of the latter. This is very far from a humanitarian appeal to privileged subjects to recognize the shared condition of vulnerability of all humans. Rather, it suggests that it is from those rendered affectable precisely through their targeting for obliterating violence that the necessary conditions for a symbolic and political architecture of immeasurable implicancy are composed.

References

Asad, Talal (2000). "What Do Human Rights Do? An Anthropological Enquiry." *Theory & Event* 4, no. 4. https://www.muse.jhu.edu/article/32601.

Asad, Talal (2007). *On Suicide Bombing*. Columbia University Press.

Atanasoski, Neda (2013). *Humanitarian Violence: The U.S. Deployment of Diversity*. University of Minnesota Press.

Bouchard, Danielle (2025). *Humanity's Ruins: Ethics, Feminism, and Genocidal Humanitarianism*. Duke University Press.

Butler, Judith (2004). *Precarious Life: The Powers of Mourning and Violence*. Verso.

Butler, Judith (2010). *Frames of War: When Is Life Grievable?* Verso.

Butler, Judith (2021). *The Force of Nonviolence: An Ethico-Political Bind*. Verso.

Ferreira da Silva, Denise (2007). *Toward a Global Idea of Race*. University of Minnesota Press.

Ferreira da Silva, Denise (2013). "To Be Announced: Radical Praxis or Knowing (at) the Limits of Justice." *Social Text* 31, no. 1 (Spring): 43–62.

Ferreira da Silva, Denise (2018). "Hacking the Subject: Black Feminism and Refusal Beyond the Limits of Critique." *philoSOPHIA* 8, no. 1 (Winter): 19–41.

Ferreira da Silva, Denise (2020). "Reading the Dead: A Black Feminist Poethical Reading of Global Capital." In *Otherwise Worlds: Against Settler Colonialism and Anti-Blackness*, edited by Tiffany Lethabo King, Jenell Navarro, and Andrea Smith, 38–51. Duke University Press.

Ferreira da Silva, Denise (2022). *Unpayable Debt*. Sternberg Press.

Ferreira da Silva, Denise (2024). "Untitled (Notes on Fascism This Time)." *South Atlantic Quarterly* 123, no. 2 (April): 418–28.

"Implicancy, N." *Oxford English Dictionary*. Oxford University Press, July 2023. https://doi.org/10.1093/OED/9331713472.

Linqvist, Sven ([2007] 2012). *Terra Nullius: A Journey Through No One's Land*. Translated by Sarah Death. Granta.

Nguyen, Mimi Thi (2012). *The Gift of Freedom: War, Debt, and Other Refugee Passages*. Duke University Press.

Spillers, Hortense (1987). "Mama's Baby, Papa's Maybe: An American Grammar Book." *Diacritics* 17, no. 2 (Summer): 65–81.

Ticktin, Miriam (2011). *Casualties of Care: Immigration and the Politics of Humanitarianism in France*. University of California Press.

Weizman, Eyal (2011). *The Least of All Possible Evils: Humanitarian Violence from Arendt to Gaza*. Verso.

8

Algorithmic Landscapes and the Raciality of Technology

Julietta Hua

A growing body of literature in technology studies examines the "automating of racism" that imposes "an epistemology based on data as the problem solver, while oppression, exploitation and dispossession are masked as innovation" (Varon and Peña, 2021, 13). Scholars like Ruha Benjamin (2019), Virginia Eubanks (2018), Brian Jefferson (2020) illustrate how digitally networked, algorithmic technologies reproduce historical and existing inequalities and systems of the status quo. Cathy O'Neil (2016) suggests that math and algorithms make it appear as if machine determinism is neutral, even while the determinations being made are highly gender and race-biased given that both the data set (history) and designers (agents) center already-privileged perspectives and positionalities. I think of this literature as providing crucial epistemological critiques of race, gender and technology, where knowledge of difference embeds technology and technological development.

While the work of identifying racial and gendered outcomes is crucial—for example, studies like Joy Buolamwini's (2017)—we need to bolster analyses that don't simply dead-end into arguments for more representational, less racist and sexist technologies and outcomes.[1] As Buolamwini emphasizes, *more accurate facial recognition technologies or their fairer uses are not the point.* Put another way, inclusion is not the desirable political outcome since better facial recognition simply expands surveillance of marginalized communities. Instead we need to undo the architectures of categorization

---

[1] See also Joy Buolamwini, Poet of Code: https://www.poetofcode.com/

schemas hidden by the (algorithmic) processes and outputs; these are data and digitization structures. An example of data/digitization structures include formats that define what even counts as data and how (Koopman 2022). As Natasha Dow Schüll points out, digitization begins by containing entities "into a binary language of ones and zeros, or 'bits' (a contraction of 'binary' and 'digits')" (2018, 42). Another way to look at algorithmic bias is to think about the terms used to sort and make information data in the first place, "Formats define, in a matter simultaneously conceptual and technical, how information is itself constituted. In specifying what data must be, formats delimit and determine the specific shapes that are allowable for any data point" (Koopman 2022, 347). Antoinette Rouvroy explains that data is worked: "Data in their proliferation are not simply given. Data are processed, ranked and so on" (Rouvroy and Stiegler 2016, 8). Kalindi Vora (forthcoming) points to how data cleaning is a kind of care work that happens even before data becomes data. These scholars highlight an arrangement of power that precedes the inputs, outputs, and user-interfaces.

Following the work of these scholars, I want to move away from simply defaulting into positions that advocate for "good," "better," "responsible" or less racist, sexist uses of algorithms and their derivatives. Instead we should be looking at the *raciality of technology*, or the architecture that embeds difference as about categorization and optimization. In other words, rather than focus on how race influences algorithmic technologies or focus on the disparate impact of digital technologies on different racial, cultural communities, I'm interested in tracing how digital technologies by design, by premise, and in situ are predicated on the elevation of users (subjects) as rational and choice-making—necessary to having a winning and losing outcome, where rational choice always equals a win. The elevation of rational choice as the principal quality of how algorithmically facilitated relations function also differentiates users. These technologies—in conception, design and function—forward modern architectures and arrangements of knowledge that unevenly value and produce population through the digitalization of life.

Ferreira da Silva's (2016) three pillars of modern thought: separability, determinacy, and sequentiality—or the *analytics of raciality*—help make a case for scholarship about technology, race, and gender to always reach beyond 1) the disparate racial, gendered impacts of technology or 2) the problematic data sets argument (history). Understanding Ferreira da Silva's intervention into how we know the world and its subjects allows us to see why it has been so easy for so-called new technologies to reassert "old" colonial modes of relating. The chapter ends with a consideration of what Ferreira da Silva describes as "virtual nonlocality" to suggest different ways of considering race/gender/difference and the digital landscape of algorithmic governance but still attend to the fact that the same poor, black, brown, indigenous communities are being unevenly, detrimentally impacted.

The Analytics of Raciality and Technology

In *The Costs of Connection: How Data is Colonizing Human Life and Appropriating it for Capitalism*, Couldry and Mejias (2019) argue that we live in a context of data colonialism. Where conventional colonialism operates through land, data colonialism operates through air (Cloud Empire). Data colonialism disparately impacts the already poor and disadvantaged who are unable to mobilize the resources necessary to blunt the impact of the Cloud Empire in dictating the terms of life. Following from their work, others like Joana Varon and Paz Peña (2021) provide examples of how US and Chinese tech companies use Latin America as both testing grounds and sites of extraction. For example, a Microsoft-facilitated machine learning experiment in Salta, Argentina leveraged the local government to predict teenage pregnancy and school dropouts. Unsurprisingly "the system was heavily criticized due to statistical errors, sensitivities of reporting unwanted pregnancies, using data inadequate to make reliable predictions, but even further, for being used as a tool for discrimination of the poor" (Varon and Peña 2021, 16). The ease with which familiar, "historical colonialism" operates in the contemporary context of digital, algorithmic landscapes is unsurprising because the key aspects of the European colonial project depended on "imposing a single universalizing narrative of values, beliefs, and politics" that ushered in the World as Singular (Couldry and Mejias 2019, 69). This Singular World, or what Ferreira da Silva describes as the Ordered World, "considers the social as a whole constituted of formally separate parts. Each of these parts constitutes a social form, as well as geographically-historically separate units, and, as such, stands differentially before the ethical notion of humanity, which is identified with the particularities of white European collectivities" (Ferreira da Silva 2016, 63). For Ferreira da Silva, the *analytics of raciality* is language she creates to describe the onto-epistemological terms of this modern, Ordered World.

In other words, the European project marked for many by 1492 is one that also conformed and consolidated the critical (intellectual, conceptual) terms through which we come to know the world—an onto-epistemological project about how we understand Subjects (subjectivation) and thus how we can become Subjects (how we live and experience the world). For Ferreira da Silva, race, racialization, even racial are all terms that are products of the onto-epistemological architectures consolidated through European colonial projects. As such, these terms are limited in what they can do; they can describe the world and they can even justify why the world works the way it does, but they cannot necessarily tell us how the world we know came to be only through these terms—that is, they cannot explain how the Ordered World is ordered. In other words, "race" can describe the differential relation between the Subject and his "others," but race cannot explain how Reason becomes the determining condition for subjectivity. Instead, race already presumes difference or separability; race is what has been used to distinguish subjects with Reason from those without.

This is why Ferreira da Silva insists on the need for alternative critical and analytic tools and language (hence *analytics of raciality*). Ferreira da Silva notes that the intent "is to address the apparatus the racial guides," which is the "productive symbolic regimen that institutes human difference as an effect of the play of universal reason" (2007, 3). As Carson Cole Arthur points out, it is important to see how "*analytics* is inextricable to *raciality.* Failure to consider the *analytics* that is *of raciality* would lead to mistaking the term as merely a discursive concept (e.g., another way of saying 'racialised' or 'racial thinking') instead of recognising it as a politico-juridical programme, a production and mode of (transcendental) consciousness" (2020, np, emphasis in original). This is what Ferreira da Silva's project to distill the analytics of raciality attends to: How is it that the (modern, rational) Subject becomes the privileged actor of the world? And in consolidating his privileged position as Subject, what kind of world does he institute?[2]

Becoming the privileged actor of the world means not only material and physical domination (taking of lands and labor), but that this domination happens always already through monopolizing how we think and come to know the world as such. Reason, for example, has become the privileged domain of modern humans. Reasoning is about formalization, notably illustrated through Descartes' "I think therefore I am": "Descartes successfully demonstrated that [the human mind alone can decipher the book of nature] when he established its existence and essence as the *formal* (thinking) thing, or *res cogito*" (Ferreira da Silva 2017: np). The elevation of the thinking, formal mind as the privileged site through which the world is not only known but made, is a metaphysical project consolidated more than 300 years ago and one that facilitates and is facilitated through colonialism. The *analytics of raciality* thus describe how our contemporary understanding of difference is anchored in the political, economic, and onto-epistemological projects of European colonial domination; what Arthur terms the politico-juridical programme signaled by the term "analytics of raciality." One can think of it this way: How is the world made into the ways we know it? What are the processes that limit our knowing the world only as the Ordered World?

That these old colonial formations find new life through the algorithmic technologies is not surprising given we have yet to attend to the architectures

[2] I think Ferreira da Silva's project is one that resonates with Bernard Stiegler's organology. For Steigler, organology is a project that profoundly rethinks the relations between desire and technology and therefore rethinks fundamentally what knowledge is in order to move us into a more radical place (Crogan 2010, 163).

of knowledge that define being an actor of the world against being something that is acted upon (affectable). This fundamental cleavage that dichotomizes Subjects from his Others, Ferreira da Silva would argue, has not-yet been undone. We are still invested in the modern knowledge program, which Ferreira da Silva describes through three movements—separability, determinacy, and sequentiality. To return to Descartes, his philosophical contributions naturalize "a separation of mind and body in which the human mind, due to its formal nature, also acquires the power to determine the truth about the human body as well as anything that shares its formal attributes like solidity, extension, and weight" (Ferreira da Silva 2016, 59). Through this modern program we have Man—the Subject who can know the world as phenomenon—and opposed to him we have the world "in nature," a priori. This makes the Subject a protagonist, acting on the world and thus moving the world. Because of Reason, the Subject is capable of apprehending cause and effect. This distinguishes him from the things of the world, what Ferreira da Silva terms "affectable" beings, or what we often describe as objects. The separation of the world into two categories (Subject and not-subject) establishes the modern subject as knowing and acting on the world. This fundamental relation—what many critics of colonialism including Cynthia Enloe (1990) describe in detail as "us" versus "them"—sits at the center of all algorithmic design, making the algorithmic world also always a colonial/racial one.

Algorithmic processing, a defining feature of the digital world, is structured for and facilitates the rational user-subject. We can see this both in the fact that algorithms operate on instructions that rationalize processing, and in the assumptions embedded in the subject-positions predicated by the algorithm. For example, algorithms work from the basic premise that there is a right and wrong. The "right" outcome is one that compels more engagement, it is the outcome where the algorithm's product is most touched by the user (this can be in the form of likes and clicks but also frequency of appearance in the data). In her study, Noble (2018) points out that the Google search algorithm is designed to rank results based on what is more and most likely to already exist online. Schüll's (2012) work on gaming and addiction illustrates how addiction is part of algorithmic design, making addiction a winning outcome of most social network algorithms. Winning and losing are predicated on rational decision-making, or subjects inhered with self-determination. Reason is the valued principle, which creates good and bad (algorithmic) outcomes.

If separability and determinacy divide the world into formal, thinking subjects and his affectable others, Ferreira da Silva also highlights how separability and determinacy, in elevating the formal mind away from the laws or forces of the universe, open up the ability to further know the world through sequentiality. The Subject, as protagonist, acts and moves the world through linear temporality (the before and after of his action).

In elevating the formal mind as rational Self, the rational Self becomes also a developmental Self who can see himself moving through time (as past, present, and future). This is the crux of history (or historical time), and as Andreia Machado Oliveira points out: "Our own historical timeline is separated by technological divisions: Stone Age, Fire Age, Metal Age ... The First, Second, Third Industrial Revolutions" (2023, 10). Our narrative of technology is developmental. While many philosophers of technology write to dislodge this formation, the "natural" inclination is to consume technology temporally and assume progress as a universal condition of the world. As Lewis Mumford (1934, 1967) describes, progress makes motion unending; progress makes movement independent and a good-in-itself-for-itself.[3] Algorithms by design are always predictive (e.g. moving properly through developmental time). If an algorithm determines that a poor, non-white community is more prone to teenage pregnancy and crime, their prior condition as poor, or of color predict the likelihood of making "bad" future choices. The algorithm maps this by transforming lives into aggregate population data. That data is transformed into a (determined) future. Algorithms are thus fundamentally about the coloniality of relations; they demonstrate the raciality of technology, as past and present are transformed into a determined future that justifies the existing conditions of domination. Is there then any algorithmic landscape that is not always already about the raciality of technology?

"Virtual Nonlocality"

In this section, I look to Ferreira da Silva's (2016) "virtual nonlocality" to think differently about how race, gender, and technology can come together. How can we talk about, analyze and consider technology in ways that are not overdetermined by temporality? How can we wrest algorithmic narratives away from "new inventions reviving old relations"? How can we conceive of the internet as other than compression of time and space (in the internet world, the long-ago is the now, the far-away is nearby)?

[3] Mumford's exploration of mechanization as the separation of organic life from mechanic regime is one that begins with the monastic clock, which regulates and standardizes production. The clock produces "seconds and minutes" that by nature is about dissociating time from human events and "creating the belief in an independent world of mathematically measurable sequences, the special world of science" (1934, 15). The clock enables time to be independent and mathematical, it mechanizes and disciplines time, which in turn disciplines humans to time, which facilitates capitalism. All this leads to a "quantitative conception of life, stimulated by the will-to-power" (1934, 210).

Writing to undo the taking-for-granted of temporality, Ferreira da Silva looks to the insights offered by the quantum world. If we take seriously insights from quantum physics, the world is both local/actual and virtual; as Ferreira da Silva explains, "nonlocality exposes a more complex reality in which everything has both actual (spacetime) and a virtual (nonlocal) existence" (2016, 64).

To unthink that world as-we-know it (Ordered World) where we may live in cultural difference, but all share humanity, Ferreira da Silva suggests taking seriously the quantum view of the world. This branch of scientific knowledge has existed alongside the Kantian program of the modern subject. It is also "western" and scientific yet offers drastically different possibilities for interpellating the world. Ferreira da Silva (2016) argues that taking the quantum world seriously can lead us away from the Ordered World and toward something like the World as Plenum. In the Ordered World there is one singular view and understanding of humanity hampered by things like "culture," "race," "gender" that force difference and separation. In the World as Plenum, the possibility for difference exists fundamentally in every singular expression of being. Drawing from the concept of entanglement, Ferreira da Silva explains: "In the nonlocal universe, neither dislocation (movement in space) nor relation (connection between spatially separate things) describes what happens because entangled particles (that is, every existing particle) exist with each other, without space-time" (2016, 64).

In the World as Plenum, difference is the condition of possibility for singularity, or any single expression (Ferreira da Silva 2016). To explain: from the smallest, quantum perspective the world is made up of particles and waves, which take on infinite compositions that result in the different expressions of matter we experience. Put simply, because everything in the world is made up of the same material on the smallest level, the fundamental components that make up a chair are ultimately the same as those that make up a human. Thus at this scale the potential for a chair to be human or vice versa exists all the time (nonlocality). As Ferreira da Silva notes, "experiments in particle physics have astonished scientists and laypeople with findings that suggest that the fundamental components of everything, every thing, could be just such, namely the virtual's (subatomic particles) becoming actual (in space-time), which is also a recomposition of everything else" (2016, 58–59). Taking seriously a quantum perspective of the world jettisons separability, determinancy, and sequentiality. While separability "considers the social as a whole constituted of formally separate parts … what if … we imagined each existent (human and more-than-human) not as separate forms relating through the mediation of forces, but rather as singular expressions of each and every other existent as well as of the entangled world in/as which they exist?" (Ferreira da Silva 2016, 63). Part of this creative alternative to writing and knowing the world takes seriously "virtual nonlocality," which concedes that there are things we cannot know. Virtual nonlocality suggests that these unknowable things are only momentarily known when we observe them (they become "local" when we measure and take account of the thing). Thus something can be neither here nor there, but exist nonetheless.

To me, the term "virtual nonlocality" evokes the internet, a virtual place that enables relation and engagement through nonlocality. Yet the insights of quantum physics insist that everything is both virtual or nonlocal *and* actual (local or situated in space-time) simultaneously. Light, for example, exists as both wave and point depending on whether it is being observed. How does this way of reading the world shift our understandings of the digitized, algorithmic scene? We already see the ways algorithms facilitate nonlocality, for instance, in making an internet that collapses our sense of space and time. We also see the ways algorithms have very local, situated outcomes, for example, in the early Google search returns of pornographic and sexual images under the category "Black girls" (Noble 2018, chapter 1). In another example, the collapse of task with worker through algorithmic management (gig work) facilitates the compression of time and space (on-demand services and goods) even while these outcomes are enabled through further fixing the economic disparities that already exist—exploiting local, undervalued populations. This is a point that drives the Fairwork Project in Brazil and Latin America as well as the concern of many other labor scholars (Nociolini Rebechi et al. 2024).

For Ferreira da Silva, nonlocality—which always brings with it locality—is one way to reimagine sociality. Nonlocality suggests that things are always inhered with the potential to be something else, even while the local or actual expressions (in space-time) may differ. This is the basic idea of being entangled, where "difference is not a manifestation of an unresolvable *estrangement*, but the expression of an elementary *entanglement*" (2016, 65, emphasis in original). If we consider the virtual nonlocality of the digital algorithmic scene, it recalls the entanglement, rather than estrangement, of the corporately owned and managed server farms and underwater cables that facilitate the internet's nonlocality (as recent works like Rachel Adams's *New Empire of AI* and Karen Hao's *Empire of AI* point out). We might consider the extractive and exploitative practices that pollute and diminish local environmental and labor conditions. We might always think of the compressions of time and space in the algorithmically driven internet as also producing disparate and uneven experiences with algorithmic governance, which constantly shift to place risk in different communities at different moments. If so, any radical sense of "the just" in the algorithmic scene could not simply be about more equitable or inclusive experiences that protect individual communities from abuses of privacy, consent, and transparency.

Conclusion

To be honest, I have never had much faith in algorithms, digital technologies, or the internet, given they tend to be spaces populated by, and processes amplifying, incels and white supremacists. I've been concerned with the addictive qualities embedded in platforms that make us want to keep engaging online trolls by trolling, while a few corporate owner-managers accumulate unimaginable wealth by accelerating climate warming. The fact that rational choice is baked into how the whole operation is set up also gives me pause. If the architecture of the internet, driven by algorithmic processes based in game theory, are already so modern, it seems impossible to expect such a scene to do other than reproduce coloniality. Yet, if Ferreira da Silva's work has taught me anything, it is that even in the most seemingly closed and confined apparatus, there is always the possibility for an otherwise. This is the point of "Difference Without Separability" (2016).

Here Ferreira da Silva goes to science—quantum physics—to illustrate how even "western scientific thinking" holds possibilities for an otherwise. As the ever-eloquent biologist Robin Wall Kimmerer (Potawatomi) puts it, despite the scientific worldview that too-often ignores Indigenous wisdoms, the practice of science can still offer useful tools to be otherwise: "Science, art, and story give us a new lens to understand the relationship that people made of corn represent … [which is] the great poem of give and take, of reciprocity that animates the world. Isn't that a story worth telling?" (2015, 344). For Kimmerer, like Ferreira da Silva, the confinement of western science and its taxonomic investment can be un-done with science. The potential for an otherwise always already exists. Stories of science can help us think about the world in other-than-modern, other-than-colonial ways, but this is work that requires critically un-doing the kinds of worldviews that prioritize separability, determinacy and sequentiality.

That the possibility to be otherwise already exists is a liberating idea. Rather than wait for an undetermined future moment, what Ferreira da Silva's articulation of sociality as entanglement gives me is a way to read and write the present in more contingent and uncertain ways. Even the certainty of modern thought, given to us through a genealogy of the Enlightenment, is not as certain as we like to think. As David Graeber and David Wengrow (2021) point out, concepts like democracy and equality are not European at all. Rather, European Enlightenment thinkers learned about principles like "equality before the law" from Indigenous American philosophers like Kandiaronk (Huron-Wendat), rather than vice versa. As they state: "Many influential Enlightenment thinkers did in fact claim that some of their ideas on the subject [of equality] were directly taken from Native American sources—even though, predictably, intellectual historians today insist this cannot really be the case" (2021, 30). Like Ferreira da Silva, Graeber and

Wengrow point to the contemporary investment in certain ways of thinking, which is an investment in "powerful modern myths. Such myths don't merely inform what people say, to an even greater extent, they ensure certain things go unnoticed" (2021, 350). Ferreira da Silva makes us notice.

The expansive span of human life, beyond the 500 to 2000 years even most academics study, offers opportunities for an otherwise. Like the quantum science that premises the world as The Entangled World, the deep span of human existence also opens up possibilities for the world to be otherwise, where archeological findings suggest that complex, technologically-minded urban centers with robust trade-routes characterized sociality in Latin America almost 2000 years ago. Such evidence upends the colonial narratives of roaming bands of primitive Others discovered by Spanish and other European explorers in the 1400s (Graeber and Wengrow 2021). Such is the gift of reading otherwise offered by Ferreira da Silva.

References

Arthur, Carson Cole (2020). "Denise Ferreira da Silva: Analytics of Raciality." *Critical Legal Thinking*, July 12. https://criticallegalthinking.com/2020/07/12/denise-ferreira-da-silva-analytics-of-raciality/

Benjamin, Ruha (2019). *Race After Technology*. Polity Press.

Buolamwini, Joy (2017). "Gender Shades: Intersectional Phenotypic and Demographic Evaluation of Face Datasets and Gender Classifiers." MIT Master's thesis.

Couldry, Nick and Ulises A. Mejias (2019). *The Costs of Connection: How Data Is Colonizing Human Life and Appropriating It for Capitalism*. Stanford University Press.

Crogan, Patrick (2010). "Knowledge, Care, and Trans-Individuation: An Interview with Bernard Stiegler." *Cultural Politics* 6, no. 2: 157–70.

Enloe, Cynthia (1990). *Bananas, Beaches and Bases*. University of California Press.

Eubanks, Virginia (2018). *Automating Inequality*. St. Martin's Press.

Ferreira da Silva, Denise (2007). *Toward a Global Idea of Race*. Minnesota Press.

Ferreira da Silva, Denise (2016). "On Difference Without Separability." In *32nd Bienal de São Paulo – Incerteza Viva. Catalogue*, edited by Jochen Volz and Júlia Rebouças, 57–65. São Paulo: Fundação Bienal de São Paulo.

Ferreira da Silva, Denise (2017). "1 (life) ÷ 0 (blackness) = ∞ – ∞ or ∞ / ∞: On Matter Beyond the Equation of Value." *e-flux Journal* 79 (February). https://www.e-flux.com/journal/79/94686/1-life-0-blackness-or-on-matter-beyond-the-equation-of-value/

Graeber, David and David Wengrow (2021). *The Dawn of Everything: A New History of Humanity*. Farrar, Straus and Giroux.

Jefferson, Brian (2020). *Digitize and Punish*. University of Minnesota Press.

Kimmerer, Robin Wall (2015). *Braiding Sweetgrass: Indigenous Wisdom, Scientific Knowledge and the Teachings of Plants*. Minneapolis: Milkweed Press.

Koopman, Colin (2022). "The Political Theory of Data: Institutions, Algorithms and Formats in Racial Redlining." *Political Theory* 50, no. 2: 337–61.
Mumford, Lewis (1934/1967). *Technics and Civilization*. Routledge.
Noble, Safiya (2018). *Algorithms of Oppression: How Search Engines Reinforce Racism*. New York University Press.
Nociolini Rebechi, Claudia et al. (2024). "Evaluating Work in the Platform Economy: The Fairwork Project in Brazil and Latin America." In *Popular Sovereignty in a Digital Age*, edited by Aaron Schneider, 65–81. Albany: SUNY University Press.
O'Neil, Cathy (2016). *Weapons of Math Destruction*. Crown/Random House.
Oliveira, Andreia Machado (2023). "Thinking About Technologies from Gilbert Simondon and Yuk Hui." *Educação & Realidade* 48: 1–22.
Rouvroy, Antoinette and Bernard Stiegler (2016). "The Digital Regime of Truth: From the Algorithmic Governmentality to a New Rule of Law." Translated by Anais Nony and Benoit Dillet. *La Deleuziana: Online Journal of Philosophy* 3: 6–27.
Schüll, Natasha Dow (2012). *Addiction by Design: Machine Gambling in Las Vegas*. Princeton University Press.
Schüll, Natasha Dow (2018). "Digital Containment and Its Discontents." *History and Anthropology* 29, no. 1: 42–48.
Varon, Joana and Paz Peña (2021). "Artificial Intelligence and Consent: A Feminist Anti-colonial Critique." *Internet Policy Review* 10, no. 4: 1–25.
Vora, Kalindi (2025). "Data Work as Care Work: Anti-Colonial Data Studies, AI and the Given World." Talk presented at Stanford University, May 12, 2025. https://events.stanford.edu/event/data-work-as-care-work-with-kalindi-vora.

PART TWO

Philosophies

9

Introduction

Julietta Hua and rashné limki

Our tools of cognition—the terms, assumptions, logics, concepts—are effects of the naturalization of eighteenth- and nineteenth-century European philosophy and the analytical foci instituted therein. These thinkers, as Peter Park (2013) explains, were deeply invested in establishing western European thought as the boundary of the discipline of philosophy. Philosophical texts tied to African and Asian traditions were dismissed as religious, lacking in their ability to separate thought from theology; they were, thus, not elevatable to the level of Philosophy (Park 2013). This act of differentiation offers an example of the investment in separability: philosophy cannot be theology. Fact cannot be Myth; Science cannot be Fiction. For Ferreira da Silva, not only do these modern philosophers of Man write themselves as transcendent thinkers, but the knowledge systems they establish also affirm the primacy of separability, i.e., the assumption that one thing cannot be another.

This is evidenced in how contemporary critical theorists take up the question of "racial-colonial subjugation." They approach this not as a central question that defines the boundaries of critical thought itself, but only as a descriptive problem that must be momentarily reconciled with it. To return to Ferreira da Silva's interview commentary from Part I of this collection,

> It's [racial-colonial subjugation] just one "thing"—one of the ways things are. Then you need a critical theoretical apparatus to account for that "thing." If that is your formulation, then you account for it [racial subjugation] but don't explain it. You name it, but then treat it as something that you include, but it's not integral to the critical tools side.

Instead, Ferreira da Silva posits that racial-colonial subjugation is constitutive of critical thought itself (akin to Park, who outlines the formation of Philosophy as secular). Thus identifying how colonial knowledge continues to be deployed in our contemporary grammar of difference is key to thinking and being otherwise.

Ferreira da Silva takes up this work by crafting what can be read as an ethnography of Modern Man. Beginning with Early Natural Philosophy, but captured most acutely in Descartes' separation of mind and body, Ferreria da Silva traces the World as Ordered (which is the world-as-we-know-it) through Kant's accomplishments in designing a system of knowing based on separability and determinacy—i.e., a description of the world as constituted through objects that are discrete and knowable through the mathematical determination of their formal attributes. Hegel adds to this sequentiality—the notion that knowledge consists of the determination of efficient causes, or that objects are knowable through a determination of the immediate cause of changes in their appearance—to establish what Ferreira da Silva describes as the three pillars of modern knowledge. Separability, determinancy, and sequentiality are thus "onto-epistemological assumptions guiding our critical work" (2020, 40). Otherness, an effect of separability, makes difference permanent and irreconcilable. For example, descriptions of the so-called "dangerous and undeserving 'Other'" are driven not only by "fear and uncertainty"—which she describes as "staples of the modern racial grammar"—but also by assumptions of an unbridgeable ethical divide (2016, 57). While fear and uncertainty are effects of determinacy (reified through the cataloguing of embodied and cultural attributes) and sequentiality (mapped through economic, juridical, and ethical descriptions), assumptions of unresolvable ethical difference are grounded in separability.

If, in this (Ordered) World, difference cannot exist without separation, then solutions to difference become tied, at best, to the inclusion of the Other, or, at worst, to their obliteration. Writing, for instance, with reference to the United Nations' Forum on Indigenous Issues, Ferreira da Silva notes how protests levied against Mexican and Canadian mining companies are rewritten by the dominant interests as "differences of culture and ways of thinking among the actors (the states, the mining companies, the communities, etc.)" (Saul Vicente Vasquez qtd in Ferreira da Silva 2020, 39). When demands for land return confront these premises of knowing, they are appropriated into a framework of cultural difference precisely because the indigenous subjects making these demands are already figured as different and subordinate. As Ferreira da Silva points out, indigenous demands are rendered epistemic and ethical differences—i.e., differences in perspectives and priorities tied to being indigenous. Such a move reduces "Indigenous and rural insurrections against state capital" into "actualizations of their cultural difference/identity without political and transformative force" (2020, 40). Ferreira da Silva asks instead whether there is another way to recompose difference. How might we read against this proclivity toward cultural difference?

Ferreira da Silva proposes a "reading method designed to capture indigenous insurgencies as anticolonial and racial critiques of global state-capital" (2020, 40). This necessitates a praxis that refuses to read indigeneity as a descriptor of difference. Our task, therefore, is to ask how we might read difference so that it may evade capture by forces looking to contain it as cultural difference. This is the decolonial center to Ferreira da Silva's work; it is an openness and centering of uncertainty and impressions. Ferreira da Silva, referencing Walter Benjamin, suggests that such methodological practice/praxis is not simply about un-doing something but about composition. Put simply, Ferreira da Silva notes that such a method presupposes that "all that happens and exists is deeply implicated. As a mode of critical intervention, it is creative in that it imagines the World as having always already been otherwise than its modern picturing" (2020, 48). Decolonial thought, for Ferreira da Silva, is thought liberated from certain, determinate, causal knowledge about difference as unresolvable investment. Instead, hers is a vision to think of difference through entanglement, as "neither the cause nor the effect of relations involving separate existents, but the uncertain condition under which everything that exists is a singular expression of each and every actual-virtual other existent" (2016, 63). It is, in other words, the abolition of categorial thinking and the pursuit of entanglement as a condition of mutual affectability.

References

Ferreira da Silva, Denise (2016). "On Difference Without Separability." In *32nd Bienal de São Paulo - Incerteza Viva. Catalogue*, edited by Jochen Volz and Júlia Rebouças, 57–65. Fundação Bienal de São Paulo.

Ferreira da Silva, Denise (2020). "Reading the Dead: A Black Feminist Poethical Reading of Global Capital." In *Otherwise Worlds Against Settler Colonialism and Anti-Blackness*, edited by Tiffany Lethabo King, Jenell Navarro, and Andrea Smith, 38–51. Duke University Press.

Park, Peter (2013). *Africa, Asia, and the History of Philosophy: Racism in the Formation of the Philosophical Canon, 1780–1830*. State University of New York Press.

10

Interview with Denise Ferreira da Silva

Julietta Hua and rashné limki

Hua: Can you place yourself a bit in terms of Black Brazilian Studies, or Latin American Studies?

Ferreira da Silva: Black Brazilian Studies is a formation that does not exist but it is about to. I can see it. It's showing up in the horizon. In that formation I do have a place for two (maybe more) reasons. On the one hand I have a place historically, because I belong to what was almost the first generation of black critical scholars in Brazil, but we were not trained as critical scholars or trained as very conventional, disciplined scholars. But we had the resources to become good at the discipline; in my case, sociology. There was an anthropologist, an historian, another sociologist. But it didn't expand because there were so few of us—four of us. Then there is a generation that comes after us, and they are also very few and also very disciplined. So there was no such thing as Black Cultural Studies [in Brazil] until the past ten years.

But in the last ten years you have this new generation. In a way they started with a concept of blackness that is informed by my work and that is only because some of them, who are artists, translated my work into Portuguese and circulated my work. The work wasn't being assigned and of course, was in English, but some of them could read in English, and they translated it. I was at the Sao Paulo biennial in 2012 and was invited to do something. By 2016 I was part of one of the programs for one of the artists. By then folks had started translating some of the work. My friends introduced me to these young Brazilian artists who are outside of the university.

So on one hand there hasn't been a thing called black Brazilian Studies or black Brazilian feminist studies until very recently. Since very recently my texts have been translated into Portuguese and that happened at the same time that the writings of black Brazilian feminists from 30 or 40 years ago were compiled and published into a collection—Beatriz Nascimento and Lélia Gonzalez primarily. These two women were well-into-life activists when I was a young scholar being trained, but they had no place in academia. Beatriz is a historian, Lélia a sociologist but they have very few publications in academic journals and were not recognized by anyone outside of the black Brazilian movement as academic. I remember reading the work and talking to them and knowing them because they were in their forties and I was in my early twenties. Now because of these publications it seems like there was this thing called black Brazilian feminist studies, but it didn't exist at the time. I know that because I was there, waiting to be trained by them, but there was no space, no opportunity for that. I met them primarily in the activist space, and then in the academic space created by the Center for Afro-Asian Studies, which was the place where I was working at the time.

Now not only do we have their work being translated, we have the work of black US feminists being translated and published in Brazil, so Saidiya [Hartman], Christina Sharpe, Dionne Brand, and they are the ones who are arriving. There are some translations of Hortense [Spiller]'s work, but not many. This is all happening in the last five years. We also have the black Brazilian feminist writers and poets—fiction writers and poets, and there are lots of them. But it's still like you can count them on two hands, and you are talking about a country like Brazil, being able to count on two hands all the black Brazilian feminist writers of this generation. You also have the artists and curators. So this "Black Brazilian Studies" formation, if we can call it that, is not only academic. Actually, the least interesting part of the formation is the academic one. They are artists, curators, publishers doing different things. That is speaking about folks in Brazil.

Of course, there has been since the late 1980s a huge number of US-American black academics who study Brazil. I don't think they have ever been able to move beyond the frontiers of Area Studies so there we have black scholars in Latin American Studies, Brazilian Studies studying black Brazil. Those folks have been doing it for 30 years or; Carol Boyce Davies who is, you know, very famous in the African diaspora. I also met her back in 1988, when Carol already had at least one book published, was an assistant professor and several others—I can't remember them.

So that's another formation that I didn't become part of because I parted ways with Area Studies very early. Now I'm fully back with them, which is very funny. Well I am. I am not. I am not in Latin American studies, but I am in the Spanish and Portuguese Language department. It's amazing how Area Studies cannot deal with Indigenous Studies, and even Ethnic Studies. The more interesting scholars are on the border, asking questions about indigeneity and Latinx Studies, and indigeneity and Latin American Studies putting pressure on these borders. So yeah, my students were, you know, raising questions about those separations and traveling these separations [disciplinary, between Ethnic Studies and Area Studies] back at UC San Diego in 2006, 2007.

Hua: Can you elaborate on the pressures you mention between Area Studies and Indigenous Studies—pressures around indigeneity?

Ferreira da Silva: The pressure between indigeneity and Latinx and Latin American Studies… One of the questions that shows up in work of folks who are looking at indigenous migrants in California—we have what, twenty years migration at least, of indigenous folks who came into the US already refusing to be identified as Chicano, Mexican or Mexican-American. Now finally, we have their children who are doing PhD research, looking at mobility, but the way they are looking at mobility is not the same as the ways Latinx Studies folks have been looking at migrants from Mexico or Guatemala. Also you have students in Latin American Studies looking at extraction and resistance, for instance conflicts with the Canadian mining companies in Mexico. They are looking at what's happening in indigenous locations and not so much concerned with Mexico and its place in the global economy. That leads to the question—for people studying mobility—what about the land? How can you talk about indigeneity without land? Are they doing Latinx Studies? If indigenous folks are in Los Angeles and not somewhere in Mexico, is that Latinx Studies?

Hua: I was actually wondering if we see some of those tensions—of Area Studies wanting to remain something, if you see that in Ethnic Studies, too? Or maybe I'm trying to ask, to what extent do you see Ethnic Studies as a formation existing as a more transnational or global formation? I ask because I occasionally find really interesting scholarship by people who think about race in fundamentally different ways than come out of the US tradition. I see your work as trying to do that [transnationalize Ethnic Studies] from an early time.

Ferreira da Silva: Well, you have two questions, one I can't really answer which is about Ethnic Studies and whether it cannot help but remain US-centered. That might be the case—that it can't because of something intrinsic to that formation, or maybe because of the centrality of racial formation as a theory. But we can also think about a whole generation of students who do not need to study Ethnic Studies in the university whose politics from high school or even before are from social justice and [for whom] social justice is Ethnic Studies. If nothing else in Canada, the social justice students in Canada are Ethnic Studies citizens. That's the sensibility they have. That creates a problem for the disciplinary formation because, you know, if those kids are going to Ethnic Studies departments, what's happening in those classrooms? For example, there is a serious political problem now at [redacted] where the department, which is part of the university, is basically at odds with its students over their pro-Palestine position. They even called the cops on these black and Palestinian students.

This has always been a part of the problem in terms of the formation, insofar as it is an academic one, inside of the university. It has always been unable to deliver what one could think it would be able to because of its content. But now it's complicated by the fact that the students are—they're much better than the professors at that. So I think it's even more complicated, more problematic an issue than just being limited to the US [as a disciplinary formation]. There has always been a problem in terms of institutionally, of being part of the institution, maybe now more than before because of the crisis in Palestine.

11

Facing Denise Ferreira da Silva

Philosophy and Black Brazilian Radical Thought

Agnes Oliveira Costa, Federico Sanguinetti, and Pedro João da Silva Bisneto. Translated by Katucha Bento

Denise Ferreira da Silva in Brazilian Academic Philosophy

If we consider the reception of Denise Ferreira da Silva in the academic field of philosophy in Brazil, it becomes evident that her influence is, to say the least, incipient. The translation of her work remains sporadic and began only very recently (her book *Toward a Global Idea of Race* was translated into Portuguese as late as 2022). Few authors directly engage with her thought in articles or book chapters.[1]

---

[1] Regarding postgraduate dissertations establishing a dialogue with Ferreira da Silva's work, we found as little as two Masters dissertations and a PhD dissertation by Abigail Campos Leal. At the 2024 National Association of Postgraduate Studies in Philosophy (ANPOF) meeting, held in Recife from September 30 to October 4, 2024, we identified only nine presentations that engaged with the author's work. See https://anpof.org.br/publicacoes/colecao-xx-encontro-nacional-anpof-2024. Our survey was conducted up until December 10, 2024.

Bretas (2022)[2] draws a connection between Ferreira da Silva and Walter Benjamin, influenced by Márcio Seligmann-Silva and discusses direct references by Ferreira da Silva to the German philosopher. The central focus of the approach concerns the need to disrupt the methodological and ontoepistemological principles that perpetuate racial/capitalist oppression. Bretas highlights similarities between Benjamin's and Ferreira da Silva's criticisms of the historical linearity characteristic of Western hegemonic thought. Ferreira Dantas (2022) employs Ferreira da Silva's Black feminist poetics alongside Antônio Bispo dos Santos's biointeraction theory and Davi Kopenawa's shamanic worldview to highlight both the violent distancing of the human being from nature and the institution, animated by the Western-colonial worldview, of a racial hierarchy between collectives that aims at the annihilation of non-white peoples. The author thus proposes examining the confluences between Ferreira da Silva, Bispo dos Santos, and Kopenawa as a path towards a counter-colonizing education (dos Santos 2023). Bensusan (2024) uses Ferreira da Silva's critique of autonomous and transparent subjectivity and her denunciation of its inextricable connection to total violence to challenge a conceptualization of the relationship between human intelligence and technologies that distribute freedom and sovereignty unevenly—freedom, qua autonomy, to human beings and servitude to technologies. According to Bensusan, the conception of the human being as autonomous is detrimental in many ways. As an alternative, the author suggests childhood as an example of a vulnerable (affectable) condition, not to be seen merely as a preparatory stage for autonomy but a source of inspiration for a different cosmopolitics, centered precisely on heteronomy. Osman (2024) bridges Ferreira da Silva and Édouard Glissant to advocate for the right to opacity as opposed to the racial metaphysics of othering, based on separation and transparency. This movement is seen as an opposition to modern text through a "(po)ethics" (Ferreira da Silva, Desideri, Döcker and Katsouraki, 2022 apud Osman, 10).[3]

In addition to these shorter texts, two more comprehensive works establish a dialogue with Ferreira da Silva's work. Galdino (2024) revisits Ferreirian themes in his extensive investigation on race, in which Mbembe figures as a main reference. In particular, Galdino retrieves Ferreira da Silva's concept of globality and her criticism of linear time (cf. Ferreira da Silva 2016) as a counterpoint to sequentiality and chronological cause-effect relationship to explain how race differentially shapes the contemporary landscape (cf. Galdino 2024, 126, 151, and 155). Additionally, Galdino connects Ferreira

[2] Bretas (2021) includes only one citation by Ferreira da Silva and does not elaborate on her thought.

[3] Each of us, as authors, also has research projects on Ferreira da Silva.

da Silva and Wilderson concerning anti-Blackness[4] (Galdino 2024, 180), addressing Ferreira da Silva's interpretation of the character Dana in *Kindred* by Octavia Butler, as well as the *Dred Scott* case (cf. Ferreira da Silva 2024, Ch. 1) to reaffirm the connection between race and property, beyond any legal framework. However, we wonder whether Ferreira da Silva would challenge Galdino's proposal of an *imaginal* investigation of race at the intersection between metaphysics and phenomenology. While citing Ferreira da Silva less than Galdino[5] and focusing more on gender issues, Campos Leal's essay (2021) seems closer to Ferreira da Silva's approach. The most explicit reference here is the critique of linear temporality to understand the phenomena of racialization and gendering and the call for the "experience of spatial-temporal crossing" (Leal 2021, 191) as an onto-epistemological horizon. However, the entire book is traversed by Ferreirian themes, such as the centrality of singularities, the search for formless materiality, the critique of the monological subject, the demand for an end to the world as we know it, the assumption of the violated body of the trans/fat/racialized person as an epistemic starting point for its dissolution against any inclusive logic, the denunciation of the war logic that informs the state apparatus, and Campos Leal's poetic-literary experimentation, manifested both stylistically–mixing diagnosis and fiction–and typographically, for instance, breaking and striking words. How can we explain, then, the relative lack of reception of Ferreira da Silva's work in Brazilian academic philosophy, despite the author having been producing for over 20 years?

In our view, this can be explained by the strong racist, Eurocentric, and sexist nature of Brazilian academic philosophy, its curricula,[6] and its funding policies.[7] Ferreira da Silva's thought undermines the very foundations of the philosophy at the core of academia, as well as the mission and configuration of the institution itself. In this regard, it is worth considering, albeit briefly, how Ferreira da Silva's work challenges the field in its current

---

[4] Translator's note: Translating race and color from Portuguese to English in dialogue with race studies is part of a dialogue with different racialization politics in different parts of the world. Considering the color-race racialization system in Brazil, I translate color and reference to skin color *black* (preta/preto) in lower case "b" and the racialized categories regarding Black (negra/negro) and Blackness (negritude) with a capital "B," causing a subtle disruption in the flow to indicate the non-hegemonic approach of what *black* and *Black* is or can be while navigating languages and contexts. There is an important negotiation of meaning regarding Blackness in this text, which would be a homogenizing loss for the reader and the political intentions of the text to translate simply as "Blackness." Therefore, the terms *pretitude*, *negridade*, and *negridão* present in this chapter will remain in Portuguese, making reference to the different ways to indicate, interpret, and situate the multifarious possibilities to experience and discuss Blackness.

[5] Leal establishes a more explicit dialogue with Ferreira da Silva in her PhD dissertation (Leal, 2024).

[6] Cf. Da Silva Bisneto (2025), and Direitoria Anpof 2023/24 (2023a).

[7] Cf. Direitoria Anpof 2023/24 (2023b).

configuration. If we examine the major fields shaping the dominant Western hegemonic matrix in Brazilian academic philosophy, along with their central references, it becomes clear that Ferreira da Silva's approach tends to completely dismantle these foundations, revealing their inextricable links to racialization. Her critique of notions such as identity, causality, mind, the understanding of the body and materiality, categorization into genders and species, and linear temporality–among others–shakes the foundations of much of the metaphysical reflections.

The field of ethics must deal with Ferreira da Silva's criticism of values derived from the idea of the autonomous subject, such as individual freedom, justice, moral rights, and so on. Political philosophy is also destabilized by her critique of the concept of the subject, as it not only undermines (neo) liberalism and its conception of rights and the state but also challenges "progressive" political philosophy and the various strands of historical materialism. Her critique of the formal notion of concepts and determinate thinking, as well as ideas of universality, necessity, and objectivity that constitute the dominant understanding of science, disrupts the principles underlying mainstream theories of knowledge and philosophy of science.

Finally, her reinterpretation of modern traditions and their (more or less "phantasmatic") ramifications in contemporary thought calls into question the very notion of history that organizes the study of the field, which in Brazil is still heavily influenced by French and Italian models, traditionally historicist. We could go on. At the same time, Ferreira da Silva's work promises to have a significant impact on areas more critical of the hegemonic Western philosophical tradition, particularly its modern and contemporary manifestations, and their respective authors. For instance, in the context of philosophical studies on race, Ferreira da Silva's radical approach offers an alternative to the so-called "critical race theory" as well as to projects that seek to include racialized non-white groups within social collectives shaped by the modern notion of autonomous subjectivity—a concept that, in various forms and degrees, haunts these analytical and emancipatory attempts.

Furthermore, with respect to critiques of coloniality, Ferreira da Silva reconfigures the premises of the debate on effective decolonization, reformulating the theoretical framework within which such demands can make sense, thus guiding emancipatory projects away from inevitable failure. It is worth emphasizing that Ferreira da Silva is working toward the complete dissolution of the frameworks of dominant academic philosophy (not only in Brazil but also in Europe and the United States), which she argues also obstruct critical and emancipatory projects addressing racialization and coloniality.

With such profound disruption, little remains within Brazilian academic philosophy as it is currently configured. What, then, remains for dialogue in Brazil? In the next section, we aim to show that there are scholars who could be described as exponents of *Brazilian radical Black thought* producing philosophical reflections *in conversation* with Ferreira da Silva, even if they are not institutionally situated within academic philosophy.[8]

The Reception of Ferreira da Silva in Brazilian Radical Black Thought

Redistribution of Violence and Blacklight: Jota Mombaça

It is impossible to discuss the reception of Denise Ferreira da Silva in Brazil without addressing the work of Jota Mombaça. We would risk saying, in fact, that no one has grasped Ferreira da Silva's proposal as profoundly as Mombaça. In *Carta à leitora preta do fim dos tempos* (Letter to the Black Reader at the End of Time), written alongside Musa Michelle Mattiuzzi as the preface to the essay collection *A Dívida Impagável* (*Unpayable Debt*, 2019), the authors articulate what we see as the central problem of decolonization according to Ferreira da Silva: how can matter be decolonized? (apud Ferreira da Silva 2019, 17). Ending the world as we know it and putting decolonization into practice as a "project of total disorder" (Mombaça 2021, 73) demands "releas[ing] ... matter from form" and "existence from knowledge" (Ferreira da Silva 2024, 167). In essence, this involves pursuing, through radical praxis, the end of the formalization through which modernity emerges as an Ordered World: the domain of total violence of value, self-justified by imposing separability between *Subjectum* and *Mundus* (Ferreira da Silva 2019, 97).[9] From this perspective, we identify three key presences of Ferreira da Silva in Mombaça's thought: a) the

---

[8] Galdino's and Campos Leal's work are at least very close to this context.

[9] In our view, the value for Ferreira da Silva is not restricted to economic value (although it encompasses it) and is closely linked to the onto-epistemological presumption of transparency that constitutes modern thought. The formalization of value, in a more comprehensive manner, is linked to the very relationship between form and matter in modernity. In this sense, with regard to the inscription, although never certain of its effectiveness, of excess (the Thing) in form, value comes to be understood as form+violence. In Ferreira da Silva (2013), Ferreira da Silva says she uses the term value "covering all its figurations, namely, judgment (ethics), measurement (scientific), calculation (economic) and appreciation (aesthetics)" (Ferreira da Silva 2019, 70). In this sense, value seems to refer to a modern form, which constitutes the sociality of the Ordered World and its total constitutive violence, much more comprehensive than its figuration in the economic scene of value. What emerges is an identification of value with transparency itself and with the very form of modern representation in its various moments, ethical, scientific, legal, economic, aesthetic and so on.

critique of coloniality as a critique of representation; b) the understanding of decolonization as the redistribution of violence and the end of the world as we know it; c) the use of black light as an epistemic tool that enables both the naming of norms and the enactment of "politics of Black opacity" in opposition to the transparency associated with whiteness.

a) *The Critique of Coloniality as Representation*: A radical change in how matter and form are approached strikes at the core of modern representation (Ferreira da Silva 2019, 37). In this sense, Jota Mombaça critiques coloniality as representation: the ways in which modernity subjects fugitive life to the transparency of representations of value, gender, the state, and so on. Mombaça goes against modern representation, urging us to think and act from and through lives shattered by normalizing violence. Lives that refuse to translate themselves "into any identitarian or representational coherence whatever it may be" (Mombaça 2021, 16, trans. KB). The *break* in Mombaça's work is not referring to mere splinters but to the force of shattering, the fugitivity of matter or life itself, *beneath and beyond representation*. It is less about an "autonomous entity than an uncapturable force": "Breaking would be that which defies definition, not out of postmodern heroism, but due to failure and insufficiency" (Mombaça 2021, 18, trans. KB). Thus, the concept of breaking has at least a dual register, or an irresolvable ambiguity, which cannot be resolved within modern representation.

On one hand, the broken life marks the event of dismantling caused by "normalizing violence," "after which a body can no longer be read as a proper body." This evokes the poetic figure of the "sexual body of the native/slave" or the "wounded captive body in the scene of subjugation" described by Ferreira da Silva (2019, 2024). On the other hand, the broken life signifies the "*fracture of the world*" (Mombaça 2021, 22, our emphasis), the limit and failure of the formalization that modernity imposes on matter and life. Thus, breaking also reminds us of the implicability and constitutive failure of a project based on the demand for wholeness and completeness, stemming from the constitution of the modern Subject as a self-determined entity. This allows us to consider the emergence of affinity politics beyond identity, politics that do not rely on demands for inclusion or greater representation.

In effect, the radical critique of modern representation inevitably requires abandoning the project of subject and identity that underpins modernity and its politics. In other words, it compels us to rethink the meaning of decolonization and emancipation in relation to the Ordered World. Furthermore, thinking and acting through *breaking* removes *negridade*[10] and gendered disobedience from the socio-scientific categorical determinations by which difference is represented and the world is ordered according to the measure of a universal reason. Mombaça asks: "what if, instead of wholeness, self-awareness, the capacity for self-determination, and self-esteem, there were a sense of breaking that would effectively displace incongruent positions to cisgender matrix" (Mombaça 2021, 22, trans. KB)?

b) *Redistribution of Violence*: A second aspect, closely tied to the first, is that the critique to coloniality as representation demands a *redistribution of violence*. Just as Ferreira da Silva urges us to remain *with/in* violence, referring both to the violence constitutive of the Ordered World and to violence as a "referent for other desires, other figurations of existence, or any other possible ways of being human in the world" (Ferreira da Silva 2013, 53). Mombaça similarly calls on us not only to stay with/in violence but to redistribute it:

> Redistribution of violence is a practical demand when we are dying alone and without any form of reparations, whether from the state or organized society. Redistribution of violence is a social justice project in a state of emergency, and it must be performed by those for whom peace was never an option.
>
> (Mombaça 2021, 65, trans. KB)

Redistributing violence, however, requires severing it from cis-masculine and white supremacist sovereignty. It is not about emulating the violence that sustains the Subject's self-determining core; instead, it arises from fragility and, as such, also implies an act of care and an ethics rooted in the vulnerability and implicability of broken lives.

c) *Blacklight*: Finally, Jota Mombaça invokes blacklight as "another way of reading the world" (Ferreira da Silva, 2019, 15). Blacklight serves as a tool that contributes to 1) dismantling modern representation; 2) redistributing violence; 3) releasing matter and, consequently, 4) releasing *negridade* from form (Ferreira da Silva 2017). According to Mombaça, blacklight redistributes violence towards whiteness while simultaneously preserving the opacity of *negridade* in opposition to the violence of transparency: "By exposing white labels, the implementation of blacklight operates as

[10] For Ferreira da Silva, as well as for Mombaça, the concept of *negridade* reinterprets blackness avoiding the category of Blackness.

> an efficient device for politics of Black opacity" (Mombaça 2021, 94, trans. KB). Blacklight accomplishes this by enabling the naming of norms (Mombaça 2021, 67, trans. KB).

Redirecting violence toward norms, in turn, makes it possible to think differently about *negridade* as a reference point for matter or life. The release of *negridade* from form, in this sense, transforms the very notion of matter. Blacklight is, precisely, the tool that makes it possible to rethink matter while ensuring its right to opacity:

> When the Black body disappears into the ultraviolet atmosphere of blacklight, the work performs its most powerful form of critique, challenging the very notion of materiality that has reproduced whiteness as the sole and totalitarian form of presence. Thus, when the lights turn black, the Black body breaks free of its containment, becoming a radically other form of presence: becoming darkness itself.
>
> (Mombaça 2021, 94, trans. KB)

Conversations in Kalunga: Castiel Vitorino Brasileiro

In her work, Castiel Vitorino Brasileiro welcomes Ferreira da Silva into *Kalunga*, a "word/force/zone/principle" with which Vitorino Brasileiro according to her own account, has been connected since the beginning of her life (Vitorino Brasileiro 2022, 56). According to Vitorino Brasileiro, "*Kalunga* designates a cosmic zone for dark-skinned people," a zone of memory, *Memories of Transfiguration*, in which *negridão*[11] shines as incommensurability (Vitorino Brasileiro 2022, 59, 60). With this in mind, we observe Ferreira

[11] Vitorino Brasileiro's use of *negridão* is akin to Ferreira da Silva's and Mombaça's use of *negridade*.

Translator's note: Translating the distinct concepts of *negritude* and *negridade* is not the the same as rendering them simply as Blackness. In both Critical Race Studies and Decolonial Studies, the capitalization of Blackness (or the lack thereof) often reflects specific political positionalities with varying, sometimes conflicting, meanings that seek to challenge the coloniality embedded in the use and stereotypical applications of the term. Blackness is far from neutral or fixed and marks a site of ongoing contestation. To convey the conceptual and affective weight that *negridade* holds in the work of Ferreira da Silva and Mombaça—where the term indicates a resignification of blackness beyond the category of Blackness—some risks are involved, especially for English-speaking audiences. Mainly, that the deliberate distinction between *negritude* and *negridade* may be flattened in translation, contrary to the authors' intentions as they suggest a neologism by playing with the sound of the words in Brazilian Portuguese. This is also why I have kept *negridão* in its original: the sound of "negro" in English carries impact, inviting a pause to reflect on its meaning.

da Silva's reception in Vitorino Brasileiro through three aspects: a) in an *otherwise* understanding of racial violence; b) in an understanding of the world without separability, which demands a critique of the exceptionality of the Human/Subject and modern formalization, which rely on race and sexual binarism for self-preservation; c) in an *otherwise* understanding of *negridade*, which does not occur through the colonial category of Blackness but through *negridão*. This last aspect also points us towards *negridão* as refusal, as incommensurability and unpredictability, in relation to colonial translatability.

a) In *When Sun No Longer Shines Here: The Failure of Blackness* (*Quando o sol aqui não mais brilhar: a falência da negritude*, 2022), Vitorino Brasileiro proposes that we think about racial violence otherwise. This involves questioning the process of *becoming Black* as an inevitable destiny (Vitorino Brasileiro 2022, 13). The author thus challenges an emancipatory route based on "racial consciousness supported by the primacy of cognition" given that racialization constitutes a Form through which modernity organizes the world, operating at "all vital levels" (Vitorino Brasileiro 2022, 23, trans. KB). This is because, according to Vitorino Brasileiro, the emancipatory proposals of Blackness are characterized as "seeking a new place in the plantation" (Vitorino Brasileiro 2022, 27, trans. KB).[12]

With this gesture, similar to Ferreira da Silva (2019, 2024), Vitorino Brasileiro understands racial violence not so much as violence against an already given difference, as a *datum* (empirical matter), but rather as a *violence of annihilation*, which refers to *negridão* as incommensurability and unpredictability, racializing it:[13]

> Coloniality is characterized by the control over darkness, it evolves in this way, and it is through this process that white supremacy develops

[12] "I am here deconstructing racial pride as an anticolonial practice, this racial pride, or the act of becoming Black, is in fact a modern act and nothing more" (Vitorino Brasileiro 2022, 25, trans. KB).

[13] Vitorino Brasileiro makes a distinction between death and annihilation. While death is understood as "an event of transfiguration of matter and transmutation of memory," annihilation is defined "as a colonial act," a management of life through racialization, a management of population control, carried out through police violence and the precarization of these people's health, for example. Annihilation interrupts personal and collective histories and announces death as a gateway to oblivion. In this sense, "modernity signs off on the promise (and the labour towards) ensuring that that life will be forgotten, along with its effects" (Vitorino Brasileiro 2022, 51–52, trans. KB).

> its programme for perpetuating its presence on a sideral[14] scale: by attempting to control the *negridão* of the seas, dark-skinned people and their civilizations, and the *negridão* of outer space. The *negrume*, the black, the dark, or a moonless night are the greatest nightmares of modern *Beings*, as they represent the materials, lives, places, and situations that expose the prevalence of relativity, chance, and ephemerality, principles that have been countered through the development of so-called human sciences or related disciplines, particularly anthropology, psychoanalysis, and psychology. (Vitorino Brasileiro 2022, 37, trans. KB)[15]

Vitorino Brasileiro identifies this modern "aversion of the unpredictability of Form" as the foundation not only of racial violence as annihilation but also of gender violence, as seen in the cases of obstetric and paediatric violence "against intersex people, who are traditionally mutilated in their early years of life under the promise of being readjusted to the *normality of the species*" (Vitorino Brasileiro 2022, 39, trans. KB). How can the cycle of this violence of annihilation be broken?

b) Against the modern formalization of the world, which claims to be eternal and feeds the "addiction to control through the desire for knowledge" i.e., the *Will to Truth*, Vitorino Brasileiro calls us to another understanding of the world, in which the principle of separability does not operate. Separability is the principle that establishes Humanity as always-already in conflict with what is produced as "nature/natural/savage/animality/uncivilized." From separability, race is produced as a "time-space of savagery that threatens Humanity, while simultaneously legitimizing the Human as a time-space where forms and ways of living are deemed genuinely correct" (Vitorino Brasileiro 2021, 64, trans. KB). Thus, among the elements of nature, the Human emerges not only as "complete" beings but as "in a state of improving their perfection" (Vitorino Brasileiro 2022, 71, trans. KB; cf. Ferreira da

---

[14] Translator's note: the word "sideral" (coming from the Latin *sīderālis*) can also be translated here as "cosmic" or "outer" space. The choice to preserve "sideral" also as it is written in Portuguese, retains the archaic English word and the somewhat ominous resonance of the word. It is an intentional reference to the multiple connotations the word received through time, such as "harmful threat" in the cosmos and something that "deserves attention," as Vitorino Brasileiro refers the sideral scale to white supremacy. My translation respects Vitorino Brasileiro's poetics, allowing the text to carry the historical and affective weight of the term and the aesthetics of the original to deepen the provocation by situating Dione Brand's reference to *No Language Is Neutral* (McClelland & Stewart, 1998).

[15] In another moment, Vitorino Brasileiro says: " the racial system is a favourable ecology to *white* fear of unpredictability, of that which they do not know—the fear of white peoples towards their own planet and the galaxy in which they live" (2022, 68, trans. KB).

> Silva 2007, ch. 5). The Black myth, within this colonial political ecology in which difference becomes a problem, is the prerogative that sustains the prosperity and continuous improvement of the Human/Subject, always-already identified with the white-European (Vitorino Brasileiro 2022, 14–15), who must reign by controlling the unpredictability identified in its Others. Dependent on separability, the prosperity of the modern Human/Subject, inseparable from colonial expansion and Global Capital, presupposes the "failure of Blackness (*negritude)*"—which, in our view, Ferreira da Silva characterized as a *negative accumulation* (2019, 2024).[16]

How can unpredictability be reclaimed without reproducing the determinations and identity fixations that characterize modern cognitive plantations? Vitorino Brasileiro conjures an *Interspecies Ancestrality* through which it is possible to understand existence without separability, but also to engage in "a crucial practice for experiencing fleeting moments of freedom in our daily lives on the *plantation*" (2022, 19). In doing so, the author also provides us with another image of sociality, based on the construction of "ecosocial interactions that ensure the integrity of vital diversity" (2020, 33). Instead of centering the world's understanding on a specific heredity or reproduction focused on human ancestry[17]—"even though the category of human never corresponds to racialized lives"—*Interspecies Ancestrality* comprehends life as the result "of the fundamental relationship between species, different realms" (Vitorino Brasileiro 2021, 96, trans. KB), encompassing plants, minerals, animals, waters, and all other existences, perpetuating unpredictability. Thus, *Interspecies Ancestrality* can also be termed the Ancestrality of Unpredictability, whose other name is also *negridão* (Vitorino Brasileiro 2022, 38).

c) Defending opacity, the mysteries of *negridão*, in relation to the violence of racialization's annihilation, is an act of refusal: a refusal of the translation of life's immeasurability within modern representation, of its ontogenesis and sociogenesis based on transparency and competition (Vitorino Brasileiro 2022, 91). The modern world, or what Ferreira da Silva (2019) calls the Ordered World, is the limit with which *negridão* interacts and in which its cosmic immeasurability is constantly translated within

[16] In this sense, the genitive "of" in the expression "failure of Blackness" is both subjective and objective.

[17] The Human/Modern Subject depends on the establishment of an (intra)species heredity, sustained through racialization and sexualization. It is through this policy of intra-human parenthood that white and cisgender supremacy ensures the perpetuation of its myth of the Eternal Form, as well as the prosperity and self-improvement of the Modern Subject. On this, see Vitorino Brasileiro (2022, 34–35).

modern representation, which does not fail to constantly delimit or position the unrepresentable. Faced, therefore, with the limits of the modern world, its representation and the violence of control and annihilation that sustains it, we see both in Ferreira da Silva (2019, 2022) and in Vitorino Brasileiro the exercise of refusing the inseparable translation of another understanding of existence in which *negridade/negridão* shines in its indefinity in relation to the claws of transparency.

Translation, Bad Encounter, and Colonial Debt: Alexandro de Jesus

The theme of translation leads us to the reception of Ferreira da Silva's thought by Alexandro de Jesus: his unique and original thinking indirectly[18] dialogues with Ferreira da Silva's production, which, in turn, strongly reverberates in his own work. What we mean by this is that reading Ferreira da Silva's work enhances the critical strength present in de Jesus's work, as it is possible to identify certain conceptual correspondences in his two main texts—*Corupira* (2019) and *Notas* (2022). We refer to these as conceptual correspondences because, until December 2019, de Jesus's thought had been developing without his knowledge of Ferreira da Silva's work.[19]

First, in his 2019 text, de Jesus attempts to recover the historiography of *Corupira*[20] by tracing the historical subdivisions of this Indigenous mythological being. This recovery follows three moments, consequently forming three *graphic-scabs*[21] that elucidate this trajectory: a) "Corupira":

[18] It is important to mention this indirect dialogue because, considering their two main texts—*Corupira: Mau Encontro, Tradução e Dívida Colonial* (Corupira: Bad Encounter, Translation and Colonial Debt) (2019) and *Notas sobre a Atualidade da Ferida Colonial* (Notes on the Persistence of the Colonial Wound) (2022)—there is only a single reference to Ferreira da Silva in the 2022 text. This occurs in a brief example, where, among the various analyses of colonial debt, Ferreira da Silva's (specifically *A Dívida Impagável*, as per the eponymous 2019 book) is noted as worth citing. Beyond this, there are no traces of a direct or significant engagement with Ferreira da Silva's approaches and concepts.

[19] Source: personal communication with de Jesus (September 18, 2023).

[20] An ancestral figure of Brazil's Indigenous peoples. The Corupira stands at the heart of the book in question, shaped by the ways in which its meaning has been interpreted, and ultimately eradicated.

[21] "Graphic scabs here translates the imprint that words, concepts, or expressions have undergone; the preoccupation of these notes on contemporaneity is to fabricate meaning(s) for the graphic scab 'colonial wound'" (de Jesus 2022, 7). The concept of graphic-scab (*casca-grafica*) was the concept used in typography to indicate the support (usually of vegetal origin) of the print. The English translation fortuitously allows us to appreciate the association between this concept and the notion of—in de Jesus's case—the colonial wound.

The first reference to *Corupira*, despite appearing in a letter by the sixteenth-century Jesuit priest José de Anchieta, was fundamentally framed as a demon, using him as a direct and absolute opposition to Christian/European divinities; b) "Curupira": The second graphic-scab introduces European epistemology, where Curupira becomes an empty name for an indigenous superstition; c) "Currupira": Following the colonial encounter and their imposed meanings, the colonizer is left to use cultural terms to frame Currupira within an anthropological context, aligning it with a certain Western representation. In other words, Currupira now needs to have an exemplary function, similar to the mythical excerpts of the West, indicating a correspondence between indigenous and western entities mediated by cultural difference. What is being done here is the formulation of a third interpretation of Corupira, not as a demon nor as a mere name for an empty representation of the natives, but rather as an anthropological justification for its existence, it being an exposition of a subordination of indigenous divinities to the principle of social division of labor and to Western European civilization.[22]

This epistemic transition between three interpretations clearly defines what de Jesus calls as "Bad Encounter,"[23] or rather, an encounter not accidental between distinct communities. This meeting, mediated by cultural difference, results in an inevitable unfolding of domination, whether through extermination or linguistic, existential, metaphysical, and

[22] De Jesus identifies here an anthropologic-economic phase and a folkloric phase.

[23] The *Bad Encounter* (Mau Encontro), as a concept of multiple definitions, needs to be dissected, especially if we consider that its genesis has always sought to frame the experience of a *mis-encounter*, or rather, the way in which linguistic, epistemological, and metaphysical tools are discovered and used to destabilize the other. This takes shape because this bad encounter "already lingers, over the power granted to a language or idiom to speak the world and the first experience, or that which comes before language" (de Jesus 2019, 25, trans. KB). It is important to highlight that this bad encounter takes on this graphic-scab form from two origins: a) The epistemological delimitation of the origin of disorder and colonial extermination. Here, a *Rectification of the Mis-encounter* would be established, or rather, the zero point where the other's path is diverted, based on cultural difference; and b) The very verbal conception of "bad" (*mau*) is distinguished by its harmful, morally reprehensible character and denotes a tendency toward doing evil, a satisfaction derived from the harm inflicted. This verbal conception highlights both the ethical violence of contact and the absence of qualitative exchange between different peoples, as well as the inherent nature that takes pleasure in the extermination it enacts.

epistemological control. This bad encounter establishes a colonial debt,[24] resembling a Christian process of sin and redemption: forsaking one's life to follow the "narrow" path leading to repentance and salvation. Based on these elements, it is noteworthy that both Ferreira da Silva and de Jesus come together to recognize cultural difference as a relevant factor in the justifications for colonial domination. According to Ferreira da Silva, acknowledging that modernity has structured cultural difference along racial and gender-sexual lines, which subjugated individuals, allows for the "delimitation of the social trajectory of exclusion and the articulation of the particular subjectivity emerging from it" (2020, 39). This underscores how raciality is a modern construct and that its resolution necessitates, also, a theoretical understanding of its dissolution. Both thinkers consider raciality as the backdrop from which cultural difference is established. Raciality mobilizes operators of violence that sustain subjugation, "occluding of the juridic-economic relevance" (Ferreria da Silva 2020, 40) of everything that is dissident to the European paradigm, or, according to de Jesus, from everything that European epistemology disregards or fails to incorporate beyond its predefined definitions.

This dissidence is significant because Ferreira da Silva, in her formulation of the opposition between the transparent-I and the affectable-I, structures a dissonance that can be characterized as the refraction of human difference produced by Enlightenment universal reason, or rather, a difference between the self-conscious and autonomous subject from a mere body, which claims to be a subject, striving for an unattainable condition assigned to the other.[25] This notion dialogues with de Jesus's framework, which outlines a contrast between:

> -white/-Black: Two fundamental enclosures—since they are arranged within the diagram of raciality—through which being, in contemporary times, is carried out. Its in-corporation marks beings inversely by raciality: the Black-being, called forth externally, for whom raciality tends towards

[24] This colonial debt takes center stage in *Corupira* only to be later expanded with greater scope in *Notas*. Initially, the debt appears as the result of an "exercise of mediation" (de Jesus 2019, 29, trans. KB), first exemplified through language but ultimately extending to the entire relationship between settler and colonized, as if the very act of non-extermination (of language, culture, traditions, ancestry, and life itself) were considered as an act of mercy, one that, at some point, may and must be repaid. This logic assumes that the preservation of life also means the opportunity of cultural assimilation and the reception of forgiveness from the Western culture's savior. In this sense, the colonial debt "is immeasurable, or since its premise functions as a counter-service for a vital favour granted to those subjected to it—a favour consisting precisely in the removal of their mis-encounter—perhaps it is better to say that its only possible measure is fulfilled in and through the consumption of that subject's life in service of the debt" (de Jesus 2019, 30, trans. KB).

[25] Ferreira da Silva's concept of the "affectable I" corresponds to the outcome of the process that de Jesus, in *Notas*, refers to as "double reduction"—see de Jesus (2022).

> a totalitarian experience (everything, or nearly everything, is racism); and the white-Being, whose racial trace is erased from the outset, so that racial issues lose density or become rarefied (nothing, or nearly nothing, is racism). In each enclosure, one of its components is eclipsed by the other: in the -white, it is the racial trace that is cast into shadow; in the -Black, it is the very being.
>
> (de Jesus 2022, 16, note 14, trans. KB)

In a singular way, we can affirm that the second key convergence between de Jesus and Ferreira da Silva lies in the suppression of the historical linearity of debt. This colonial debt is not confined to a purely historical framework but extends into a relationship of affectability that surpasses generational succession and familial ties. It deploys mechanisms that go beyond the linearity of racial subjugation—adapting what Hortense Spillers describes as historical immobility (Wilderson 2021), an understanding that acknowledges a certain reflex of "narrative of violence that enslavement itself has been preparing for a couple of centuries" (Spillers 1987, 79) or even the extension beyond the temporal limits of racial subjugation. It is no longer simply a "historical debt" but rather a debt that goes beyond the limits of history, metaphysics, epistemology, ethics, and economy as we know them.

This conceptual trajectory in de Jesus's texts resonates with and is amplified in Ferreira da Silva's analysis of racial subjugation as a reality that transcends the boundaries of time and lineage, particularly in what she terms the *Unpayable Debt*. This debt is not purely economic, as it lacks an interest rate or a definitive means of repayment, nor does it have historical or pain-related limits. Given this, we gain an understanding of how the extrapolation of historical limits permeates the works of these two Brazilian thinkers, especially while analyzing how the *colonial wound* and *unpayable debt* maintain a persistent presence across present, past and the erasure of affective domains of racialized bodies. Moreover, they share the concept of *necessity* as an organizing principle of this condition, albeit with a broader application in Ferreira da Silva's work—considering that she interprets it as the regulatory and functional mechanism of the modern world: "In the shapes of force and order, it constrains, regulates or limits. It acts as the exterior power (as law or form) that composes and destroys the things of the universe" (Ferreira da Silva 2009, 214).

Social Death and Anti-Blackness: Osmundo Pinho

The dialogue between Ferreira da Silva and Osmundo Pinho is established through their understanding that their initial works, at least within the context of the 1980s and 1990s, shared a return to the classics of Brazilian sociology while simultaneously engaging in a "metaphysical" critique of slavery. Both were influenced by the need to rethink the obstacles that persist in the formation of Black Brazilian thought. In particular Pinho has more recently drawn direct influence from the Afro-pessimist movement[26] (Pinho 2024, Introduction), through his critique of the myth of racial inclusion mediated by the urgency of diversity and the failure to centralize the persistence of the metaphysical effects of slavery. According to Pinho, there is a legitimate argument in Wilderson's Afro-pessimism, as there is no clear historical line that marks the end of slavery. Instead, its continuity is maintained through the very existence and formation of Black identities, imposing an ontological mark on the constitution of non-subjects and is inseparable from this type of existence. This structure results in two inevitable effects: social death (cf. Wilderson 2021, 119; also Patterson 2008), a structure of social antagonism marked by the annulment of racial subjects' citizenship, and anti-Blackness, the fundamental antagonism that sustains the incompatibility of Black people in the world as we know it (Pinho 2021, 22). Due to these two elements, non-subjects are left in a state of fungibility,[27] where their very existence serves as evidence of their inferiority. These bodies are entirely encased in a tragic symbolic triangulation based on "the objectivity of historical forms, the volatility of subject constitution, and aesthetic objectification as self-conception" (Pinho 2024, trans. KB), binding them to the image of beings made to die.

This reality is reinforced by the normalization and erasure of racial violence, which transforms the Black body into a totemized object—as the fabricated representation of an essentially mixed-race nation—formulating a "great phantasmagoria, organized according to the same racial categories of the nineteenth century, revealing the sad colonial aspect of Brazilian racial ideology" (Pinho 2021, 77, trans. KB). This phantasmagoria is rooted in the myth of racial democracy, voyeuristically framing the "brown, mixed, national body, adorned with French or English ideas, and displaying a willingness to use charm or flattery to climb the steep peak of social ascension" (Pinho 2021, 79, trans. KB), while simultaneously destroying and dismantling them. Pinho identifies a direct correlation between the genocide of the Black population and the defense of miscegenation, which

---

[26] We do not have sufficient space here to fully explore the intersections between Pinho's Afro-pessimism and elements of Ferreira da Silva's thought.

[27] This fungibility can be interpreted as a feature of being a commodity, as the condition to be substituted or exchanged according to the master's will. This feature is shared by enslaved people. Fungibility enables the transformation of the enslaved body into an abstract and empty vessel, worthless beyond its exchange value and the profit in ownership that the master acquires through trade.

is based on a mythicization of the "song of the three races,"[28] positioning it as a formulation of Brazilian success while perpetuating "the discourse of racial difference production as the foundation of a residual logic that renders Blackness the dregs of the (de)stabilization process of stable identities and subjectivities" (Pinho 2021, 80, trans. KB).

This strategy operates through "differentiation and colonial hierarchy of bodies, demanding their regulation through mechanisms of racialization and sexualization" (Pinho 2021, 83, trans. KB). It reverberates in a model of life that recognizes Brazil as both a transformer and multiplier of social death's metamorphoses. Social death is validated by a system that places Blackness in direct opposition to humanity, rendering the non-subject killable and exterminable. The Black body, as the visible product of miscegenation and its supposed moral and intellectual inferiority, is thrown into the realm of social death and anti-Blackness, indicating its self-evident inferiority. This body becomes the ultimate representation of "devastation, dispossession, and death. Attributes of a structure of antagonism that defines the conditions of possibility for the formal articulation of meanings and subjectivities" (Pinho 2021, 110, trans. KB). The author argues that this body is marked by gunfire, symbolizing "the daily coexistence with death and violence" (Pinho 2021, 110, trans. KB), a fact that denotes the deepening of a triad of affectability, in which social death—as the irreconcilable impossibility of life—, anti-Blackness—as the incongruent opposition between Blackness and humanity—, and genocide—influenced by Abdias do Nascimento's *Genocide of the Black Brazilian*—delineate the juridical right over the life and death of these bodies. This triad sustains an absolute negativity that enables the necessary viability to racialized bodies as a pile of worthless flesh.

When approaching Pinho through Ferreira da Silva's lens, we perceive that Ferreira da Silva's work provides an intensification of these formulations. Ferreira da Silva asserts that the subject is inherently false and cannot adequately represent racialized bodies, as race becomes a strong factor of anti-modernity, demonstrating an intrinsic contradiction to the white world. This contradiction manifests through the dichotomy between the *transparent-I* and the *affectable-I*, produced by Enlightenment universal reason as the distinction between the self-conscious, autonomous subject in opposition to a mere body, striving in vain to attain the condition of subject. However, let it be clear, this opposition goes far beyond a simple reproduction of the white/Black-European/African opposition. It necessitates an understanding of how these positions were defined and, crucially, deciphering "how whiteness came to signify the transparent I, and blackness to signify otherwise?" (Ferreira da Silva 2007, 8).

[28] "Samba" by Paulo César Pinheiro, popularized by the singer Clara Nunes. The song lyrics criticize the idea of harmonization amongst white, Black and Indigenous people in Brazilian society.

This contraposition is deeper than it appears because, as Ferreira da Silva argues, the value assigned to Blackness is encased in a valuation indicating the nature of flesh,[29] thingness, and excess. As a consequence, racialized bodies are placed within social, economic, political, ethical, symbolic arrangements that falsely naturalize their corporeality based on inferiority. Such constructs infer the arrangement that subordinates the enslaved body under the domain and control of the masters, naturally holders of reason and superiority, fostering a "juridic arrangement capture[d] through the juridic concept of property" (Ferreira da Silva 2019, 89), determining *flesh* as the result of negativity.

This excess resonates with Pinho's mobilization of social death and anti-Blackness, yet it extends beyond these concepts. The racialized body, qualitatively inferior, is marked by deprivation, whether of social contracts, the benefits of globalization, or even the viability of its own existence—deepening social death and anti-Blackness. Therefore, the body-flesh, recognizing its inadequacy within rationality and consciousness as employed by philosophy, perceives itself as mere excess, that which is left over, without value or function, and thus as disposable. This negative excess signifies waste, authorizing its elimination without suspicion or concern. This representation of an already-authorized-premeditated death is identified by Ferreira da Silva as the establishment of an obliteration logic, describing "the trajectories of the others of Europe as a movement toward annihilation" (Ferreira da Silva 2007, 154). This is not merely a cultural difference but an acknowledgment of the epistemological/metaphysical/ethical/symbolic/juridical limits of modernity, and their lethal effects on Black populations based on the right to exercise the transparent I to kill and exterminate them. This always-already realized possibility of death is a factor of affectability in racialized bodies, which are not only exterminated but also exist in a constant state of always-living with the imminence of murder. Clearly, this proximity to annihilation is a reverberation of the construction of modern rationality, which has always been lethal to racialized bodies, such that:

> Black death is implicitly understood within the psychology of integration for everyone who is not Black. Black death functions as form of national therapy, even if the rhetoric that explains and mourns these deaths, it does not express this psychological dependence directly but rather symptomatically. It is complex, yet also simple .... I know I am human because I am not Black. I know I am not Black because when and if I

[29] This definition of flesh in Ferreira da Silva's work is influenced by the North American philosopher Hortense Spillers, particularly her classic text "Mama's Baby, Papa's Maybe" (1987), in which racial subjugation is not only essential to the development of the modern state but also functional to it.

experience the kind of violence that Black people experience there is a reason, a contingent transgression.

(Wilderson 2021, 255, trans. KB)

Furthermore, Ferreira da Silva moves beyond the authorization of extermination as a natural condition of the modern framework and applies this notion of excess to another understanding—one that uses excess as justification for racial violence, regardless of how it is enacted. This violence ultimately becomes "a figuring of excess" (Ferreira da Silva, 2013, 50), exemplified, for instance, by police forces shooting unarmed Black youths, children, or even Black men and women who, when meeting the demands of state repression, are cast into operations designed for them to kill or be killed. Here, she reintroduces her image of the wounded captive body- in the scene of subjugation to illustrate how racialization is instituted as excess-flesh. It is crucial to highlight that *excess* also takes on another dimension—one that represents the wounded captive body in the scene of subjugation through what Ferreira da Silva defines as "the descriptor for a cosmic (because unmeasurable) excess (to juridical, economic, and symbolic production)" (Ferreira da Silva 2013, 56), carrying with it the contradictions of materiality tied to modern substantiality: the female sexual body. This body embodies the sexual desire of the (female) slave as an impossible cry. This descriptor, in turn, is mapped onto a tripartite structure comprising three productive positions within the modern framework: a) the enslaved labor—framed in Brazilian society as act of redemption; b) the (female) domestic worker, the service sector worker, factory worker, and cleaning lady—who constituted the nuclear formation of the Brazilian family as always an "almost-already" family member; c) the (female) reproducer of workers.

This sexual framework is particularly significant because, as Ferreira da Silva argues in her article "*À Brasileira: Racialidade e a escrita de um desejo destrutivo*" ("The Brazilian way: Raciality and the writing of a destructive desire"), the relationship between *mestiçagem* (racial mixing), as a defining feature of Brazil's supposed racial democracy, and sexuality is intrinsic to the gendered determinations of the slave-based system. This occurs both through the historical naturalization of racial difference and its associated attributes—including the sexual attributes assigned to Black men and women, respectively—and because colonialism itself is a mode of desire control, including sexual desire. To substantiate her point, Ferreira da Silva traces the genealogy of this sexuality framework through two direct influences: sexuality in George Bataille and the connection of sexuality and miscegenation in Gilberto Freyre. From Bataille, she draws upon the dichotomy of erotic meaning, manifested in a desiring subject framed by historical and sexual contexts, what he describes as a "return to animality" (Ferreira da Silva 2006, 72) and "a return to nature without the mediation of rules that extract from it, yet also exist only as a transgression of the very rules that define humanity" (Ferreira da Silva 2006, 72). Regarding Freyre, she observes his methodological approach to *excess*, particularly in his articulation of "the erotic sites at the core of the narrative of the Brazilian subject" (Ferreira da Silva 2006, 73, trans. KB) and the sexual function of enslaved people. In this framework, the enslaved woman was positioned as the object of desire for the white man, perpetuating *mestiçagem* through rape and violence, producing "bastard" children. Meanwhile, the enslaved man functioned as a reproductive agent, generating an "industrial reserve army" of new enslaved individuals, thereby increasing the property holdings of his Master-Rapist-Father-of-the-Sold-Bastard-Children.

Ferreira da Silva explores this topic more broadly in the third section of her masterful *Toward a Global Idea of Race*, but in "*À Brasileira*" she highlights Freyre's predisposition to maintain a particular construction of the Brazilian subject through his classic claim: the assimilation of *mestiçagem* as a natural characteristic of Brazilians, framed as a learning process from the other, ultimately culminating in an acceptance of whitening tools as a principle of civility. Pragmatically, Ferreira da Silva positions Freyre's narrative as one in which racialized bodies are reduced to non-subjects, inherently incapable of driving history, development, or freedom forward. Their sole role, according to this narrative, was as reproductive vessels of *mestiçagem*, whose primary function was transmitting through whitening—regardless of whether this process was the result of violence, control, rape, or extermination. Thus producing a generation that was progressively less irrational and, consequently, more submissive to colonial effects, resulting therefore in the idea that "the only relevant contribution of Africans was the body of the slave" (Ferreira da Silva 2006, 76, trans. KB).

This logic ultimately determines a threefold configuration of Brazilian social order: a) The master of the casa grande (master's house[30]) holds an unquestionable juridical/economic position of control and power. He is the measure and reference of the social model; b) racialized bodies participate in reproducing corrective generations for the flawed colonial social model and must be subordinated to the master, both for the urgency of whitening and for the necessity of providing support—food and reproduction; c) women, both white and non-white, are naturally available to the master. Here, power and control eliminate the possibility of attraction. Sexual and servile obligation prevails over women, even if it involves exploiting a body perceived as inferior, associated with death and corruption. The master's desire for

[30] Translator's note: This is a reference to Gilberto Freyre's book *Casa Grande e Senzala* originally published in 1933 and translated as *Masters and Slaves*. The term "casa grande" means the geo-political position of the master's house and "senzala" the enslaved people's headquarters. The translation here opts to situate the meaning of the "casa grande" to respect the authors' juridical-economic critique of ownership, instead of following the translated book title, also an important dialogue established by the authors on this point.

this body exists alongside a complete disregard for its own lack of desire toward him. Thus, the establishment of this distinction regarding sexuality led to the perception that "the Portuguese man and the enslaved woman ... were the primary agents of miscegenation" (Ferreira da Silva 2006, 78, trans. KB)—even though the enslaved woman had no legal or social control over her offspring or their future. This portrayal falsely implied an equality of conditions, thereby framing the enslaved woman as a representative of active and uncontrolled sexuality. This served only to "mask the inherent violence of slavery" (Ferreira da Silva 2006, 78, trans. KB).

Ferreira da Silva and Pinho share a categorical understanding of racial subjugation through the formulation of the inferiority of the Black corporeality, reverberating in political-ethical-symbolic-juridical mechanisms of negation, a fact that reverberates the effects of racial oppression and the situation of vulnerability through the justification of violence. Their work highlights the *affectability* of racialized bodies—the congruence between fungibility and Blackness—sharing an enduring performativity for survival, in the attempt to escape the shooting and also from the logic of obliteration, searching for the continuity of life. They fundamentally oppose the idea of miscegenation as a humanitarian corrective for the so-called moral deficiencies of non-subjects. Instead, both authors carry out this reading through a contradiction to Freyre's position. In fact, what we find here is the formulation of a concern directed at the violent and bloodstained forms of socio-political control, highlighting genocidal measures against the Black population by effectively maintaining raciality as an instrument of absolute negation and obliteration.

Conclusion

What we observe is that, beyond the shared grammar, this radical Black Brazilian thought weaves a critique of modernity, constructed as a patchwork quilt composed of different fabrics and patterns, yet forming a cohesive artistic image with an undeniably consistent aesthetic. This aesthetic points toward the end of the world as the overcoming of coloniality and the persistence of racial subjugation.

This critique is at the core of Ferreira da Silva's proposition. To bring about the end of this world as a task of decolonization, Ferreira da Silva reminds us that "it is necessary the un-knowing and un-doing of the World, reaching its core" to unbind knowledge and action from a specific mode of thought, as a condition to radically distance ourselves from "a certain kind of World" (Ferreira da Silva 2014, 86). Such un-knowing and un-doing, a mode of radical praxis, thus targets modern grammar as a whole. This very praxis is what we observe in the radical Black thought produced in the territories occupied by the Brazilian nation-state. This radical distancing—or refusal—compels us to a reconsideration not only of how racial subjugation is described and explained beyond its mere exclusion from modern universality but also of the radical potential harbored by *negridade*: nothing less than the End of the World as we know it, along with the categorical determinations enforced through the (violent) subsumption of existence into the form dictated by racial and cis-patriarchal capitalism.

This point explains the absence of absorption of Ferreira da Silva's work into contemporary academic philosophy, which remains strictly tied to the structures of racial and cis-patriarchal capitalism. At the same time, it also highlights a risk, of which Ferreira da Silva appears fully aware. As de Jesus argues, the risk is that Ferreira da Silva's work may itself be "engulfed" by traditional academia, subjected to frameworks and logics that overlook the radicality of her proposal and diminish its dissolutive and transformative core.

References

Bensuasan, Hilan Nissior (2024). "Intelligence Beyond Emancipation: From the Childhood of the Machines to Assemblages of Affectability." *Cosmos and History: The Journal of Natural and Social Philosophy* 20, no. 1: 1–23.

Bretas, Aléxia (2021). "1822, 1922, 2022: Imagens dialéticas de uma contramemória brasileira." In *Dimensões do estético*, edited by C. M. Damião et al., 53–61. Goiânia: Cegraf UFG.

Bretas, Aléxia (2022). "Lendo imagens dialéticas contra a flecha do tempo: Walter Benjamin com Denise Ferreira da Silva." In B. A. Guimaraes, *Hoje, Walter Benjamin*, 10–21. Belo Horizonte: Relicário.

da Silva Bisneto, Pedro J. (2025). "A Morte e a morte de Quincas Berro d" Água: uma crítica ao cânone filosófico." *Revista Estudos Anarquistas e Decoloniais* 5, no. 8: 1–26.

de Jesus, Alexandro (2019). *Corupira: mau encontro, tradução e dívida colonial.* Recife: Titivillus.

de Jesus, Alexandro (2022). *Notas sobre a atualidade da ferida colonial.* Recife: Titivillus.

Direitoria Anpof 2023/24. (2023a). "Alguns dados para pensar currículo e excelência na área da filosofia: por uma filosofia pluriversal." https://anpof.org.br/forum/curriculo-e-excelencia-na-area-de-filosofia/alguns-dados-para-pensar-curriculo-e-excelencia-na-area-de-filosofia-por-uma-filosofia-pluriversal

Direitoria Anpof 2023/24. (2023b). "Pela ampliação da excelência: uma radiografia das bolsas de produtividade em pesquisa do CNPq." https://anpof.org.br/forum/bolsas-de-produtividade-em-pesquisa-do-cnpq/-pela-ampliacao-da-excelencia-uma-radiografia-das-bolsas-de-produtividade-em-pesquisa-do-cnpq.

Dos Santos, Antônio Bispo (2023). *A terra dá, a terra quer*. São Paulo: UBU.

Ferreira da Silva, Denise (2006). "À brasileira: racialidade e a escrita de um desejo destrutivo." *Estudos Feministas* 14, no. 1: 61–83.

Ferreira da Silva, Denise (2007). *Toward a Global Idea of Race*. Minnesota Press.
Ferreira da Silva, Denise (2009). "NO-BODIES: Law, Raciality and Violence." *Griffith Law Review* 18, no. 2: 212–36.
Ferreira da Silva, Denise (2013). "To Be Announced: Radical Praxis or Knowing (at) the Limits of Justice." *Social Text* 31, no. 1 (114): 43–62.
Ferreira da Silva, Denise (2014) "Toward a Black Feminist Poethics: The Quest(ion) of Blackness Toward the End of the World." *The Black Scholar* 44, no. 2: 81–97.
Ferreira da Silva, Denise (2016). "Fractal Thinking." aCCeSsion. https://accessions.org/article2/fractal-thinking/. Accessed March 1, 2024.
Ferreira da Silva, Denise (2017). "1 (life) ÷ 0 (blackness) = ∞ – ∞ or ∞ / ∞: On Matter Beyond the Equation of Value." *e-flux journal* 79.
Ferreira da Silva, Denise (2019). *A dívida impagável*. São Paulo.
Ferreira da Silva, Denise (2020). "Reading the Dead: A Black Feminist Poethical Reading of Global Capital." In *Otherwise Worlds: Against Settler Colonialism and Anti-Blackness*, edited by Tiffany Lethabo King, et al., 38–51. Duke University Press.
Ferreira da Silva, Denise (2024). *A dívida impagável*. Rio de Janeiro: Zahar.
Ferreira da Silva, Denise, Valentina Desideri, Georg Döcker, and Eve Katsouraki (2022). "Another Image of Existence." *Performance Philosophy* 7, no. 1: 132–45.
Ferreira Dantas, Luís Thiago (2022). "Confluências afro-pindorâmicas: por uma formação humana contra-colonialista." *Praxis educativa* 17: 1–12.
Galdino, Victor (2024). *Imagens da noite. Ensaios sobre raça e racialização*. São Paulo: GLAC.
Leal, Abigail Campos (2021). *ex/orbitâncias. Os caminhos da deserção de gênero*. São Paulo: GLAC.
Leal, Abigail Campos (2024). *A transição é uma fuga: as poéticas do infinito y o fim da ontologia*. PhD dissertation, Universidade Católica de São Paulo.
Mombaça, Jota (2021). *Ñ vão nos matar agora*. Rio de Janeiro: Cobogô.
Osman, Elzahra M. R. O. (2024). "Metafísica da raça." *Perspectiva filosófica* 51, no. 3: 23–47.
Patterson, Orlando (2008). *Escravidão e morte social. Um estudo comparativo*.. São Paulo: EDUSP.
Pinho, Osmundo (2021). *Cativeiro. Antinegritude e ancestralidade*. Salvador: Segundo Selo.
Pinho, Osmundo (2024). "*Negritudine* poética: modernismo e masculinidade." *Revista Z Cultural*. https://revistazcultural.pacc.ufrj.br/negritude-poetica-modernismo-e-masculinidade/
Spillers, Hortense (1987). "Mama's Baby, Papa's Maybe: An American Grammar Book." *Diacritics* 17, no. 2: 64–81.
Vitorino Brasileiro, Castiel (2021). *Tornar-se imensurável: o mito negro brasileiro e as estéticas macumbeiras na clínica da efemeridade*. M.A. thesis, Psicologia Clínica da Pontifícia Universidade Católica de São Paulo.
Vitorino Brasileiro, Castiel (2022). *Quando o sol aqui não mais brilhar: a falência da negritude*. São Paulo: N-1.
Wilderson, Frank B. (2021). *Afropessimismo*. São Paulo: todavia.

12

On the Impact of Denise Ferreira da Silva's Scientific Thought (Humanities, Brazil, and Elsewhere)

Alexandro Silva de Jesus.
Translated by Thuani Queiroz

Introduction (Violence as a Criterion for Projecting the Impact to Come—of the Thought of Denise Ferreira da Silva)

To attempt, now, to assess the impact of Denise Ferreira da Silva's thought on the Humanities—whether in Brazil or elsewhere—is, unquestionably, an untimely gesture. It is an inquiry that is, at once, too early and/or too late. It is too early if the investigation is driven at its core by the desire to see Ferreira da Silva's thought established within the disciplinary landscape in a way that grants it the status of a classic for the Humanities. In that case, we would have to contend with two issues or circumstances: First and foremost, the fact that the publication and translation of her works are still relatively recent[1]—that is, they lack time. Furthermore, one must bear in mind the dynamic that the Humanities in general—and Philosophy in particular—have established between thought and its tradition. That is to say, whatever novelty a given emerging thought may propose or respond to, its relation to tradition must translate either into a form of ratification (as Gilles Deleuze [1972] did with Spinoza, Proust, and Foucault) or of rectification (in the manner of Giorgio Agamben, in his reflections on the loss of experience among moderns). In either case, it is a matter of adhering to and/or preserving a certain state of affairs that tradition upholds, whether in full communion or through critique.

The operation that unfolds in *Homo Modernus* and in the unpayable debts that Ferreira da Silva envisions and theorizes suggests to me the impossibility of making her thought an integral part of the tradition of the Humanities. And if that is the case—which is assumed here as yet another hypothesis of this brief essay—then the word "impact," which orients and weaves together the various inquiries gathered in this collection, aligns more closely with her idea. For according to the analogical tradition of the Portuguese language, its meaning is established in proximity to other terms that signal, among things, their non-relation (dissociation, disconnection, or that which is forcibly imposed), the impossibility of confusion between one and the other. Precisely for this reason (for the way thought traverses or rides through Ferreira da Silva's work) it becomes necessary to consider her work as already too-late for tradition—which is to say that one day, it will stand accountable for the twilight (dissolution) of the Humanities as we know it.

Under this hypothesis, centered on the violent meaning that the idea of impact gathers in its graphic scab, what follows here is an attempt to outline a framework that demonstrates how violence founds, permeates, and organizes the Humanities—just as it, in turn, founds the ordered world itself—to project the possibilities of the reception to come for Ferreira da Silva's thought.

[1] In 2019, Ferreira da Silva published *A Dívida Impagável* through Casa do Povo—the result of her time at the Oficina de Imaginação Política (English title: *Unpayable Debt*). *Homo Modernus* was translated in 2022 by Cobogó (English title, *Toward a Global Idea of Race*), and *A Divider Impagável: Uma Crítica Feminista, Racial e Anticolonial do Capitalismo* was published by Zahar in 2024.

On the Ambivalent Relationship Between the Humanities and Violence

In a 2022 essay,[2] I draw attention to the dual articulation of violence inherent to the colonial wound with that inflicted through Western Humanities. There violence figured as at once 1) a condition upon which Western thought advances, seizes, and capitalizes; 2) as an impediment, an unavoidable obstacle to this very thought that is in solidarity with it; it is the matter that resists, that brings it to collapse, and that exposes its politics (26–28). There is no shortage of examples across the disciplines that makes both the solidarity and the embarrassment explicit, and in anthropology, it is indeed a genetic relationship. For example, in a brief text included in Claude Lévi-Strauss's *Anthropologie structurale deux*, Lévi-Strauss acknowledges the fundamental relationship between the radical asymmetry that the bad colonial encounter produced among peoples and the emergence of anthropology:

> It is the outcome of a historical process which has made the larger part of mankind subservient to the other, and during this millions of innocent human beings have had their resources plundered and their institutions and beliefs destroyed, whilst they themselves were ruthlessly killed, thrown into bondage, and contaminated by diseases they were unable to resist.
>
> (1983, 54–55)

The anthro-structuralist went further by linking violence and epistemology:

> Anthropology is daughter to this era of violence: its capacity to assess more objectively the facts pertaining to the human condition reflects, on the epistemological level, a state of affairs in which 1 part of mankind treated the other as an object.
>
> (Ibid., 55)

It should also not be forgotten that the first anthropological effort to define the concept "culture" inscribed, upon its graphic scab, its programmatic exercise of world dissolution:

> In every society, there exists the customary element, the element of habits and traditions, of the technique of adaptation to the environment; perhaps it would be possible to use a particular term for this element, culture, for

[2] Book: *Notas sobre a atualidade da ferida colonial*. Recife: Titivillus. (free translation: *Notes on the Present Relevance of the Colonial Wound*. Recife: Titivillus.)

> example ... This element completely assimilates human societies to those of lower animals, not only those close to humans in morphological type, but also to a very different type, that of invertebrates ... This element opposes progress and tends to immobilize all social forms. It is the anthropological element of every civilization, the residue of the past of society.
>
> (Lavroff apud Leclerc 1973, 28–29. Free translation of the Portuguese edition)

Indeed, there will be those who argue that this relationship between violence and anthropology, though fundamental to the advent of the discipline, was confined to only a part of its trajectory, and that the relativism it later achieved—or the perspectivism it more recently uncovered and which it, at least in part, subscribes —attest to its recognition of and political alliance with the perseverance of the Others of the West. However, arriving late—that is, when worlds were already shattering—relativism blew gently where evolutionary anthropology had once bitten, and the renewed attention to indigenous peoples that perspectivism has stirred in recent years accounts for some of their latest misfortunes. Such is the case with the circulation of images of Yanomami killed by miners and, as a result, the impossibility of carrying out communal mourning. In anthropology, everything unfolds—its theory, its methodology, and even its academic or activist practice—under the domain of violence. Its machinery is responsible for the beauty we perceive in the other, but at the cost of that beauty being the beauty of the dead, and its very affections serving as signs of a disappearance yet to come. It is what Davi Kopenawa sensed upon encountering Yanomami objects displayed in a museum in Paris: "Finally, having seen all these things in the museum, I began to wonder if the white people had also started acquiring Yanomami baskets, bows and arrows, as well as feather ornaments because we are already in the process of disappearing ourselves. Do they want to get them in anticipation of our death?" (Kopenawa and Albert 2013, 348).

Throughout almost its entire course, what was criticized in philosophy was its conceptual operation of uncovering the world. We should not dismiss this exercise. It was for a long time the fundamental element of many of the original choices that shaped the West.[3] Today, we know that it was a partial critique, since as fundamental as what philosophy uncovers is what its operation conceals and casts into shadow (see Dussel 1993). In what follows I elaborate on some of the gestures of concealing violence. Of these, Hegel's dialectic of the master and the slave has been the most pregnant and nefarious in its consequences for the ongoing racial operations in the

[3] By original choice, as Michel Foucault clarified: "I do not mean simply a speculative choice in the realm of pure ideas, but a choice that would delimit the entire set constituted by human knowledge, human activities, perception, and sensibility" (2002, 234).

world. But since the fabrication of this dialectic is thought in juxtaposition to the events that occurred around the same time as its production, in Saint-Domingue, the concealment of its worldly determination and its value as a security device—that of revolutionary violence—accumulates the conditions for its own dissolution. Ferreira da Silva's analysis in *Homo Modernus* and *Dívida Impagável* are, to me, the most consistent examples of this dismantling. For what I wish to demonstrate, it will suffice to suggest that the violence traversing Hegel's dialectic—its life-or-death struggle—neutralizes the meaning of the violence carried out by the Haitian revolution— which is anti-dialectical and, therefore, anti-recognition.

Contemporaneously, Slavoj Žižek sought to elucidate violence. Departing from analyses that only translate it in its most apparent form—"Directly visible 'subjective' violence, violence performed by a clearly identifiable agent" (2008, 1–2) as the philosopher puts it—, his operation consists of integrating this dimension with another, of an objective nature, and a bifurcated disposition or orientation: namely 1) a symbolic one, exercised in the domain of language; 2)and a systemic one, which consists, he clarifies, in "the often catastrophic consequences of the smooth functioning of our economic and political systems" (2008, 1–2). However, this elucidation was compromised by Žižek's methodological choice, insofar as he departs from a frontal analysis of violence and from a "direct confrontation" with it. The sidelong gaze leading to the direct consideration, is grounded in a certain intrinsic mystification of violence: "the overpowering horror of violent acts and empathy with the victims inexorably function as a lure which prevents us from thinking" (Žižek 2008, 4). So intransigent is this mystification—the intrinsic mystification to direct consideration stands as an inescapable condition—that I dare say Žižek's very premise advances a trap—meaning, before violence, the only fate is a certain paralysis of both body and mind—while also releasing the philosophical gesture from the symbolic exercise of violence.

Jacques Rancière (1999) thought about violence while considering the role of dissent within the political community. His perception of the state or political condition reveals the primacy of a state or condition of policing. He notes: "Politics is generally seen as the set of procedures whereby the aggregation and consent of collectivities is achieved, the organization of powers, the distribution of places and roles, and the systems for legitimizing this distribution. I propose to give this system of distribution and legitmization another name. I propose to call it the police" (1999, 28). Two passages—one of them defining and developing the state or political condition—help to outline the limit of its program:

> The paradigm of the slave war is one a purely war-generated achievement of equality between the dominated and the dominator. ... What they cannot do is transform equality in war into political freedom. This

> equality, literally mapped out over the territory and defended by force of Arms, does not create a divided Community. It cannot be transformed into the improper property of that freedom that establishes the demos simultaneously as both part of and as the Whole of the community (1999, 13). … Politics exists when the natural order of domination is interrupted by the institution of a part of those who have no part. This institution is the whole of politics as a specific form of connection. Outside of this institution there is no politics. There is only the order of domination or the disorder of revolt.
>
> (1999, 11–12)

The first limit is the assumption of something like a "natural" order in the experience of domination. I note that this assumption arises after the evaluation of the parts that make up the democratic agreement in its exercise (merchants, aristocrats, and the people)—which would imply the recognition of a historically forged order of domination. Then, the limit extends over the two states or conditions which are anthitetical to the political condition, namely the order of domination and the disorder of revolt. It is important to stress that Rancière does not mark any effective difference between these conditions of impossibility for the enactment of politics. For now, a fundamental difference suffices, regarding how domination can transmute into the form of voluntary servitude—thus avoiding the trauma of rupture and the maintenance of order—, something impossible for the disorder of revolt, which is the recourse for those whose servitude is an ad-hoc imposition. The programmatic limit is thus completed by the misunderstanding of democracy's eugenic character. On the contrary, Fabián Ludueña Romandini (2012), intervening in the contemporary debate on biopolitics, highlighted Plato's perception of biological difference as the origin and foundation of civil war and the inability to overcome this condition, which disqualifies any violence that would deliver democracy to dissolution, relying on the conviction that no communal experience could emerge after the fulfillment of a program of absolute disorder.

At a time when it still overlapped with social psychology, sociological analyses sought to exorcize or control violence, since revolutionary fervor—alongside all the original choices that supported it—was simultaneously responsible for the dissolution of the old world and the emergence of the modern world. Gustave Le Bon (2001) was among those who sounded the alarm. He saw that, for the first time in history, one of the most violent agents of historical change (the crowds) existed in a predominant yet unrestrained form, detached from its containment by the sacred double: the Monarchy and the Church. This placed democracy and its public sphere under threat of dissolution or non-realization. Faced with this premonition—and the need to exorcize it—the sociological effort would consist, after understanding the psychology of the crowds, in classifying them according to the psychological types revealed by their socio-historical manifestations.

Operating from a different perspective on who should hold dominion over the era, Gabriel Tarde (1901) envisioned a social landscape less susceptible to violence, given the emergence of public opinion, which, unlike the crowd, does not require physical gatherings to assert itself. There would then have to be a psychology of the public to be uncovered, "as a purely spiritual collectivity, as a dissemination of physically separated individuals whose cohesion is entirely mental" (Tarde 1901, 5). However, this "spiritual" nature of public opinion, far from dissolving violence, updates it through other means. This debate has had a long career in the sociological tradition.[4]

On Violence in the Black Radical Tradition

Regarding the relationship between the humanities and violence, I seek to demonstrate that a fundamental relation exists where, 1) violence is the foundation of the humanities; and 2) humanities, as an epistemological exercise itself, is an ongoing form of violence. The concealment of this fundamental relationship between the humanities and violence seems as necessary as the relationship itself, in step with its function of exorcizing "revolutionary" violence or violence which originates from the racialized. In contrast, what guides a certain black radical tradition is a hopelessness toward this ordered world—hopelessness here in its most literal sense, contrary to despair as anguish. The reason for hopelessness already indicates the differential relationship of black radicalism with violence. Its conviction regarding the fundamental role of violence in the structuring of the colonial world and the ongoing presence of its wound is presented here through reference to several influential thinkers, both contemporary writers situated in Brazil (myself, Mombaça) as well as "global" philosophers of the black radical tradition (Glissant, Fanon). As I write elsewhere:

> Against this backdrop of blood, of appropriation and expropriation of energy—but also of its expenditure, depletion, and perverse dissolution—the colonial apparatus formalized matter (the master, the slave), produced the becoming-skin (that is, it articulated the world and experience through the lens of race), and in doing so, made race into an ontological enclosure (the being-Black, the Being-white). It brought forth certain complexes (the master's house & the slave quarters / interracial relations), and set into motion diagrams and dispositifs (especially those

---

[4] For example, see Le Bon (2001); original 1896; Tarde (1901); Canetti (1984); original 1962; Ortega y Gasset (2007); Sloterdijk (2002).

> of debt, in a structuring way) that sustained the colonized subject as an expropriated subject.
>
> (de Jesus 2022, 15. Free translation of the Portuguese edition)

This violence is fundamental to the production of some of its subjects, as Glissant expresses:

> What is terrifying partakes of the abyss, three times linked to the unknown. First, the time you fell into the belly of the boat. For, in your poetic vision, a boat has no belly; a boat does not swallow up, does not devour; a boat is steered by open skies. Yet, the belly of this boat dissolves you, precipitates you into a nonworld from which you cry out. ... This boat is your womb, a matrix, and yet it expels you.
>
> (1997, 6)

As described by Mombaça, this violence is exaggeratedly without measure toward black bodies, an excess intrinsic to the production of public security:

> It is especially in the systemic control of the movement of free Africans and Afro-descendant people that the police will come to operate, as an arm of the colonial project in its modern version, ensuring the safety of the white and mixed elites and the terror of impoverished and racialized communities. Racism against Black and poor people, therefore, is in the DNA of the police and the networks of control and extermination that are articulated around them.
>
> (2021, 64. Free translation of the Portuguese edition)

Violence persists in the most everyday moments or seasonal of experiences, politically compromising even the erotic scene. Laferrière discloses:

> The great Negro of Harlem has the delirium of screwing the daughter of the owner of all the unhealthy shacks at 125 (his neighborhood), fucking her for all the repairs that her naughty father never did, fornicating with her for the horrible winter of last year that killed his younger brother of tuberculosis. And so the young white girl enjoys it too.
>
> (Laferrière 2012, 19. Free translation of the Portuguese edition)

On the indifference and/or (juridical and academic) impossibility toward the racialized of achieving remission or reparation, Rodríguez states:

> In the discursive and philosophical currents of the academic regime on genocide, the ideal subject, (potentially) endowed with rights, is almost entirely articulated through the genealogies of the white Western liberal subject, whose rational, self-determined sociality unfolds alienated from

> the conditions of acute vulnerability (physiological, cultural, spiritual, and subjective), and perpetual violence, and from the exterminatory logic of the New World and the broader Modern West.
>
> (2017, 17–18. Free translation of the Portuguese edition)

For this reason, the disobedient, anticolonial, and gendered redistribution of violence stands as unavoidable to any program aimed at overcoming this fundamental asymmetry, in whatever dimension it manifests. To return to Fanon:

> At the risk of arousing the resentment of my colored brothers, I will say that the black is not a man. There is a zone of nonbeing, an extraordinarily sterile and arid region, an utterly naked declivity where an authentic upheaval can be born. In most cases, the black man lacks the advantage of being able to accomplish this descent into a real hell.
>
> (1967, 8)

Similarly, Mombaça asks, "What kind of ethic must we develop to embrace our own violence without thereby restructuring the global design of pure violence against which we mobilize? What forms of political care must we generate to heal the wounds that violence (against us, and our own) inflicts upon ourselves?" (2021, 60). To which Fanon replies:

> National liberation, national reawakening, restoration of the nation to the people or Commonwealth, whatever the name used, whatever the latest expression, decolonization is always a violent event. At whatever level we study it—individual encounters, a change of name for a sports club, the guest list at a cocktail party, members of a police force or the board of directors of a state or private bank—decolonization is quite simply the substitution of one "species" of mankind by another. The substitution is unconditional, absolute, total, and seamless.
>
> (1963, 35)

Mobilized by violence, Ferreira da Silva's work shares this same desire expressed by the black radical tradition, of dissolving this world.

The Violent Genesis of Ferreira da Silva's Thought

Another hypothesis: If violence—what it injures, its discomfort—pressures thought to think, the black woman is ontologically the being N-1 (being-lesser, partial) destined to operate it (to pressure it, to merge with it, to dissect it, or to dissolve it). In its quality of happening thought, *Homo Modernus* [*Toward a Global Idea of Race*] is triggered by strata of violence operating its limit-experience, homicidal, from at least two orders or registers. The first order or register is factual; it operates on the black and brown *res extensa* (the order of racial subjugation), it holds scientific truth value, and forces thought to react to the horror of the experience of being dead—in a mob, group, gang, it doesn't matter. It will always be collective death even before it can be conceived. Around this event, where its decisive moment lies in its before,[5] militant gestures and the sociology of social relations (political and epistemological effects) are organized. Their different shades are sustained by the theory of socio-historical exclusion (it does not make racism the decisive and organizing element of modern experience).

The second order, dissolution, lies in the ontoepistemological register, precisely, the death of the Subject, an event from which *Homo Modernus* shifts quickly, suggesting first this Death of the Subject as a false or near-event. That is, offering his dissolution as poorly established evidence. There is also the suggestion of the irrelevance of the Subject's death, since, in its aftermath, the tools and conditions of its production persevere. The Death of the Subject is not the abolition of the original choice by history, science, and the nation—a choice that inaugurates and sustains the modern text—from which the subject is only one of its effects, one of its actualizations. In any case, accounts of his death have produced genealogies capable of mapping places of origin and points of emergence, and foretelling disappearances.

Now, it happens that, in the architecture of the text, the death of the future—laid out by a prior impossibility—and this other death, which seemingly led to the dissolution of the subject, are not, in the architecture of *Homo Modernus*, immediately connected; between them lies the Glossary with which the author operates to address the (global) problem of raciality, and about which it will be necessary to make some considerations. To begin, we must consider positionality. The Glossary's content (it does not contain all the terms with which Ferreria da Silva thinks, but only those she gave birth to in order to think), affirms Ferreira da Silva's desire to decide on the present through "her own" terms—using some already existing and forging new ones—and it gathers only the terms that the author gave birth to. My suggestion is that this novelty be taken as a path for a thought-event. This is because, situated between deaths as it is, the first operation of the Glossary is mimetic, even before our appropriation of its lexicon becomes possible. And in a way that allows thought to replicate, theatrically, the disarticulation of these two deaths [thus, the book, before speaking or

[5] The preface of *Homo Modernus* [*Global Idea of Race*]—titled "before the event"—is grounded in the economy of the enunciated epigraph that I record below: "my generation died when our parents were born."

stating the disarticulation, makes it a material experience, a physicality], to indicate, against the grain, the effort—decisive in her thought—to overcome the incommunicability between the death of the subject and the problem of racial subjugation.

But there is something else separating the two deaths: the scandal of the ontological claim of black death's is excluded from the scene of value. Although the death of the subject is theoretical—that is, a death that does not imply disappearance, but the remodeling of its formalizable matter—it is only this that counts as an event. Concrete death, the ultimate disappearance of black bodies, is the non-event that sustains the catalepsy of the modern subject. For this reason one of the fundamental gestures of *Homo Modernus* is to articulate the genealogy of the Subject—up to the limit of presuming his death—to the death and evisceration of black flesh, to uncover that raciality is what connects what has event-value (the birth and death of the Subject) to what lies outside and before it—and thus has always been disposed to inhabit the horizon of death.

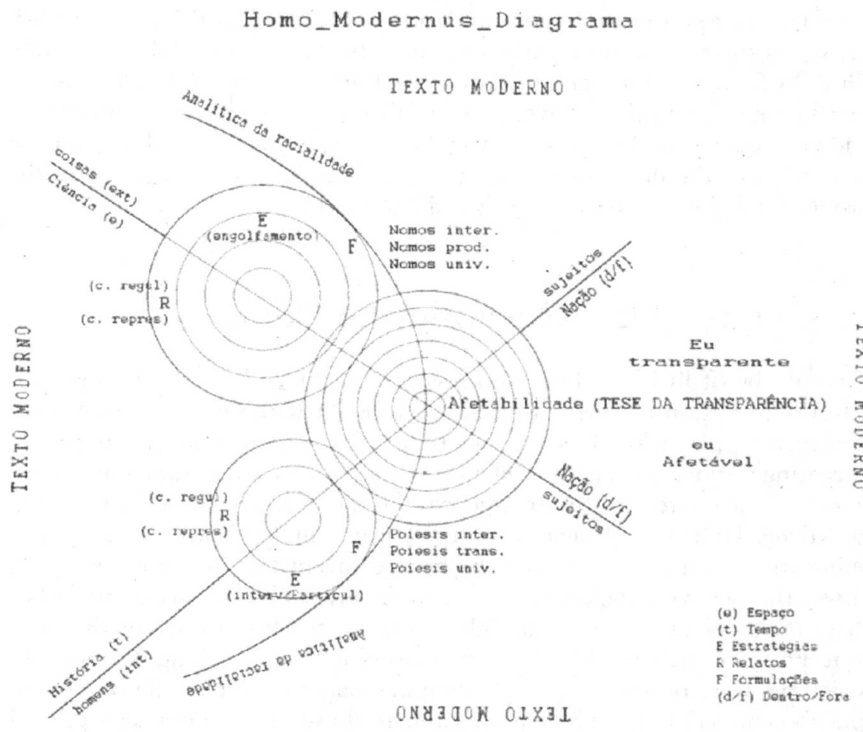

FIGURE 12.1 *Diagram of the Modern Text (*Homo Modernus*) by Alexandro Silva de Jesus.*

Certainly, much theoretical effort was required for black radical thought to reflect on the fundamental issue of the colonial bad encounter—namely: colonial persistence and the contemporaneity of its wound—with the consequences now unfolding (the shift from structural racism to global raciality). What makes Ferreira da Silva's thought one of the rare points of enunciation of this insight? *Homo Modernus* itself suggests some conditions of possibility in articulating 1) The new capture of raciality by political economy. That is, the imbuing of multiculturalism and cultural difference with the value of an ethical imperative marks the point at which the politics of recognition encounters its aporia: to include that which, ontologically excluded, sustains and gives meaning, from the outside, to the economy of politics. And it is here that theory begins to undo, and lose, its solidarities. Another condition of possibility lies 2) with prominence, or the refusal to think raciality with the same tools that forged the Subject (the sciences and the humanities) and determined its fabric (its ontological descriptors: universality and historicity). This refusal makes the thesis on socio-historical exclusion (for there lies the denial of the ontological gesture that makes black skin an abyssal surface) account for the displacement of raciality from its strategic function and foundation of (modern) politics, to establish racism as the exclusion or pathology that afflicts it and/or dulls its march. Thus, by fixing the horizon of death as the foundation of the modern text—that is, uncovering the analytics of raciality as elemental to epistemology and politics, and no longer as an accident—*Homo Modernus* allows for the projection of the death or disappearance of the humanities as part of the program for the dissolution of this ordered world.

On a Reception to Come

It would be of little or almost no use if I concluded this effort to project a future reception of Ferreira da Silva's thought without noting that there is something, in what I point out, that reflects more than a narcissistic mirroring. And once again, Deleuze (1988) offers us an opening, if we return to the context of the emergence of the theses on power, inaugurated by Michel Foucault: "When Foucault returned in 1975 with a theoretical publication, he must have been the first to invent this new conception of power that we were looking for but could neither find nor articulate" (34). I can then say that Ferreira da Silva must be the first to invent this new conception of raciality, which (some among us) were seeking. Correction: which we were on the verge of finding or imagining and in the process of (partial) enunciation. And if she was able to do so, it was because it proved decisive for thought to weave the genealogy of the Subject—not only his death: his points of origin, emergence, trajectory, and dissolution—into the death and evisceration of black flesh. Raciality is what links every event (the birth and death of the Subject) to that which lies outside and before it (to dwell always already within the horizon of death).

This has allowed Ferreira da Silva to mark the violence resulting from our bad colonial encounter as that which founds and infuses the humanities—including, as we know today, all efforts of a sociology of racial relations—and that imposes the function of guarantor of our ordered world. By holding the value of "congresses of culture," its exercise of violence operates by covering up or repressing itself, alongside its effect of damming all violence that does not monopolize it. Her critique thus becomes definitive since in one direction it collapses—which is the same as saying: it racializes—the modern text, and with it, any possibility of a politics of recognition. Ferreira da Silva's critique is definitive also because it sets the framework within which critique, henceforth, must operate. Definitive, still, in a final sense or drive: it necessarily suggests the dissolution of the humanities as one of the conditions of possibility for the undoing of the fabric of the modern text.

Hence, it is only seemingly that Ferreira da Silva gathers her thoughts within the philosophical tradition. She is certainly engaged in contemporary debates, but it is less about updating the conditions for handling the philosophical apparatus and more about assigning it a final use (unveiling the *analytics of raciality*)—somewhat akin to what Rousseau did in his *Discourse on the Sciences, Letters, and Arts*. Thinking, then, about the forthcoming reception of one whose proposition implies dissolving tradition, two possible paths for the work of Ferreira da Silva within the Humanities exist. First, its engulfing, in the same way the Haitian Revolution was engulfed by Hegel's dialectical thought. In Ferreira da Silva's terms, the "strategy of engulfing" consisted of the production of scientific concepts that explain other human conditions as variations of those found in post-Enlightenment Europe. Here, I suggest that her graphic shell bare an additional meaning, one that accounts for concepts explaining other epistemological conditions as variants of those produced by pre- and post-Enlightenment Europe. This engulfing would function as a device of rarefaction, burying the original choice found in Ferreira da Silva's thought. This fate may be sensed through the poetics of editorial disposition[6] that will cover, with each publication, her thought.

[6] An expression Frantz Fanon (1963) uses to highlight the colonial strategy of retreating from the use of physical violence while advancing through the legacy of its spiritual values: "When the colonized begin to reflect on their chains, to disturb the colonizer, they are sent good souls who, at cultural congresses, expound to them the specificity and richness of Western values. They propose solid values, explain abundantly that decolonization must not signify regression, that it is necessary to rely on tried, solid, and cited values" (179).

Diagram's vocabulary			
Portuguese	**English**	**Portuguese**	**English**
Analítica da Racialidade	analytics of raciality	Nação (d/f)	Nation (Interior/ exterior)
Coisas (ext)	things	Eu transparente	transparent I
Ciência (e)	Science (space)	Afetabilidade (TESE DA TRANSPARÊNCIA)	affectability (TRANSPARENCY THESIS)
(c.regul)	(scene of regulation)	eu Afetável	Affectable I
(c.repres)	(scene of representation)	Poiesis inter.	Interiorized poesis
(interv/ Particul)	(Intervention / Particularization)	Poiesis trans.	transcendental poesis
História (t)	History (time)	Poiesis univ.	universal poesis
homens (int)	Men (interiority)	(e)	(space)
E (engolfamento)	STRATEGIES (engulfment)	(t)	(time)
Nomos inter.	Interiorized nomos	E	Strategy
Nomos prod.	productive nomos	R	Descriptions
Nomos univ.	universal nomos	F	Formulations
Sujeitos	Subjects	(d/f) Fentro/ Fora	(i/e) Interiority/ exteriority

FIGURE 12.2 *A Table of the* Homo Modernus *Diagram's Vocabulary by Alexandro Silva de Jesus.*

The second path for Ferreira da Silva's work in the Humanities lies with its subcommons use or use by the under-commons (Moten and Harney 2024). This is a criminal and dissolute use that, from the center of the mechanism, imagines the counterforce of resistance. Here we can forge her thought as a tool for accomplishing work (fundamental) beyond work—an excess that resists being priced, and that only fulfills itself insofar as it constitutes in itself a certain refusal of work. This refusal is one of the aspects that configures the relationship of the under-commons with the university as a criminal relationship. Its use would not be tasked with conserving the university—there would be nothing in it to restore or reform—but from its underground, it would gestate the abolition of this ordered world.

References

Canetti, Elias (1984). *Crowds and Power*. Translated by Carol Stewart. New York: Farrar, Straus and Giroux.

de Jesus, Alexandro Silva (2022). *Notas sobre a atualidade da ferida colonial*. Recife: Titivillus.

Deleuze, Gilles (1972). *Proust and Signs*. New York: G. Braziller.

Deleuze, Gilles (1988). *Foucault*. Translated by Seán Hand. Minneapolis: University of Minnesota Press.

Dussel, Enrique (1993). "Eurocentrism and Modernity (Introduction to the Frankfurt Lectures)." *boundary* 2 20, no. 3: 65–76.

Fanon, Frantz (1963). *The Wretched of the Earth*. New York: Grove Press.

Fanon, Frantz (1967). *Black Skin, White Masks*. Translated by Charles Lam Markmann. New York: Grove Press.

Ferreira da Silva, Denise (2022). *Homo Modernus: para uma ideia global de raça*. Rio de Janeiro: Cobogó.

Ferreira da Silva, Denise (2024). *A dívida impagável: Uma crítica feminista, racial e anticolonial do capitalismo*. Rio de Janeiro: Zahar.

Foucault, Michel (2002). *The Archaeology of Knowledge*. Translated by A. M. Sheridan Smith. London: Routledge.

Glissant, Edouard (1997). *Poetics of Relation*. Ann Arbor: University of Michigan

Kopenawa, Davi and Bruce Albert (2013). *The Falling Sky: Words of a Yanomami shaman*. Cambridge: Harvard University Press.

Laferrière, Dany (2012). *Como fazer amor com um negro sem se cansar*. São Paulo: Editora 34.

Le Bon, Gustave (2001). *The Crown: A Study of the Popular Mind*. Kitchener: Batoche Books.

Leclerc, Gérard (1973). *Crítica da antropologia*. Lisboa: Editorial Estampa.

Lévi-Strauss, Claude (1983). *Structural Anthropology. Volume 2*. Translated by Monique Layton. Chicago: University of Chicago Press.

Mombaça, Jota (2021). *Não vão nos matar agora*. Rio de Janeiro: Cobogó.

Moten, Fred and Stefano Harney (2024). *Sobcomuns: planejamento furtivo e estudo negro*. São Paulo: Ubu editora.

Ortega y Gasset, José (2007). *A rebelião das massas*. São Paulo: Martins Fontes.

Rancière, Jacques (1971). *Sobre a teoria da ideologia: a política em Althusser*. Barcelos: Portucalense Editora.

Rancière, Jacques (1999). *Disagreement: Politics and philosophy*. Minnesota: University of Minnesota Press.

Rodríguez, Dylan (2009). *Suspended Apocalypse White Supremacy, Genocide, and the Filipino Condition*. Minnesota: University of Minnesota Press.

Romandini, Fabián Ludueña (2012). *A comunidade dos espectros, 1. Antropotecnia*. Florianópolis: Cultura e Barbárie.

Sloterdijk, Peter (2002). *O desprezo das massas: ensaio sobre lutas culturais na sociedade moderna*. São Paulo: Estação Liberdade.

Tarde, Gabriel (1901). *Opinion and the Crowd*. Translated by T. Newbigging. London: Kegan Paul, Trench, Trübner.

Žižek, Slavoj (2008). *Violence: Six Sideways Reflections*. New York: Picador.

13

Shine: On Hegel, Marx, and the Non-appearance of Blackness in Denise Ferreira da Silva's Raw Materialism

Sara-Maria Sorentino

In Denise Ferreira da Silva's writing, conceptual thought undergoes a transformation. Reckoning with the grammar through which the "modern text" writes its racial subjects into existence, Ferreira da Silva stretches old concepts, devises new neologisms, and experiments at the edges of what it is possible to think. By inventing "poethical tools," drawing from mathematics to the visual arts, her work assiduously decomposes and recomposes the relationship between race and world, blackness and its forms of appearance. In 2017, interfacing with the work of Nigerian artist Otobong Nkanga, Ferreira da Silva added a new concept-tool to her lexicon: "blacklight," which reappears under and is disseminated through the transitive verb "to make shine." As Ferreira da Silva writes this "black feminist reading device," blacklight is activated for the purposes of searching over that which is "already known" (2017a, 245). This searching is necessitated by the fact that racial violence is simultaneously obvious and opaque. When roaming over the "primal scene of capital" (2022, 229), blacklight "de-emphasizes" Marxist bread and butter concepts like "value," which determines which labor counts, in order to make "luminous" the inseparability of "raw material" and the commodities they compose (2017a, 248).

Insofar as Ferreira da Silva's blacklight activates the Marxist idiom, there is an obvious interpretative asymmetry. Marxists can take her decompositions and return them to Marx's "laboratory," where they can be recomposed internal to a well-established, if internally fraught, series of philosophical questions concerning historical method and political practice. But when Ferreira da Silva's tools are wielded to communicate what is already seen (spectacles of violence) but can never be consolidated ontologically or epistemologically (what David Marriott calls the "*n'est pas*" (2023, 77), they produce a kind of shadow critique opaque to, and in excess of, Marxist methods. This chapter gives space to the shadow emergent in Ferreira da Silva's use of "shine," as it illuminates both the different valences of "appearance" in German Idealism and Ferreira da Silva's critical project. By attending to Ferreira da Silva's conversion of the problem of appearance into that of *non*-appearance (carrying with it competing conceptions of plenitude and negativity), we will be poised to better appreciate how her "strategically naïve" (2022, 200) presentation of Marxism simultaneously enables "blacklight" to figure the outline of blackness and the problem of slavery. Ferreira da Silva's strategic misreading of Marx shines a spotlight on the non-appearance of the slave, despite slavery's ubiquity in Marx's texts, and moves through and beyond her earlier theorization of "affectability" (2007) to relay a truth about blackness—a "negativation" (Ferreira da Silva 2022, 55) that, alongside infinity, refuses the subsumption of non-being and, in so doing, profoundly complicates critical thought.

Capital's Appearance

The German "*schein*," central to Hegel and Marx's speculative and critical inquiry, gets translated variously as "semblance, seeming, show, shine, guise, mere appearance, surface appearance, illusion, illusory being, etc." (Abazari 2020, 16 n. 2; Yeomans 2012, 47 n. 10). George di Giovanni's 2010 translation of the 1832 edition of *The Science of Logic* opts for "shine" (lxxii), deliberately engaging light as a metaphor, a choice Robert Pippin believes "takes on as many problems as it avoids" (2018, 230 n. 25).[1] While Hegel's own wrestling with *schein* does deploy light as metaphor, shine more properly names a sort of appearance that is less false than it is "one-sided" ([1832] 2010, 512). Shine appears at the moment that the logic of being—guided by being's immediacy, equality, and independence—gives way to the relational and hierarchical categories of essence. From the backwards looking

[1] But see Hegel effectively using light as a metaphor: "Just as the light of nature is not a something, nor is it a thing, but its being is rather only its shining, so manifestation is self-identical absolute actuality" ([1832] 2010, 489).

standpoint of essence, the stark separability and immediacy of being is an illusion ([1832] 2010, 342). This gathering of reflection does not, however, necessarily reveal a truer reality beyond shadows and caves, nor does it insinuate phenomena forever cast off from noumena. For while essence, as Hegel writes, "must appear" ([1832] 2010, 418), it is essence's own non-coincidence with its appearance that both gives it its dynamic character and sets critical inquiry in motion.[2] At the same time, shine is not falsely opposed to essence, as with surfaces obscuring hidden depths, such that speculative reason uncovers the true of essence below false appearances (i.e., "false consciousness"). Instead of a process of unveiling, Hegel's "task is to demonstrate that the determinations which distinguish [shine] from essence are the determinations of essence itself" ([1832] 2010, 343). Thought, in thinking itself, provides the determinants for apprehending more concrete appearance, actuality as such.

Hegel's shine finds its structural fulfillment in Marx's investigation of ideology (Abazari 2020, 15–43). For what better way to apprehend the meaning of shine than to turn to those beliefs that are both false *and* "socially intuitive and plausible" (Pepperell 2010, 193)? In the shine composed through capitalist critique, commodities appear on the marketplace alienated from the labor they crystallize. And yet, Marx writes, their distorted form of appearance nonetheless expresses a certain truth. Take the famous formula of commodity fetishism: "To the producers ... the social relations between their private labours appear [*erscheinen*] as what they are, i.e. they do not appear as direct social relations between persons in their work, but rather as material relations between persons and social relations between things" (Marx [1867] 1976, 165–66).[3] In this topsy-turvy world, social relations between things don't simply veil material relations between persons; rather, capital's inverted forms express a contradictory unity of appearance and essence (Reichelt 2005). Commodities really do take on social lives of their own, while producers really are atomized from themselves, their fellow laborers, and the objects they produce. Likewise, at the same time that capitalism compels new forms of unfreedom and inequality (familiar enough from the Marxist vantage) capitalism also makes available new forms of freedom and equality—the freedom to sell one's labor on the market for

---

[2] Indeed, writes Marx, "all science would be superfluous if the form of appearance of things directly coincided with their essence" ([1894] 1981, 956).

[3] On the difficulty of translating "*erscheinen*" in Marx, see Hanzel's instructive remarks: "While the noun '*Erscheinung*' corresponds to the verb '*erscheinen*', and the noun '*Schein*' to the verb '*scheinen*', the latter verb is used primarily in the common-sense meaning of, for example, '*Es scheint, als ob* ... ', that is, 'It seems as if ... '. Marx, at least in my view, therefore used not only the verb '*scheinen*', but also sometimes the term '*erscheinen*' in order to give an epistemological characterisation of the knowledge attained at the level of appearances and given in everyday consciousness; in this case the translation should be 'to appear'" (2014, 226).

a contract premised on equality in exchange. These one-sided freedoms, recomposed, supply the material, for Marx, for many-sided revolutionary freedoms.

In this way capital unleashes an "ambivalent regime of possibilities": "the actualization of labour in the service of capital" and the simultaneous "deactualization of the worker" (Zambrana 2018, 88). Historically and politically, however, interpretations almost exclusively emphasize Marx's deactualizing critique of objectification. Any reader of Marx can identify how, "In ordinary awareness [*Vorstellung*], individuals are freer under the dominance of the capitalists than before, because their conditions of life are contingent; in actuality, of course, they are less free, because they are to a greater extent governed by objective coercion [*sachliche Gewalt*]" (Marx [1867] 1976, 719). But fewer attend to how Marx's Hegelian methods ground the actuality of this unfreedom in the distinct form of freedom and equality thrown up by capitalism.[4]

In Marx's complex Hegelian staging of capital's many guises, the immediate force of characteristics of slavery means the slave does not become a "*dramatis personae*" (Marx [1867] 1976, 280).[5] Understanding the mediations of capitalism through Hegel's doctrine of essence has the effect of cordoning off non- and pre-capitalist social relations to being's realm of immediacy. The slave, in this arrangement, becomes unable to contribute meaningfully, theoretically or otherwise, to the project of freedom and the movement of the concept. Until converted into a seller of labor-time, the figure that Ferreira da Silva calls the "*wounded captive body in the scene of subjugation*" has, she writes, "no place in the plot" (2022, 277).[6] Despite the slave appearing, as James Ford III has noted, "in nearly every chapter of *Capital*" (2011, 22), these appearances do not, from Marx's perspective, constitute *schein*, though it is possible the Hegelian framework may be stretched to reconstruct the slave thusly. Following Ferreira da Silva's own methodology of "refusal," her "refusal to engage, to maintain thinking within the limits of the very distinction between matter and form, which cannot but request the onto-epistemological pillars of modern thought in order to assemble its grounds" (2020, 42), in this section, I mimic and in the

[4] Writes Marx, "Equality and freedom are thus not only respected in exchange based on exchange values but, also, the exchange of exchange values is the productive, real basis of all equality and freedom. As pure ideas, they are merely the idealized expressions of this basis; as developed in juridical, political, social relations, *they are merely this basis to a higher power*" ([1939] 1973, 245, original emphasis).

[5] On how the problem of force (slavery) and form (capitalism) informs Marx's incomprehension of slavery, see Sorentino (2019).

[6] This phrase is inspired from her piercing use of Hortense Spillers's reading of "flesh" as a "praxis and a theory, a text for living and dying" (2022, 25–39), Saidiya Hartman's theorization of "fungibility" (2022, 96–99), as well as, more obliquely, Gayatri Spivak's "native informant" (2022, 26 n. 5).

next refuse an incorporative move that would bring the slave into the light of dialectical criticism.[7]

First, the possibility of reconstruction. Although Hegel's *Phenomenology* and *Lectures on the Philosophy of History* are centralized across Ferreira da Silva's critical body of work (see 2007, 69–90; 2022, 40–43), the *Logic* can in many ways provide a useful lens through which to grasp the movement of her thought. Like Hegel and Marx, Ferreira da Silva deciphers how the social determinants of concepts participate in their own contradictory reality-making—the relationship between the "onto-epistemological pillars (separability, determinacy, and sequentiality)" of modern thought (2022, 58) and "analytics of raciality" (2007). Not related to onto-epistemological pillars as mere scaffolding, race expresses a particular way of seeing (a "political-symbolic tool") that hasn't yet caught up to the problems it produces. In excavating the "logical circuity" of the "racial dialectic" (2022, 66), Ferreira da Silva ends up sounding a good deal like Hegel, for whom the gap between concepts and world participates in the movement of the world. This gap then conditions Ferreira da Silva's blacklight to trace over "correspondences that expose how the juridical and economic architectures of colonial/racial violence enter into the very construction of the analytical tools available to critiques of global capital" (2017a, 245). And, like Marx, for whom "vulgar economics" gets trapped in its own hall of mirrors, doing "nothing more than interpret, systematize and turn into apologetics the notions of agents trapped within bourgeois relations of production" ([1894] 1981, 956), Ferreira da Silva targets "the leading account of racial subjection" (in her parlance "the sociohistorical logic of exclusion") for how it "merely describes how the racial, along with other social-historical categories, produces exclusion without really explaining how or why it does so" (2007, xxiv). The analytics of raciality are, in this sense, determinative: they produce what they posit and posit what they produce.

Yet it is precisely on the question of determinacy that Ferreira da Silva, in her only direct address to Hegel's *Logic*, tasks Marx with the "most intractable aspect of determinative knowledge," that which, in her writing, "demands that concepts and categories neatly and flawlessly comprehend, that is, determine the diverse aspects, of datum or the empiricum manifold they were deployed to comprehend" (2022, 183).[8] Hegel would likely disagree with being purposed for such an un-dialectical demand, as would Marx. Ferreira da Silva's corresponding footnote (2022, 183 n. 27), quoting

---

[7] See also her thinking through Fred Moten's "common refusal" (2022, 50–56). In another work, I have opened a different corridor: the "immanent critique of immanent critique" (Sorentino 2024).

[8] Ferreira da Silva does cite the *Logic* elsewhere (2015, 35 and 2017b), in order to describe the development of world history, but leaves the connections between historical development and Hegelian necessity so implicit as for the *Logic*'s inclusion to be irrelevant.

from the "Preface to the Second Edition" of the *Logic*, cites Hegel's interest in "the thought determinations that instinctively and unconsciously pervade our spirit everywhere—and remain non-objectified and unnoticed even when they enter language" ([1832] 2010, 19). But moving, as Hegel does, to a "reconstruction of those determinations which reflection has already abstracted and fixed as subjective forms external to a material content" ([1832] 2010, 19) means, *pace* Ferreira da Silva's reading, that concepts do not demand a neat and flawless comprehension of the empirical world. Rather, a case can be made that Hegel's logic discloses how reflection *retrospectively* grasps forms of common sense, contingency, and contradiction *as part of its own actualization.*[9] Indeed, for some Hegelians, it is through effecting a "tightness of fit" between concepts and the world, the possible and actual, that we can point "to the fact that other tight fits are available" (Yeomans 2012, 157; Zambrana 2018, 86). The external world doesn't simply submit to the march of the concept; the concept finds itself in the world as part of the transformation of the world itself. Reflection then confirms which possibilities have been actualized and which have been deactualized, in turn confirming the contingency of essence as concretized in the appearances of any actual moment, especially the present.

This reading of Hegel (also extending to Marx's "human anatomy contains a key to the anatomy of the ape" (Marx [1939] 1973, 105) undermines any strict developmentalism, but the question as to whether a "radical, negative, nonteleological, 'left' Hegel" (Terada 2023, 21) would actually target the problem of race remains at large in academia. Ferreira da Silva's answer is pessimistic. Historical materialism's commitment to "exteriority"—the space-time extension that makes us affectable beings—smuggles in what she earlier calls the "transparency thesis, the ontological assumption that writes self-consciousness as a self-determined thing" (2007, 190; 2022, 225). "Because man neither is nor exists without his body," she writes, "exteriority would remain a ghost haunting every later refashioning of self-consciousness" (2007, 44).[10] This ghost takes the form of an "affectable other" in the body of race, the remnant of a stage of exteriority that cannot be banished.

But if capitalism's mystifying standpoint involves a gap between concept and world, then does a forward-looking social logic, in which "the full and

[9] Hegel: "Reflection, in positing, immediately sublates its positing, and so it has an *immediate presupposition*. It therefore *finds* this presupposition before it as something from which it starts, and from which it only makes its way back into itself, negating it as its negative. But that this presupposition is a negative or a positedness is not its concern" ([1832] 2010, 349, original emphasis).

[10] For the outline of a theorization Ferreria da Silva might call a "radical gesture that would turn modern representation on its head ... a social ontology premised on globality (exteriority-spatiality)" (2007, 190), see Garba (2023).

free development of every individual forms the ruling principle" (Marx [1867] 1976, 739), require their unification? While the transparency thesis seems to represent the actualization of being over the threat of non-being, there exist versions of the dialectic configured around the continued persistence of non-being and distortions effected by a non-recuperable negativity (Žižek 1993, 125–64). If Ferreira da Silva misses this retroactive twist to the dialectic, then is her critique of the analytics of raciality in Hegel-Marx unfounded?[11] In the next section, I will investigate how Ferreira da Silva's activation of blacklight takes her to new terrain, making shine the indeterminacy between infinity and negativity.

Raw Materialism

In many of the deeper registers of Ferreira da Silva's thought, the shine of self-determinacy involves actuality. When understanding the social universe (the "modern text" (2007) that makes such human ascendence plausible, self-determination can be considered ideological in the Marxist-Hegelian sense of *shine*—not as false consciousness but as one-sided revelation. The self-determined I would not simply be *at the cost of* the affectable other (false consciousness); the affectable other would be a necessary product of the self-determined I, one whose disavowal at the same time conditions the illusion of the self-determined I and forms the actual barrier to its realization. The impossibility of transcendence then propels this I into newer and newer registers—in Sylvia Wynter's reading, from a theocentric *homo religiousus* to Man$_1$ (*homo politicus*) to Man$_2$ (*homo oeconomicus*) (Wynter 2014, 35; Ferreira da Silva 2014a, 92–96). When, in *Unpayable Debt*, Ferreira da Silva returns to transparency "in the guise of the ethical and the economic subject" (2022, 24), we might read the economic subject's "guise" as a translation for *schein* and involving some substantial bearing in the world.[12] We could through this partial truth interpret Ferreira da Silva's engagement with labor as a "*conceptum*," an "economic category that captures both modern bourgeois society as a specific historical moment and unity (the arrangement or order of relations) and the specific operations

[11] See, for an affirmative response, Best's rejoinder to *Unpayable Debt* that "it's not that Marx-as-theorist effaces the violence of value-forms. Marx's point, rather, is that capital *is* the process of this effacement" (2023, 262).

[12] I focus on the "economic," but Ferreira da Silva's reading of the slave at the intersection of Human and Thing exposes an "in/distinction" (2022, 56) between the economic and ethical, insofar as the slave figures as an "object without the ethical (because partly Thing) and economic (because not a productive Human)" (60).

of the other economic categories under the capitalist mode of production" (2022, 196). In materialist fashion, it would be through the "conceptum" of the economic subject that one retroactively confirms the movement of a more generic self-determination to begin with.

This sublation of historical materialism is not, however, the direction Ferreira da Silva's refusal takes.

Ferreira da Silva rejects the above approach because it renders the slave "comprehensible by the same conceptum that constitutes the subject within the totality from which she would have been excluded" (2022, 284). Against (and alongside) what she calls "interpretative" and "determinative" readings, which correspond loosely to liberal and Marxist vantages, Ferreira da Silva offers a "delimitative" critique, tracking how given descriptive statements function to "distinguish between what falls under a particular concept (as opposed to that which is determined by a given category) and what does not fit under (negative) and exceeds (infinite) it (which is not the same as what contradicts it, its negation)" (2022, 211). Her refusal of sublation has reverberating effects on thought: while interpretative (liberal) and determinative (Marxist) readings, tethered to the dialectic of appearance/essence, can register the various forms of slavery's *dis/appearance* under capitalism, delimitation's refusal to stay within a given onto-epistemological framework also toggles the slave's *non-appearance*, where the "particle *non*" refers to "the quality of what is unknowable" (2022, 291). As another name for a delimitative reading, blacklight, as we will see, makes shine the non-recuperable excess and negativity that supports affectability.

Ferreira da Silva illustrates limitations of interpretative and determinative readings through a quotation from *Capital*: "All [the slave's] labour appears as unpaid labour. In wage-labour, on the contrary, even surplus labour, or unpaid labour, appears as paid. In the one case, the property-relation conceals the slave's labour for himself; in the other case, the money-relation conceals the uncompensated labour of the wage-labourer" (Marx [1867] 1976, 680; Ferreira da Silva 2022, 190, 211, 232). Here slavery forms the negative basis for what Marx considers of "decisive importance": "the form of appearance" of the wage ([1867] 1976: 680). At least one prong of this argument should strike contemporary readers as misguided. Eighty years downstream of Eric William's *Capitalism & Slavery*, this descriptive distinction is both lacking common sense, for of course slaves contribute to wealth creation, and seems distinctly un-Hegelian, dispersing any interest in how slavery itself actualizes as a concept. Unfolding under the banners of racial capitalism and Black Marxism, the interpretative response is content with either reporting the disappearance of slavery, or making slavery's productivity reappear, neither challenging Marx nor contributing theoretically beyond descriptions of slavery as production through brute force (Ferreira da Silva 2022, 169–82).

To move beyond this dead-end, a Marxist determinative reading would have to reconstruct how the bad fit between labor and slavery, a conjunction that conditions slavery's incomprehensibility, is socially plausible in some manner. In *The Price of Slavery*, Nick Nesbitt lambasts interpretative approaches that substantialize labor and wealth without attending to their forms of appearance (2022, 13–61). Taking into account Marx's *schein* means, in Nesbitt's reformulation of the problem of the unpaid, that "in the case of slave labor, unlike wage labor, which appears to be paid in full, it is ironically the very visibility of the violently extracted, unpaid labor that hides the impossibility of the commodity's producing surplus value" (2022, 93). Here, slavery is disappeared not, as we will see with Ferreira da Silva, because the truth of slavery's production is disavowed. In Nesbitt's reading, the reverse is true: slaves cannot produce value directly because their labor is not bound by a wage and thus cannot appear in monetary form. Unable to increase relative surplus value, slavery's actual subsumption by the wage hastens slavery's conceptual irrelevance. In fact, in Marx's journalistic mode, slavery's continued persistence is important precisely as false consciousness: because the very self-evidentiary nature of the slave's violation is thought to obscure the more "suprasensible" (Hegel [1832] 2010, 444; Marx [1867] 1976, 165) problem of value, Marx believes (formal) abolition would help workers clarify the nature of their own exploitation—the disappearance of obvious violence would mean those "in white skins" could finally see their own exploitation.[13] Of course, this does very little to describe racial slavery's conceptual life, which in Marx's hands either remains in the realm of the descriptive or becomes a generic referent for past modes of production (the ancient world and feudalism) that disavows racialized conditions for the abstraction of slavery to begin with.

To fully appreciate the delimitative reading's foundational account of this disavowal, we follow Ferreira da Silva's tracking of infinity (that which exceeds a given category) through raw material and the *plenum*, in the next section, relaying blacklight's "negative" (that which falls out—not negation, which would be that which contradicts). On the side of excess is the "creative (*material*) capacity" Ferreira da Silva retains from the historical materialist text (2022, 235), signifying the continued importance of affectability in her work. For Marx, this creative material—the transcendent category of species-being—can only be realized as a generic possibility that has been thwarted *because* of the specific operations of capital (one-sided freedoms and so on).

[13] For a critique of Marx's version of abolitionism, see Sorentino (2019, 27–34).

Rather than seeing labor as a power, for Ferreira da Silva, labor is the transference of raw energy, meaning the distinctions governing raw material, instruments of production, and labor do not hold (Ferreira da Silva 2022, 249). Though arguing that "Marx's equation disappears the creative capacity of 'slave labor' and 'the colonies' into/as raw material" (Ferreira da Silva 2022, 238), and that raw material disappears into commodities (cotton vanishes into yarn, tobacco into cigarettes, etc.), she does not then seek to differentiate the slave from cotton, further humanizing the enslaved as "person." Instead, Ferreira da Silva's "raw-materialist approach" (2022, 263) tracks cotton in the "same position and performance" (2022, 287) as blackness, not only rendering indeterminate the juridical difference between slave labor and wage labor but also incorporating an indistinction inclusive of the wider universe, the quantum "*elementa*" comprising solid, liquid, gas, and plasma (2022, 248; 261–62; 292).

But does rejecting the "conceptum"—the fact that "labor," as an "immeasurably ancient relation valid in all forms of society, nevertheless achieves practical truth as an abstraction only as a category of the most modern society" (Marx [1939] 1973, 105)—in favor of the "elementa" not mean "exteriority" has become internalized as a new transparent principle? Does Ferreira da Silva's raw materialism not accord creative activity a horizon of transcendence that repeats the gestures she critiques in historical materialism? By desiring release from the grip of capital, we seem to be losing sight of what Marx's dialectic *does* reveal—how equality and freedom emerge from capitalism's history of separability, and how self-determination becomes real through its figuration—along the way missing ongoing determinants of violence.

These questions intensify in Ferreira da Silva's uptake of an interlocuter she shares with Hegel: Gottfried Wilhelm Leibniz. When Ferreira da Silva draws from Leibniz's *plenum*, quoting, "For everything is a plenum, which makes all matter interconnected" (Leibniz [1714] 1989, 221; Ferreira da Silva 2020, 41), she hopes to dissolve modern pillars ("separability, determinacy, and sequentiality") by returning us to ways of relating that have always been available: "existents and events considered not as separate entities but as deeply implicated *pars*, as elementa, as singular compositions, would regain their orientation toward the infinitum" (2022, 264). But in returning to the *plenum*, Ferreira da Silva seems to mire us in an even more ahistorical, non-critical view of the universe—the same sort of dogma that Hegel was at pains to dispel by dialecticizing the divide between appearance and essence (Ingram 1985, 434; Pippin 2018, 219). For in Leibniz's Platonic theology, the universe is composed of monads, simple substances that then create aggregates we would recognize, ranging from atoms to rocks to humans. While the aggregate appears only ephemerally, the monad is actual and eternal, coming into being as a reflection of God's perfection, this world being the most perfect of all possible worlds.[14] As Hegel writes, disparagingly, "The Leibnizian *monad* develops its representations from itself but is not their generating and controlling force; they rise up in it as a froth, indifferent, immediately present to each other and to the monad as well" ([1832] 2010, 334). Because monads are limited—reflecting God but not divine themselves—Leibniz considers their perceptions "confused" ([1714] 1989, 219) and distorted along a perceptual spectrum, with humans having more reflective capabilities than animals and so forth. What results is a "monadic hierarchy" (Jolley 2017, 121) in which some monads generate better and more perfect assemblages. And because perfection also means the most possible variation and order among monads (Leibniz [1714] 1989, 220), there can be no void, as any vacuum would be filled with more and more infinitely indivisible substance. The *plenum*'s built-in "metaphysical optimism" (Costreie 2011, 216) not only involves a dogmatic theory of essence that both disavows the void and makes of appearance something insubstantial (including death (Leibniz [1714] 1989, 223), its perfectability is intimately connected to Leibniz's theodicy, and ultimately unresponsive to suffering. Why, then, would Ferreira da Silva turn to the *plenum*, with all its baggage? In my reading, it is because blacklight can illuminate new registers to infinity *by also* taking up negativity.

Slavery's Non-appearance

Because raw materials, for Ferreira da Silva, *really are* productive of surplus value, the conceptum that makes them appear "unproductive" seems more akin to false consciousness than Marxist-Hegelian *shein*, a "blind spot ... inscribed in the *symbolic* (social-scientific) assembling of Capital as a totality" (2022, 170). But if the disappearance of slavery has any real weight—if it signals its own violence—then labor's appearance also has to have real effects. The shine of labor (an appearance constituting essence) corresponds in some fashion to the shine of the slave (a non-appearance that manifests as disappearance, reappearance, and opacity). The energy of the slave transfers latent potential, "the infinite self-energy of the elementary particles that compose their bodies," into "excess" for the slave owner at the same time that this excess accrues what Ferreira da Silva calls "*negative* accumulation" to the body of the slave (2022, 250).

The negative in negative accumulation is not negation. The total violence accumulated "(x)" corresponds to a "(-)" productive capacity constitutive of

[14] Leibniz: "Thus there is nothing fallow, sterile, or dead in the universe, no chaos and no confusion except in appearance" ([1714] 1989, 222).

blackness (2022, 250). As (x), negative accumulation does not (only) work to register the disappearance of existing entities, as in the genocidal "case of Indigenous Americans," through the theft of land and appropriation of the means of production. Rather, Ferreira da Silva writes, the impossibility of imagining an industrial revolution without slaves meant blackness comes to register an "incapacity to comprehend or enact the principles and procedures that distinguish the modern ethical and scientific program" (2022, 53). In this sense, the slave's non-appearance shines through the analytics of raciality and the various compositions of the racial body. In short, "the Negro is not presented as *negation* (having attributes that compete with and threaten white persons) but as the *negative*, that is, a Human existent, a person who lacks what is specific (*unique*) to the white person (the Owner, trader, or overseer)" (2022, 148). This negative gets filled in in a variety of ways, from racial science to the sociology of race. In promising to link skin color and moral attributes, the upper-case "Category of Blackness" (2022, 37–38) expresses a kind of closed circuit, where the negative, appearing as negation, becomes both cause and effect of its own violation. In such deranged fixity, every new discovery of the problem, every new interpretative and determinative reading, condemns the problem of blackness further.[15] What I am identifying as non-appearance targets how the unknowable link between the appearance of race (Blackness) and its "essence" (blackness) necessitates violence to confirm its presuppositions. As Ferreira da Silva writes, "the Category of Blackness is revealed in racial violence, which exposes it as a referent 'The Thing'" (2014b, 90).

Already, this reading of the negative clarifies some elements of Ferreira da Silva's use of the *plenum*. In his unpublished remarks, Andrew Santana Kaplan (2023) detects a "tacit desire for redemption" in Ferreira da Silva's "likely unwanted affiliation" with Leibniz's theodicy. Ferreira da Silva's account of energy, as exceeding determinants that separate things into space and time, value and raw material, does share a good deal with what has been called "Black optimism," but given the reading of negative above, this optimism is less metaphysically optimistic than it is ambivalent and indeterminant, and increasingly so. In *Toward a Global Idea of Race*, Ferreira da Silva recognizes the ways Leibniz disavows "outward determination" in favor of a self-determining/transparent account of the monad's "interior (exclusive) force" (2007, 57). In an endnote that sets the stage for her recuperation of the *plenum* a decade later, however, she is more admiring of the "boundless

[15] See one of Ferreira da Silva's more reflexive passages: "it is impossible to avoid the problem of staying with total violence without reproducing its effects, which results from how the tools of raciality (and the inherently perverse dialectic they set up) fail to comprehend as political the refusal to comply to the logic of obliteration" (2022, 77).

creative force" (2007, 284 n. 10) that emerges from Leibniz's themes of contingency and infinity. In returning to the *plenum* in 2017, excess is now paired with the negative as a "referent of undeterminacy," one that hails "blackness's capacity to release the imagination from the grips of the subject and its forms" (2017b), but without necessarily setting the stage for any movement that follows.

It is not incidental that Ferreira da Silva's appreciation of the *plenum* comes hand-in-hand with her registration of blacklight. When first introduced, blacklight is speculated to be no "more than a trick, an analytical ruse," one that can offer important new imaginative incursions but, she continues, "does not need to be much more" (2017a, 251). In another piece published the same year, blacklight opens up beyond mere heuristic; because it "works *through* that which it makes shine," blacklight's "ultraviolet radiation" gains objective force and "has the capacity to transform at the DNA level, that is, it reprograms the code in the living thing exposed to it, and causes mayhem in their self-reproductive capacity at the cellular level" (2017b). This concept-tool continues to transform the more it becomes entangled with *Unpayable Debt*'s (non)protagonist: "the *wounded captive body in the scene of subjugation*." Shining from within her own position—a position not reducible to the forms of othering and abjection of a white logic—the *wounded captive body* returns "the total violence (the overseer's and the whip's potential energy transduced into wounds)" done to her at every conceivable scale and register and overwhelms Marx's delimitation of capital (2022, 284). Following the "*what* (elements) and *how* (arranging) of its configuration," the wounded captive body becomes her own monad (2022, 96).

This captive body cannot rise to the status of black subjectivity which, as Ferreira da Silva's reading of scenes of subjugation makes clear, "is not retrievable from historical records of enactments of slavery's scenes of total violence" (2022, 144). Rather than closing off suffering, as with Leibniz, the slave's de/re/compositions in scenes of terror induce in Ferreira da Silva a "cosmic perspective": "Her wounded (marked and raped) body, as well as her shrieks—and the love and terror she might and does feel—echo from without the sociological scene but also—as *elementa*—from within every tiny little particle (of signification and exchange) that constitutes the world to which it is applicable, the world in which the racial dialectic makes sense" (2022, 154–55). The indeterminant activity of blacklight, its relative "materialist" relation to the world it "transduces" (2022, 154), reflects the terrifying non-separation of its user from its act—itself reflective of the incomprehensibility of blackness.

Blacklight's roving between plentitude and the negative, everything and nothing, ends up repeating the anoriginal scene of primitive accumulation, Hegel's doctrine of being and its collision between being and nothing. A final sweep through Hegel's *schein* shows it is intimately linked to the nature of non-being it subsumes and that its reflecting forgets. Non-being doesn't disappear; instead, it returns in shine: "What constitutes the shine is the immediacy of *non-being*; this non-being, however, is nothing else than the negativity of essence within essence itself" ([1832] 2010, 344; Pippin 2018, 221). In its historical materialist configuration, shine composes the being of labor through alienation (negation) and activity (essence). This Marxist essence here retains reference to non-being, insofar as full-sided creative activity remains thwarted, but it promises being through a transcendental I that, even if just a revolutionary promise, elides its own entanglement with an affectable other. For Ferreida da Silva, the slave's negation is also active, a "negativation" posed also as a "negativ(e active)ation" (2022, 55). As negativation, Ferreira da Silva's "wounded captive body" registers the non-being disappeared in the first instant Hegel's dialectic of being and non-being prioritizes being and, in the next step, registers determinacy as "something." "Not as a constitutive outside," blacklight enables a jump, like a singularity, between "nothing and everything" (283).

From this singular vantage, freedom cannot then return to slavery to properly conceptualize it. While the overcoming of slavery itself is, at one register, necessary for the very movement of freedom, the shine of being more profoundly activates the actualization of slavery through the upper-case Blackness that secures the being-ness of the "not."[16] Here, slavery is "not economically identified or determined because it is not comprehensible by a quantitative category"; blackness, Ferreira da Silva writes, is "that which remains undetermined, that is, not that which is *not* (thereby determined as such) but that which is merely *non*" (2022, 189). Returning to Marx's illustrative quote, we might say "all slave labor appears as unpaid labor, all wage labor appears as paid. It is the immediacy of the slave's labor that hides the non-comprehensibility of the slave." As the shadow of the beginning in being that, instead of becoming more and more determinate, becomes more and more indeterminate, racial blackness concentrates the slave form, necessitating unrelenting violence to secure its own inadequacy with any Idea. Slavery is a concept made actual but whose existence shimmers through the plane of non-being. In this murky half-light, the wounded captive body articulates a dehiscence internal to the Idea—an exposed inquiry into what to make of concepts when the concept approaches non-determinancy or nothing, and to track the violence that emerges from the failure to remain nothing.

[16] "I say absolutely that the n'est pas does not constitute a concept—it is the dark *invisable* of reason—for it is not *determinable* or *meaningful*" (Marriott 2023, xiii, original emphasis).

Conclusion

In 2014, Ferreira da Silva was preparing a different ground of refusal, asking "methodological" questions, rather than "ontological" ones, which trap us in the same circular reasoning. "Instead of the question of who and what we are," she writes, "we need to go deeper into the investigation of how we come up with answers to the question" (2014a, 104).[17] For Marx, certainly, one cannot separate his method from his sense of social ontology, concept from actuality. Insofar as the "ideal is nothing but the material world reflected in the mind of man, and translated into forms of thought," Marx's dialectic strives to represent "the life of the subject-matter," "now reflected back in the ideas" ([1867] 1976, 102). If done right, flexibly and rigorously, the Marxist concept of labor would separate from slavery not because of an idealist error but because Marx had reconstructed a rift that expresses how emerging forms of wealth and labor had dissolved alternate arrangements of being, power, and violence. With blacklight, Ferreira da Silva also seems to reconverge method and ontology. But the blacklight that *makes* shine involves a distinctly different order of operation than Hegel and Marx's *schein*. Instead of involving an activity of thought propelling itself, with reflexive vision, towards an ever more mediated and relational worldview that "freely discharges itself" (Hegel [1832] 2010, 753) in the realm of communism, the shine of slavery imaginatively takes what is seemingly obvious and inert—"raw material"—and illuminates the hidden correspondences and gaps that return, in higher frequency, violence to its whitened source. Blacklight's relation to blackness and the *elementa* reveals an ontology whose indeterminacy follows neither the descriptive sort of revelation nor the determinant kind of *schein*. Illuminating the translucent superimposition between Hegelian-Marxist "forms of appearance" and Ferreira da Silva's strategic misreading of the historical materialist in/distinction between labor and slavery, the indeterminacy between the negative and excess might still manifest an account of the world incomprehensible to even the most rigorous of historical materialists.

[17] Given that this distinction was levied against Wynter, it makes sense that by the time of *Unpayable Debt* Ferreira da Silva is charging her with a "separation between truth and ideology" (2022, 68). Building on her early skepticism of Wynter's reliance on science (103–4), Ferreira da Silva now detects in Wynter, like Marx, the smuggling of "universalism—the Human's capacity to produce and hide from itself both its collective existence and accounts of it, or 'descriptive statements'" (2022, 68–69). But Wynter's writing can also be made legible from the perspective of the negative in ways that complicate any purported universalism. See Garba and Sorentino (2025).

References

Abazari, Arash (2020). *Hegel's Ontology of Power: The Structure of Social Domination in Capitalism*. Cambridge University Press.

Best, Beverley (2023). "The Commune Is Out Payable Debt." *Cultural Dynamics* 35, no. 4: 258–66.

Costreie, Sorin (2011). "Leibniz on Void and Matter." In *Vanishing Matter and the Laws of Motion: Descartes and Beyond*, edited by D. Jalobeanu and P. R. Anstey, 215–34. Routledge.

Ferreira da Silva, Denise (2007). *Toward a Global Idea of Race*. University of Minnesota Press.

Ferreira da Silva, Denise (2014a). "Before Man: Sylvia Wynter's Rewriting of the Modern Episteme." In *Sylvia Wynter: On Being Human as Praxis*, edited by K. McKittrick, 90–105. Duke University Press.

Ferreira da Silva, Denise (2014b). "Toward a Black Feminist Poethics: The Quest(ion) of Blackness Toward the End of the World." *The Black Scholar* 44, no. 2: 81–97.

Ferreira da Silva, Denise (2015). "Globality." *Critical Ethnic Studies* 1, no. 1: 33–38.

Ferreira da Silva, Denise (2017a). "Blacklight." In *Otobong Nkanga: Luster and Lucre*, edited by C. Molloy, P. Pirotte, and F. Schöneich, 245–51. Sternberg Press.

Ferreira da Silva, Denise (2017b). "1 (life) ÷ 0 (blackness) = ∞ – ∞ or ∞ / ∞: On Matter Beyond the Equation of Value." *e-flux* 79. https://www.e-flux.com/journal/79/94686/1-life-0-blackness-or-on-matter-beyond-the-equation-of-value/.

Ferreira da Silva, Denise (2020). "Reading the Dead: A Black Feminist Poethical Reading of Global Capital." In *Otherwise Worlds: Against Settler Colonialism and Anti-Blackness*, edited by T. L. King, J. Navarro, and A. Smith, 38–51. Duke University Press.

Ferreira da Silva, Denise (2022). *Unpayable Debt*. Sternberg Press.

Ford III, James E. (2011). "From Being to Unrest, from Objectivity to Motion: The Slave in Marx's Capital." *Rethinking Marxism* 23: 22–30.

Garba, Tapji (2023). "On Materialism, Freedom, and Self-Consciousness." *Philosophy Today* 67, no. 4: 833–50.

Garba, Tapji and Sara-Maria Sorentino (2025). "Blackness Before Race and Race as Reoccupation." *Political Theology* 26, no. 3: 227–48.

Hanzel, Igor (2014). "'The Circular Course of Our Representation': 'Schein', 'Grund' and 'Erscheinung' in Marx's Economic Works." In *Marx's Capital and Hegel's Logic*, edited by F. Moseley and T. Smith, 214–39. Brill.

Hegel, Georg W. F. ([1832] 2010). *The Science of Logic*. Translated by G. Di Giovanni. Cambridge University Press.

Ingram, David (1985). "Hegel on Leibniz and Individuation." *Kant–Studien* 76, no. 1–4: 420–35.

Jolley, Nicholas (2017). "Plentitude and Mirrors of God in Leibniz." In *Tercentenary Essays on the Philosophy and Science of Leibniz*, edited by L. Strickland, E. Vynckier, and J. Weckend, 111–29. Palgrave Macmillian.

Kaplan, Andrew (2023). "Afropessimism's Anagrammatical Liturgics of Renunciation as the Im/possibility of Care." *Political Theology Network Conference*, September (unpublished).

Leibniz, G. W. ([1714] 1989). "The Principles of Philosophy, or, the Monadology." In *Philosophical Essays*, translated by R. Ariew and D. Garber, 213–34. Hackett.

Marriott, David S. (2023). *Of Effacement: Blackness and Non-Being*. Stanford University Press.

Marx, Karl ([1939] 1973). *Grundrisse: Foundations of the Critique of Political Economy*. Translated by M. Nicolaus. Penguin.

Marx, Karl ([1867] 1976). *Capital: A Critique of Political Economy, Volume One*. Translated by B. Fowkes. Penguin.

Marx, Karl ([1894] 1981). *Capital: A Critique of Political Economy, Volume Three*. Translated by D. Fernbach. Penguin.

Nesbitt, Nick (2022). *The Price of Slavery: Capitalism and Revolution in the Caribbean*. University of Virginia Press.

Pepperell, Nicole (2010). "Disassembling Capital." PhD thesis, RMIT University, Melbourne.

Pippin, Robert B. (2018). *Hegel's Realm of Shadows: Logic as Metaphysics in the Science of Logic*. University of Chicago Press.

Reichelt, Helmut (2005). "Social Reality as Appearance: Some Notes on Marx's Conception of Reality." In *Human Dignity, Social Autonomy and the Critique of Capitalism*, edited by W. Bonefeld and K. Psychopedis, 31–67. Ashgate Publishing.

Sorentino, Sara-Maria (2019). "The Abstract Slave: Anti-Blackness and Marx's Method." *International Labor and Working-Class History* 96: 17–37.

Sorentino, Sara-Maria (2024). "With What Must Slavery Begin?" *differences* online forum, April 3. Available online: https://differencesjournal.org/writing/with-what-must-slavery-begin.

Terada, Rei (2023). *Metaracial: Hegel, Antiblackness & Political Identity*. University of Chicago Press.

Wynter, Sylvia (2014). "Unparalleled Catastrophe for Our Species? Or, to Give Humanness a Different Future: Conversation." In *Sylvia Wynter: On Being Human as Praxis*, edited by Katherine McKittrick, 9–89. Duke University Press.

Yeomans, Christopher (2012). *Freedom and Reflection: Hegel and the Logic of Agency*. Oxford University Press.

Zambrana, Rocío (2018). "Actuality in Hegel and Marx." *Hegel Bulletin* 40, no. 1: 74–91.

Žižek, Slavoj (1993). *Tarrying with the Negative: Kant, Hegel, and the Critique of Ideology*. Duke University Press.

Acknowledgements

The author would like to thank Seb Franklin and Andrew Santana Kaplan for their illuminating conversations that shaped the course of this writing.

PART THREE

Speculations

14

Introduction

Julietta Hua and rashné limki

How can we think, and thereby make, "the World otherwise"? (Ferreira da Silva 2015a, 81). How do we imagine the world anew when our tools of analysis are precisely those that present the world to us as we know it? Ferreira da Silva's founding proposition is that our tools of analysis are always already limited because they are constitutive of the very onto-epistemic system that is to be abolished. Or as Audre Lorde has poignantly and memorably stated, the master's tools cannot dismantle the master's house. This is the primary concern that drives Ferreira da Silva's elaboration of recomposition, a method of doing that proceeds as un-doing. Can difference be disordered so that justice is not about inclusion nor about universalization?

Shifting our epistemic frame away from an ordered to a disordered world allows for a reading of the World as Plenum, where everything is present all at once: "An infinite composition in which each existent's singularity is contingent upon its becoming one possible expression of all the other existents" (Ferreira da Silva 2016, 58). That is, from indigenous science as well as physics, we learn that order is mere appearance; the world is composed of particles, the arrangements and interactions of these particles manifest the appearance of separate(d) objects, or existents. However, the fact that our compositional material (particles), or the material of the universe, is singular means that the potential to manifest as one particular appearance exists in each existent at once. It is only through *intra-action* that existents become expressed into one form rather than another. This is the World as Plenum; it is a world composed through difference, but without separability. Given that all matter in the universe is composed of the same material, every appearance is a different expression of the same, and the potential for multiplicity is inherent in everything. This resonates with Joanne Barker's (Lenape) sentiment that "beings [who] see one another ... do whatever it takes to take care of one another, even if it means changing the very purpose of their existence. It is about the power of transformation and reciprocity. It is about our origins in the stars and our connections and travels between the worlds of ground and space" (2018, 211). Similarly, Ferreira da Silva suggests nonlocality over separability where,

> beyond the surfaces onto which the prevailing notion of difference is inscribed [literal skin], everything in the universe co-exists in the manner Leibniz (1646–1716) describes, that is, as a singular expression of everything else in the universe ... When nonlocality guides our imagining of the universe, difference is not a manifestation of an unresolvable *estrangement*, but the expression of an elementary *entanglement*. (2016, 65, original emphasis).

Thus, Ferreira da Silva offers a way to think about ethnic, racial, national difference that is not about inclusion nor universality; rather this perspective recomposes difference as the (shared) potential inhered in every being to be otherwise.

The method of recomposition indicates and facilitates epistemic revolution. Such a project necessarily reaches beyond our existing, colonial horizons of language and knowledge. Accordingly, Ferreira da Silva offers readers new terms that recompose existing vocabularies. For example, in both "Hacking the Subject: Black Feminism and Refusal beyond the Limits of Critique" (2018) and "1 (life) ÷ 0 (Blackness) = ∞ – ∞ or ∞ / ∞: On Matter Beyond the Equation of Value" (2017) Ferreira da Silva reconfigures algebraic signifiers and formulations to demonstrate her conceptualization of power in shaping subjectivity and specifically blackness. In these pieces, signifiers (terms) and formulations (principles) derived from algebra can work outside the restrictions in place in our usual mathematical grammar. Yet Ferreira da Silva's use of algebra is to work out of it, rather than to use it as a tool of direct translation. While such moves may be disorienting, they represent radical possibilities.

In another example, the method of hacking follows from Ferreira da Silva's argument that our knowledge of the world is an effect of the tools of measurement developed to access it (intra-action). Moreover, these tools of measurement are instituted as separated from what is being measured, so that there is no assumed relation between the two. Blackness exists in this schema as the object being measured, a descriptor in the world. As such, blackness always already threatens to expose the limits of our mechanisms of measurement, to reveal the inseparability of knowledge (what) and method (how); this is blackness' radical potential. Ferreira da Silva substantiates this argument by recomposing mathematical reasoning as follows.

In a scene of opposition or dichotomy, positive life represented as 1 produces negative life as -1. In this modern and dialectic formulation, blackness is written as "life that does not matter" or -1. When this form of blackness (-1) is added to life (1), the result is 0, or nullification. However, blackness as 0, Ferreira da Silva demonstrates, has the power to obliterate life, "In negativity (Blackness) engulfs value," but "as nullification Blackness destroys value (as added or multiplied with life)" (2017, np). She further postulates that because it is impossible to divide any value by 0 (i.e., to diminish nullification) such an equation can also be signified as ∞ (indeterminacy). As ∞, blackness is a refusal of dialectics and becomes "content without form or *materia prima*—that which has no value because it exists (as ∞) without form" (2017, np). Here Ferreira da Silva deploys blackness as "a guide to thinking, a method for study," which makes the World in Plenum and becomes a "referent of another mode of existing in the world" (2017, np). Through algebraic recomposition Ferreira da Silva illustrates the radical potential of blackness (as indeterminacy) to always exceed its predetermined function (as negative life).

Ferreira da Silva continues to explore this in "Hacking the Subject," where hacking is "refusal as a mode of engagement. ... It consists in a series of moves ... to transfigure 'woman' (and with her the female and feminine), to deface her, and release her to accomplish what she alone can perform, which is the dis/ordering of the modern grammar in which the patriarch remains the presupposed bearer of self-determination" (2018, 22). X, as marked absence, is taken up in a series of equations so that Ferreira da Silva can demonstrate how, even in those texts that conscript our notions of the human subject, there is still a latent potential to un-do those very texts. The challenge is in lacking tools that can express that potentiality. Ferreira da Silva offers us X as one method to locate that potential, a referent without determination and therefore without opposition or violence, where the \X "explodes the male-form XY" (2018, 31). Here, a black feminist tool, X can hack (\) operations of racial patriarchy to suggest the possibility of something otherwise. Like the equations she uses to demonstrate the \X, Ferreira da Silva's works suggest that the potential to be otherwise is always with us but may require the reassembly of the tools we already have to unleash that potential.

The methodological importance of recomposition is perhaps best understood through Ferreira da Silva's engagement with the work of artists like Otobong Nkanga, from whom she draws inspiration, as well as artists who have used Ferreira da Silva's work for their own. It is in the practice of art that Ferreira da Silva finds some of her most productive engagements. Rather than the scholarly exercise of translation and citation, the referential relations centered in artistic engagements hold radical potential. Noting the indeterminacy of art, Ferreira da Silva writes: "What if one approached each and every work of art as a composition, that is, as an imaging, an assemblage of bits of representation: the already said, the already seen, the already written, the already imaged—or rather, words, images, texts, gestures, scenes?" (2015b, np). That art exists only as it confronts us—puts us in relation to not only the art, but all those referents evoked through the art—foregrounds an orientation to the world that is "as plenum" (2015b, np). Just as recomposing the World as Plenum insists on a release of order, Ferreira da Silva's understanding of artists' engagements with her work foregrounds relation, response and feeling—referential rather than citational engagement. This releases our engagement with her work from the certainties of knowing and the utility of citation. Instead we are allowed to work with or imagine through uncertainty. Artists, to frame it another way, engage recomposition by working in referential, abstract ways that are often more uncertain. We hope this mode of being in conversation with Ferreira da Silva captures the contributions of this collection.

References

Barker, Joanne (2018). "Decolonizing the Mind." *Rethinking Marxism* 30, no. 2: 208–31.

Ferreira da Silva, Denise (2015a). "Toward a Black Feminist Poethics." *The Black Scholar* 44, no. 2: 81–97.

Ferreira da Silva, Denise (2015b). "Reading Art as Confrontation." *e-flux journal* 65, SUPERCOMMUNITY (May–August). http://supercommunity.e-flux.com/texts/reading-art-as-confrontation/

Ferreira da Silva, Denise (2016). "On Difference Without Separability." In *32nd Bienal de São Paulo - Incerteza Viva. Catalogue*, edited by Jochen Volz and Júlia Rebouças, 57–65. São Paulo: Fundação Bienal de São Paulo.

Ferreira da Silva, Denise (2017). "1 (life) ÷ 0 (blackness) = ∞ − ∞ or ∞ / ∞: On Matter Beyond the Equation of Value." *e-flux journal* 79.

Ferreira da Silva, Denise (2018). "Hacking the Subject: Black Feminism and Refusal Beyond the Limits of Critique." *philoSOPHIA* 8, no. 1: 19–41.

15

Interview with Denise Ferreira da Silva

Julietta Hua and rashné limki

limki: To me there's something about the ways in which Spinoza thinks about affection that feels very tied to quantum physics. Would you say that there is some Spinoza in the feminists who work with quantum physics? Implicitly or explicitly?

Ferreira da Silva: Well, if Spinoza had not begun with the assumption that there is that one substance that connects everything and hence makes affection possible, then yes. But he begins with God—he begins with the One. But if you think without that one [God], which is what those quantum feminists are doing (I think Karen [Barad] more than others), then, yes, there is something like Spinoza [in the work of quantum feminists], but without his presupposition of that final, you know, transcendent substance.

What I'm trying to do is to collapse everything into the material. For Spinoza God is a formal efficient entity; for Leibnitz it is a final efficient, but definitely a final entity. And in a way you can read modern philosophy in terms of this: they alternate, they go from the former to the final, and the efficient. Kant is the formal and the efficient; Hegel is the final and efficient. But those are the causes.

Now their answers, their formulations of the question of why and how, and the relationship to the material, is always that which can never be the beginning of anything—that was a move that we find in Aristotle's Metaphysics, after he goes over the physicists, the pre-Socratic philosophers, and then the question is the question of being. You know, that's one possible place where we can trace how the material could not, would not, become the organizer of a question, the question of why. Yes, the question of why. So, I'm interested in the material but as I was saying before, I'm not interested in the question of what—because that's the ontological question. It's given—who knows, who cares [about the "what"]? I'm also not interested in the question of why—which is the ethical, the general ethical, human question. I'm interested in the "how." Existence is "how." You know, existence is about the how, given compositions and the parts of that composition that change right? I mean they [the compositions of existence] transform, transduce, whatever, but they are always the same. Insofar as existence is concerned, the question for me is the how of existence. How, in terms of the composition, the image, or the shape, in that material sense. But also the how of processes.

Hua: So for instance are you thinking not about subjects and things, but on the processes that make things things in one moment and something else in another—like the composition of water that is also both the same and different from ice and vapor? Is this difference without separability?

Ferreira da Silva: The "how" of, you could call them processes, but whatever that is (we may call it transformation) if it is a shift in form, or transduction, when the shift is beyond form, the shift is at the level of energy. That is "how," too. The "how" of how things look and the "how" of how they become. But it's inherent to the things. It's not outside of their existence. It's a matter of change in pressure and temperature, and changes in pressure and temperature come out of how things move in relation to each other. And then there are conditions, the context within which they move. So if there is a squeeze, there will be more pressure, and you know, whatever is in there will become solid. But if the pressure keeps going, eventually it's going to explode and only because of that change in pressure. There's nothing that happens beyond what happens in that context. You can ask the question of what that context is, but then you begin with the question of "what" and "why" rather than "how."

I think the question of "why" is relevant because modern philosophers, following their thinking and writing and militating against the Aristotelian orthodoxy, the medieval thought, made it relevant. They [modern philosophers] were busy creating space so that Reason could proceed without the Divine. But we don't need to do that [create space for Reason, continue asking the question of "why"] because this is not the problem. We don't need to ask the question of "why" of everything. Or at least we don't need one answer, only one answer, for that question, but we have one answer, which is the question of the "the universal"—the one God.

limki: Given everything that you've said, do you think the theory of everything is actually part of the problem? Even the possibility of a theory of everything, the search for the theory of everything is part of the problem of the world as it is?

Ferreira da Silva: Yes, in terms of the question that gives you the final "why" and the final "what" of the world, it is at that level [a problem]. But then there is that famous phrase from Einstein—it's telling that he says that God doesn't play dice [on uncertainty]. So there's an order. It is impossible that uncertainty, and in that sense disorder, is what it is [the final "what" of the world]. But quantum physics makes something else possible (and because Einstein is dead this is possible). The findings of quantum physics run against precisely the presumption of order being given, being the natural state of things. And saying that order is natural is, you know, redundant because natural and order mean the same thing in this line of thinking.

The weirdness of quantum physics, of particle physics—all the weird things they find, they're only weird because the tools we use for describing what happens, they presuppose space-time as the context. These weird things that happen are assumed to occur in time and they are assumed to occur in space. This is a limitation since the one thing that cannot happen in space is that things that are not in the same place affect each other or even communicate with each other. If they're not in the same place, the presumption is that there must be a channel through which they communicate. And the fact that we assume that is then what makes entanglement seem weird. But that assumption: 1) that things happen in space; and 2) that because they are in space things are separate from each other—without those assumptions, then it's just what it is; it just happens. Why it happens—when you ask that question, then you go back to this impulse to be able to provide another answer that is not the answer that they had before, which was the divine. So yes, the answer is kind of complex, but I think so.

There is this physicist [Ludwig] Boltzmann from the late nineteenth century, early twentieth century [1844–1906]. [Boltzmann] was dealing with entropy because the universe, everything tends toward disorder; because heat, right, because internal energy passes from a place with lots to a place with less. This transference of internal kinetic energy always happens, and then that's how things happen, and that's why we have the sense of time passing because you can't undo heat, you can't turn heat back. If we could, we wouldn't have this problem with global warming. But anyway, what Boltzmann says is, "yes, the universe (talking about the cosmos), the physical universe is where entropy rules. But even in that condition there will be pockets of order." What happens is that when you have disorder, it means that everything is possible. This means order is also possible out of that generalized disorder. And that's what explains the fact that this planet appears to be, you know, totally governed by order. However, he went even beyond that saying this also explains the human brain [why such an ordered/ordering thing as the human brain exists]. And then he [Boltzmann] has some extrapolation that it wouldn't be a surprise if you could find some huge brains somewhere in the universe. You know, some configurations that are just like the human brain, out of this order. I mean, it's a crazy proposition, but it's a proposition that's in the attempt to explain, of giving order, of giving an answer to the question of why: The "why" of order, while all their [scientists'] observations and calculations would only show no order. The "why" ends up saying, yes, of course, there is order at the end of the whole thing [even with disorder]!

I think the point is just that order is the preoccupation. We are preoccupied with it. And then everything, when it comes to thinking, even my thinking is so organized it's insane. This is the problem. I think that's why we turn to thinking about other dimensions, in terms of existing and communicating and going back to some kind of established connections. So I keep trying ... like okay, how do you present something with this limitation [the preoccupation with order]? We have this limitation to thinking and the ways we think, so how do you open up to something else? That is where I move to the artistic. There [the artistic] you don't say anything, you just put the thing together. It [the artistic] doesn't explain anything; it's not about teaching anything. It's no longer about understanding. It's about, you know, inspiration or whatever happens when somebody sees the work: whatever it is and how it elicits response.

limki: I was writing something about what decolonization or decoloniality means, and I was thinking about how colonial and anti-colonial scholars ask us to reclaim those things that have been abandoned by contemporary conceptions of the human. For instance, things like the erotic, emotion, and so, on if you think of writers like Audre Lorde. I was also thinking about your work and especially your "Difference without Separability" piece. Would you say that what you do there is similar in terms of how we should be thinking? In other words, you suggest that disorder should be part of the new world that we need to inhabit. Would you think of your work as about reclaiming disorder?

Ferreira da Silva: I think so, both in a more abstract and less abstract way. On the one hand, in the more abstract way, it is a reclaiming of something that I don't even know if we humans have ever had. But you can think of it as the reclaiming of a certain trust in that fundamental thing that characterizes everything. Trusting it, which also means trusting existence without order. Trusting that—which is existence without something that would have been imposed by some divine entity or by universal reason. Is that disorder, in the general sense? Maybe not, because disorder presupposes some idea of order, that there is something that a certain situation departs from. So that's why I don't think it is disorder.

But definitely just trusting that existence, for the most part, unfolds without order, right? Without order that we impose onto the world so that we can make it [the world] more comfortable for the human. Order, you know, makes it comfortable for the human. Order makes the world available and accessible to the human. That's on the one hand. On the other hand, in the less abstract sense of disorder, I think that embracing, ethically embracing—not affectively or emotionally embracing, but ethically embracing—that trust means that some out-of-order-ness will take place. It is refusal: the refusal to follow the order of things.

Disorder is, by its very definition, its very formulation, order to the human. Order is controlling; it's constraining. At some point the embracing of that which is not will also entail some kind of confrontation, whether that is a confrontation that is direct, like disobedience, or a confrontation that attempts at enforcing the existing order. You know, like law enforcement, policing. More generally, I think disorder—you know, dis-order, which is not "other" because it is opposed to what we have, but it's not order, because it's not known, it is not what we have—requires that other mode of making sense of actually existing. There are some fundamental shifts that are needed, even for us to contemplate and even to begin to think—not only thinking, because that is what happens at another level—probably it's the imagination, imagining. The image of existence that difference without separability invites, is one that I think needs to be rehearsed in the same ways that this existence with order has been rehearsed for 200 years. And that includes shifts at different levels. One, because it's an image, and as such it is by definition, abstract: something has to take place at what we would call the metaphysical level, which is the level of that image. If knowing, if asking the question of knowing is important, is needed, is relevant, then that question would have to be reformulated, because the very basis of the question will have to change.

If asking the metaphysical question of being (from Aristotle) is also relevant then that has to change. And that question of Being, I think, is the one that will have to go—the ontological question will have to go insofar as it is about establishing a separation, you know, in terms of beings. Or also if it is about having a sense of one whole Being in which everything participates. That I think has to go.

The most important moment, and to me a fundamental shift, is the one marked by a move from the descriptor of experience to the descriptor of existence for the human. Right? Because modern philosophy and its social conditions begin with experience, right? Because they [modern philosophers] begin in the world—you know, the settler world of space-time, asking the question of experience. Because they begin already separated from everything else, between the angels and the roots. So that turn mediates everything, even when it is not explicit. Experience only makes sense from that position that Man was made to occupy [the position of a World in a state of order, a state of separability]. I think the main shift is existence. It's not a question of experience, but of existence ... but not the Sartre existentialism because that question [of existence] goes back to that figure of Man immediately.

Just like, the coyote [I just saw], we share the space. How do you move? Do you move with it arrogantly, getting close to the coyote, or telling the coyote not to be close to you. Or do recognize that the coyote got there before you, so you better move and find another way for yourself if sharing the way is not desirable or possible?

limki: You're saying that your thinking is very ordered or organized, but the fact that we are all constantly repeating the same thing in different ways, doesn't that actually indicate that there is a lot of disorder, because we're never actually quite able to pin anything down?

Ferreira da Silva: I agree with you, all that there is, is disorder. But it's the movement, it's how we frame things and how we image the things that are happening, that is the law or the mandate, which is order. Then, when you fail, when you fail in your performance, are you crazy? Are you criminal or is it just you can't understand things? But at the same time we have this increased anxiety and fear and sadness and madness that comes from being out of order. This mandate that if you are out of order, there is something wrong with you, but we are always out of order. Always. All the time. Because all there is is out-of-order-ness. But then the failure is individualized—you know, into that process [of subjugation, pathologization].

99.9999% of all that happens escapes our Kantian and Lockean understanding and any controlling tool that's been designed after that [Kantian and Lockean] understanding. But we live as if, and it is a totalizing "as if," that situation is necessary, we live as if there is only order and understanding. But there is always an "if." And now I'm sounding like, not even Hume, I'm sounding like something worse than Hume! What I was highlighting is the question of how do we live with this limitation? A limitation that even is in the escape routes we design and are contaminated by this thing [preoccupation with order] and we have to live with it. That's part of the condition, too. It's another element in the general disorder of things.

16

Tikal Futura

Central American Futurities, Latinx Studies, and Other Possible Narratives (¿ensayito futurista?)

Cecilia M. Rivas

How is the study of Central America globally significant? How are the communities, cultures, literary legacies, migrations, histories of violence and resistance, postwar processes, and many other facets of the isthmus understood? This chapter seeks to highlight some ideas about the isthmus, to read its locations in time and space, and to consider how the study of Central America must be part of conversations with and about Ethnic Studies, Latinx Studies, and the global scope of Latinidades. I refer to the posthumously published novel *Tikal Futura: Memorias para un futuro incierto (novelita futurista)* (2012) by Franz Galich (Guatemala, 1951–Nicaragua, 2007) as a way to begin to broadly address some of these questions.

In *Tikal Futura*, Galich presents a landscape of violence and resistance set in the spatially, socially, and politically divided (yet inseparable) worlds of Ciudad Miseria and Ciudad Superior, also known as Ciudad de Arriba and Ciudad de Abajo. These dual worlds—one "superior" and the other in misery; one above and the other below—reveal questions of power, struggles, and difference.

The world of *Tikal Futura* combines, merges, and recurrently refers to dualities and themes of the Mayan creation story, the *Popol Vuh*, the centuries-spanning genocidal violence against the Indigenous civilizations of Guatemala (and other regions of the Americas), and modern urban spaces of consumption (such as shopping malls). Spanish colonization, the massacres and displacements during the Guatemalan 36-year civil war which ended in 1996, and the postwar forms of violence that characterize the late twentieth and twenty-first centuries carve the novel's landscape. As Greg Grandin has noted, the massacres of the civil war were no longer colonial responses to a "*motín de indios*" but now "distinct [...] prefiguring more deadly forms of counterinsurgent violence that were soon to come" (2004, 2; emphasis in original). Violence is historical, cyclical, and intense.

Creation myths, memories, and references to historical events combine in the novel. In *Tikal Futura* the stories of centuries of genocide and of the forced disappearance and diminishment of cultures, languages, literatures, written records, and codices exist simultaneously. Events are forgotten by many in Ciudad de Arriba and Ciudad de Abajo, yet remembered and preserved by Abuela Cané, who writes and keeps records for an uncertain future. She can see what is to come, including the destinies of the other characters—importantly, of Namú and Ix, a young couple central to the future of their struggle.

References to the postwar neoliberalism of twentieth- and twenty-first century Central America abound. One of the main characters of *Tikal Futura* is Juan, also known as el Apocalíptico, who lives in Ciudad de Arriba, enjoying power and profitable connections as he fulfills his political ambitions. He began his career in a *zona franca* or *maquiladora*, dutifully supervising, "el más atento y cumplidor de los empleados" (the most attentive and compliant of the employees) (Galich 2012, 63). His compliance has benefitted him politically and materially. Although his marriage is unhappy, his wife Proserpina remains with him as his influence grows and his political future begins to seem more promising— el Apocalíptico might become a *diputado* (a lawmaker), or even the president, of his conflicted country. He is, as his name makes obvious, the end. Meanwhile, Proserpina hides her true identity and origins (she is from Ciudad de Abajo). It should not surprise us that el Apocalíptico and some other characters of *Tikal Futura* have multiple, changing names. The "linguistic disintegration" of the names of many of the novel's characters is a sign of "social, economic, and environmental degradation produced by neoliberalism" (Caña Jiménez 2014, 71; my translation).

The protagonists inhabit worlds where nearly everything is for sale and commercialized, worlds of opportunism and extractivism. In this neoliberal reality, some inhabitants of Ciudad de Abajo are reduced to expendable status; they are *los descartables*, the disposable ones. Their expendability is regarded as their most notable quality. The poor are displaced and disappeared. El Apocalíptico saw his opportunity to exploit and leave other workers behind in order to achieve his political aspirations. Militarization and restrictions are normalized; it is a state of exception. In the worlds of *Tikal Futura,* where power is concentrated and authority is repressive, resistance and popular discontent against these forms of control grows, even if gradually. Here the capacity for communication, for alternative narratives, and for keeping memories becomes important.

As we move away from *Tikal Futura*, we can see how these thoughts may be relevant to the study of Central America, to its diasporas, to Ethnic studies, and to Latinx studies. We must continue to pay attention to literature, dualities, histories, and languages. We must question concentrations of power and wealth, forms of control, propaganda, and how narrative control becomes repression.

Scholars of Central American studies must be connected with the fields of Indigenous Studies, Afro-Latinx Studies, and Ethnic Studies, be engaged in pushing the borders and boundaries of various disciplines, and work to expand the scope of these fields into a global study of Latinidades. The Central American isthmus is dynamic, has great cultural and ethnic diversity, and grapples with legacies of violence and socioeconomic inequality. Overall, we must be able to recognize how our study of Central America expands our critical thinking and understanding of migration studies, cultural studies, media studies, and other areas of research.

This must include the study of new mobilities, diasporas, and critical studies of transnational communities. For instance, how much do diasporas live and know about the realities of the isthmus they left years ago? How much of this knowledge is mediated? As this dialogue is constructed, this is part of the task of Central American studies: to remain in touch with the issues of the isthmus, and to revisit and revise diaspora and transnationalism discourses. To look for unlikely histories, to write for the uncertain future and for what is on the horizon. Narratives of safety and control must also be questioned. As people in the isthmus and beyond continue to voice their struggles and fight for their dignity, they continue to lose their fear. People must have the ability to hope and to reflect on these many questions and issues in order to envision Central American futurities.

References

Caña Jiménez, María del Carmen (2014). "Vida resurgida y neoliberalismo en *Tikal Futura* de Franz Galich." *Latin American Literary Review* 42, no. 84 (July–December): 68–87.

Galich, Franz (2012). *Tikal Futura: Memorias para un futuro incierto (novelita futurista)*. Guatemala City: F&G Editores.

Grandin, Greg (2004). *The Last Colonial Massacre: Latin America in the Cold War*. Chicago: University of Chicago Press.

17

Anastácia's Eyes

Nathalia Carneiro

In Anastácia Livre [Free Anastácia], a metamorphosis is produced as artist Yhuri Cruz strips away the steel mask and iron collar from the famous lithograph Escrava Anastácia [Slave Anastácia]. In their stead, a gilded necklace and a mouth emerge. The Escrava Anastácia [Slave Anastácia] image wearing the punishment devices has been a long-present image in Brazil. On the one hand, she has been used as a common representation of the horrors of slavery, such as in school books. Anastácia has also rotated as a sacred figure. Conceição Evaristo highlights the mask demolition as a collective endeavor. For her, Anastácia had been speaking "through the orifices of the mask," as her image is appropriated "in situations which do not imply silence," for example, when a group of hip-hop girls calls themselves The Anastácias when the samba school pays homage. "I imagine it happening gradually, you know?

FIGURE 17.1 *Palavras, "Anastácia Livre," Monument to Anastácia's voice by Yhuri Cruz, 2019.*

You force it, push it, and keep pushing until one day that mask explodes" (Cruz and Hartman 2020, np).[1]

I encountered Anastácia Livre in 2020 when the artist shared on his Instagram the celebratory news that she (the unmasked Anastácia) was now in a school textbook. Touched, I messaged the artist, thanking him for the work. At the time, I was reading the recent Brazilian Portuguese translations of Octavia Butler. I mentioned *Kindred*'s main character Dana, and our power to return in time "because we know it is not linear." He replied: "Butler, great inspiration!" As a possibility that has always been there, in Anastácia's eyes, Escrava Anastácia is now Anastácia Livre. Something happened. In this text, as part of the collective endeavor of destroying the mask, I aim to produce a reading of Anastácia in the key of refusal. That is, I read her openness not as a resolution but as Anastácia Livre's ongoing work of her open secret and demand. With Denise Ferreira da Silva's "Black Feminist Poethics," I read the excess of violence in the torture devices as a sign of infinity, as a cosmic force present in Anastácia's eyes. The excess embedded in Escrava Anastácia is evident in scenes of racial/colonial violence such as the whipping of individuals already handcuffed or the killing of people already situated in the peripheries and favelas.[2]

Cruz's gesture of re/de/composition discloses Anastácia's rebellious existence signaled by the torture devices imposed upon her. The iron collar, heavy by design, was used on fugitive slaves to hinder further attempts at escape. It also served as a symbolic marker of enslavement. As depicted in the portrayal of Escrava Anastácia, the steel mask concealed the slave's mouth or, in some cases, the entire face.[3] A component of the steel apparatus was inserted into the enslaved's mouth, effectively preventing her from eating, drinking, and speaking. This measure was often employed to prevent suicide by soil ingestion but was also used for other punitive purposes (Assis 1906, np). These torture apparatuses highlight a dual dynamic pointed out by Ferreira da Silva in *Unpayable Debt* (2022). On the one hand, they underscore the enslaved to the status of property or production tool, as a Thing, pointing to the legal-economic framework enabling exploitation through violence. Indeed, the mask and the collar

---

[1] These translations, including the subsequent ones, have been undertaken by the present author.

[2] "The police use of excessive force (I should say, bullets) in aggrieved communities of colour and against black and brown people is probably as ubiquitous as was the excess (of power) signified by the use of the whip against already shackled bodies of slaves" (Ferreira da Silva 2001, 422).

[3] As depicted in another renowned illustration by Debret, "Iron collar punishment for fugitive slaves," from "Voyage Pittoresque au Bresil," 1816.

were designed to prevent the loss of property, whether through escape or self-harm. On the other hand, they also reveal that the enslaved were recognized as possessing will and desire requiring taming, that is, as Human. As Ferreira da Silva writes: "When total violence is deployed, her possession of this exclusively human mental trait is exposed, that is, her capacity to refuse (to work, to laugh, to dance, to cry)" (2022, 43–44). Excessive force, then, was applied because the owner could never be entirely certain of having subdued her desires.

Nevertheless, the violence inherent in these torture devices and actions that marked her simultaneously as Thing and Human also obliterates any acknowledgment of her as a being of will or desire, as everything she says or does can be interpreted as a consequence of this imposed coercion on her (Ferreira da Silva 2022, 44). This dynamic continues to mark blackness, and, as Ferreira da Silva states, stereotypes and racial categories "hold her hostage as a symbol with the same intensity as the lash held the slave as a laborer" (2022, 101). Neither the names nor the whipping or even the mask, however, annul what she might want, her unknown desire, at the exact moment when they detain her.

To unravel this excess, Ferreira da Silva employs the racialized female sexual body not as a category but as "the most prolific signifier of excess within modern knowledge" (2019, 62). This can be demonstrated in Ferreira da Silva's observation that while feminist scholars and critical race studies have since the 1980s elucidated the interplay of gender and race, illustrating how "when coupled with gender, race produces additional gender exclusion and, when coupled with race, gender produces additional racial exclusion, and so on" (2007, xxix), the very logic shaping the construction of these categories as exclusionary principles and their intersection, formed within the "patriarchal hell" has impeded the theoretical work necessary to comprehend the production of the female of color as a subaltern subject (2007, xxx). From this place, Ferreira da Silva assembles black feminist poethics, a radical praxis tasked with bringing about the end of the world *as we know it*, fostering decolonization.

What I read in the assemblage of the black feminist poethics or in Cruz's gesture is the mobilization of this un-known-ness. In what follows, I will consider how Ferreira da Silva's black feminist poethics mobilizes the troubles that the feminine subaltern of raciality poses to knowledge in order to release blackness as a sociological category, thereby opening its creative potential. And how this poethics unravels the excess as the "violence already resolved," a violence never exposed of categories because it resides within the very colonial architectures of Understanding, the State, and Capital. First, I explore how Ferreira da Silva mobilizes the Brazilian text in constructing this poethics. Then, I will consider Anastácia's rebellious existence and freedom, producing a raw materialist reading of the demand that she poses. Certainly, given Ferreira da Silva's incisive critique of the figure of the

Human and its attributes, such as equality and freedom, reading Anastácia Livre along with black feminist poethics might appear strange—and perhaps it is. I will remain with and mobilize that tension. Some texts debate Anastácia's existence. Here, it is not important whether Anastácia lived and died, because, drawing from Ferreira da Silva's approach to Dana's burden in *Unpayable Debt* (2022), Anastácia will lead us to a reconsideration of reality and existence.

Anastácia as Venus, Brazil as Excess

Because this text involves translating Anastácia Livre into "Free Anastácia," I will begin with the online performance "Anastácia as Venus, Venus as Anastácia" created by Cruz and his collective Pretofagia (Bezerra et al. 2020). Cruz recounts that while translating Saidiya Hartman's article "Venus in Two Acts" (2008), Anastácia "bothered" him, urging him to translate her as Venus. Anastácia says to Cruz: "Yhuri, Venus' story—or the non-story of Venus—is very similar to my non-story. Yhuri, you need to create a scene where you somehow relate me to Anastácia" (Cruz and Hartman 2020). Nevertheless, Cruz also asserts that the narratives surrounding Anastácia are not critical fabulations, nor is he Hartman. Hearing this, I could not help but agree with Cruz, yet I was left questioning: How is this dispositive, which refuses to fill the gaps in their stories with invented narratives while also rejecting their erasure, different from Anastácia's own layered (hi)stories?

In her most famous narrative, Anastácia is a slave who refuses to be raped by her owner and is then punished by the collar and mask. But her story is far from singular or fixed. At times, she is an African princess teaching captives in Brazil to syncretize *orixás* with Catholic saints. In others, she is a healer and eloquent speaker who mobilizes the enslaved. She is also portrayed as a woman born in Bahia, the daughter of rape, planning an escape for the enslaved, only to be captured and tortured to death. In another rendition, she is Brazilian, the daughter of Yemanjá, who instructed her to flee but was caught and punished. In yet another, Anastácia is Angolan, brought to Brazil as a captive, resisting her owner's attempts to rape her. Aware of the risks (and perhaps inevitability) of being misunderstood—as in Pretofagia's translation of Nina Simone's song—I will not attempt to answer my own question, nor could I. Instead, I will take a detour and consider it as a starting point to study Ferreira da Silva's comparison between the United States and Brazil. In this section, I will also examine the assemblage of black feminist poethics, which, like Anastácia, born on Brazilian soil, has always been global and cosmic.

The Brazilian text[4] can be interpreted as a figuration of *excess* in Ferreira da Silva's work, eluding the frameworks typically governing analyses of race. In her "Facts of Blackness" (1998a), she highlights that racial inequalities in Brazil are often viewed as a puzzle, emerging without the widespread acceptance of racial separation or explicit segregation mechanisms. Within this logic, Brazil is perceived as characterized by a lack of clear racial divisions or a strong racial consciousness or identity. However, Ferreira da Silva reads this perceived lack as *excess*[5] when she argues that Brazil's puzzle cannot be attributed solely to the country's empirical configurations. She identifies that Brazilian and US scholars often overlook the specificities of the former when it comes to racial subjugation; the US, initially serving as a term of comparison, becomes a model. This issue, however, is not simply a matter of ethnocentrism but reflects the broader functioning of modern knowledge as a productive tool. Ferreira da Silva argues that overcoming this reductionism requires an "analytic perspective which works through, rather than rejects, the presuppositions informing modern knowledge" (1998a, 214). In this critical soil, we read the assemblage of the black feminist poethics.

Drawing on Foucault's *The Order of Things*, Ferreira da Silva interrogates the assumption that "the empirical realm is an expression of a transcendental domain" (1998a, 213). She critiques the tendency to treat concepts like race and nation as separate, abstract entities or "ontological trajectories" as if their histories and meanings do not overlap. In such frameworks, race becomes a natural subtraction, and the characteristics of multiracial societies are reductively explained as stemming from the distinct physical traits of their populations, disregarding the fact that these traits held no racial significance prior to the production of racial difference by modern systems of knowledge. In "Facts of Blackness" Ferreira da Silva states that "multiracial social spaces are not isolated empirical expressions of abstract notions of race and the nation, neither are they isolated entities whose histories have developed unaffected by the historical and cultural developments of other societies" (1998a, 204). In "Revisiting the 'Racial Democracy'" (1998b), she argues for the necessity of linking Brazilian national construction with racial theories, analyzing how Brazil as a modern nation was made possible through a specific construction of race as miscegenation.

Since abolition became imminent, Brazil's large black population became a problem to its viability as a modern nation due to the "scientifically proven" inferiority of black people. In the post-abolition era, Brazilian theorists introduced an innovative perspective by proposing the thesis that

[4]This notion of text is developed by Ferreira da Silva throughout her writings and points to the productivity of knowledge, to non-fundamental separation between the empirical and abstract.
[5] She does not use this word here.

miscegenation would ultimately lead to the whitening of the population, an idea that also supported state policies promoting European immigration. However, the racial theories circulating internationally still viewed miscegenation negatively and thus cast a negative light on Brazil's national identity. According to Ferreira da Silva, it was only with the impact of World War I, the destabilization of Europe, and the concurrent rise of Brazilian nationalism in the 1930s that Gilberto Freyre restructured these notions on more positive terms (1998a,). Ferreira da Silva traces how Freyre's ideas, widely recognized as the foundation of Brazil's racial democracy (a term he himself does not use), were not entirely new. The "three races myth" (Africans, whites, and natives) had already been developed, along with the notion that these races coexisted in a kind of racial paradise and that miscegenation was a necessity given the absence of white women and easy access to Native and later black female bodies. However, Freyre succeeded in reframing these ideas, introducing an important inversion: The real inequality of Brazilian society is resolved on a mythical level, suggesting an original equality in which the "three races" have contributed to the nation's construction. However, for Ferreira da Silva:

> What constitutes the core of the Brazilian text is a teleology of assimilation, where Africans and Indians are sublated to the narrative of the always-already (white) national subject, the mestiço, which moves towards its full realization, whitening, in the always-postponed (white) future.
>
> (1998a, 218)

The notion of miscegenation is the mechanism through which this national subject is constructed. Thus, in this discourse, the racial is deeply intertwined with the sexual, positioning the European man as the active agent of miscegenation. The male Portuguese and the enslaved black woman are cast as the primary figures in this dynamic. The black woman is reduced to "collective (male) property, to whom basic (patriarchal) moral rules do not apply" (1998a, 221).

The relation between the temporal trajectory of black erasure, modernity, and the Brazilian text is better understood through Ferreira da Silva's analysis of soap operas. *The Reverse of the Mirror: The Role of Color in Modernity—A Study on Myth and Racial Ideology in TV Globo's Prime-Time Soap Opera* (1991) is a study of prime-time soap operas with high viewership during the 1980s, through the statements of actors, authors, and the scripts. Drawing on the Lévi-Straussian concept of myth, Ferreira da Silva posits that the soap opera functions as "a myth of modernized Brazilian society" where soap operas symbolically actualize the concrete exclusion of Brazil's black population. Like a myth, the soap opera is not interpreted as a faithful reproduction of reality but as a language that reaffirms a particular representation of black people in Brazilian society (1991, 136). However, the movement here is not denouncing the underrepresentation of black individuals on Brazilian television. Instead, she interrogates how their (limited) inclusion is constructed to perpetuate erasure.[6]

With this Ferreira da Silva manages to state that modern ideals of freedom and equality are completely compatible with racial violence. First, a discussion on the myth of Brazilian racial democracy, which, as the author defends, is predicated on the idea that through miscegenation, black individuals will ultimately disappear. Second, an elaboration on the modern individual and the inherent incompatibility between modern subjectivity and race (viewed as traditional, non-modern), and black persons being marked by the latter must succumb for modernity to prevail. Analyzing soap opera scripts, she shows how these representations are placed in a peripheral context within the plots. The black character is constructed to be on the periphery of modernity and, in fact, is positioned to eventually disappear. Another myth addressed in *Reverse of the Mirror* is the dichotomy of tradition versus modernity, which surfaces in telenovelas as a recurring tension between familial obligations and romantic love, with the latter ultimately prevailing (1991, 30). This triumph represents the ascendancy of the individual, the celebration of free will, and the prioritization of personal desire (1991, 125). However, we also learn that this same modern engineering assumes that to unfold the racial, others have to perish. Ferreira da Silva unravels this complicated relation between blackness and humanness, where she ties together black erasure, the absence of "interiority," and the subjective richness that defines the modern individual.

Through her interviews with black actors and actresses, Ferreira da Silva reads that the issue in the soap operas extends beyond the stereotypical roles often assigned to them—such as domestic workers or doormen. The deeper problem lies in their lack of complexity and multidimensionality. Thus, there is a connection between the lack of subjective complexity and erasure. According to the author, unlike their white, multifaceted and subjectively complex counterparts, black characters become conflated with their race, which is viewed in modern discourse as an unchanging, natural essence. To be sure, even the racial issues and a certain critique of racism only surface in the scenes in the black characters' presence. Hence, whiteness is equated with modernity itself. As Ferreira da Silva observes, black characters "lack a human side; they do not truly exist; they are not people" (1991, 148).

Once again, she highlights the intertwining of symbolic and material erasure. Ferreira da Silva weaves theories of Max Weber, Louis Dumont, Georg Simmel, Marcel Mauss, and Hannah Arendt, assembling a discussion

---

[6] With erasure I am calling attention to the inequalities, but not the violences that the racial establish, a point that will be stressed in Ferreira da Silva's later works.

about the modern individual, differentiating the tangible level but also the conceptual level, as the "subject of reason, moral value, and the normative subject of institutions" (1991, 30). This individual is defined by three dimensions: first, the juridical-moral aspect of universality; second, the private sphere of familial relations; and third, the psychological dimension of interiority and subjectivity (1991, 35). However, in this framework, racism appears as a vestige of the past, an atavistic remnant, and something to be erased in the name of progress such as those theories and policies of Florestan Fernandes (1991, 16). Ultimately, putting the racial and the modern individual in two different plays reinforces the narrative that blackness must disappear for modernity's ideals to be fully realized.[7]

While her master's thesis focused on the modern notion of the individual, *Toward a Global Idea of Race* (2007) elaborates on notions of interiority and exteriority within scientific and philosophical modernity. She traces consciousness and interiority, where "I come to know myself through time," which also requires mediation (space) to know. One of the key moments in the problem of exteriority and interiority arises when the play of reason unfolds within world history, a concept deeply influenced by Hegel. According to Ferreira da Silva, Hegel situates the social configurations of post-Enlightenment Europe as the apex of Spirit's development, portraying Spirit as a violent, dynamic process. As this process unfolds, "self-consciousness recognizes that nothing is exterior to itself because, like itself, every existing thing is a moment, an actualization of Spirit" (2007, 71). Hegel describes Spirit as a temporal movement, a process of self-realization, and History as its trajectory, privileging time as the domain where epistemologies and ontologies locate ultimate truth (2007, 42). Ferreira da Silva argues that the transparent self—self-determined and capable of knowledge—emerges only in opposition to affectable selves, who are externally determined, bound to natural conditions, and situated in particular global regions (2007). As Ferreira da Silva explains with the *analytics of raciality*, this framework created the racial subject as both an ontological and epistemological category, producing "the raced consciousness as a fundamentally mediated, determined, and spatial condition" (2007, 208). It effectively separated regions and bodies.

[7] In her later work, *Toward a Global Idea of Race* (2007), Ferreira da Silva develops a vocabulary that enables her to picture how in the *play of universal reason* (of which universality and raciality are producers), its characters (the affectable-I and the *self-determined I*, or the *transparent I* and its racial others) are placed in different scenes (the scene of representation and the scene of regulation) facing each other. The affectable self—the racial others—situated toward the horizon of death, and the self-determined I situated before the scene of life, are safeguarded by the universal principles of justice and its institutions. One of Ferreira da Silva's central questions is how black individuals can be killed at the hands of state agents without provoking an ethical crisis. This question becomes a philosophical inquiry into modern representation.

As Ferreira da Silva defends, the transition from race as a biological concept to its framing as cultural difference or as a sociological category does not dissolve its effects but reshapes and perpetuates them. Ferreira da Silva argues that blackness, as a sociological category, is deeply tied to the United States' configuration, which establishes a fundamental separation between racial groups. According to the author the national identity constructed in the nineteenth century viabilized the US as embodying modern principles such as freedom, equality, and individualism, with African Americans, Native Americans, and Asians positioned at the boundaries of this national identity (Ferreira da Silva 1998b). By the beginning of the twentieth century, the sociology of racial relations would have constructed racism as an instinctive response to difference. Following World War II, this sociology began addressing racism as a social construct rather than a natural response. However, as Ferreira da Silva observes, even within constructivist approaches, racial difference continued to function as an assumed foundation upon which social meanings and relations were constructed (1998b). Dislocating the biological framework, racism in the sociology of race relations was reconceptualized as an instinctive reaction to the "other," with racial difference redefined as a pre-political and pre-social essence. In that transformation, the black body becomes evidence.

Blackness as a sociologic category underpins the socio-logic of exclusion that governs the explanations of racial subjugation. This framework asserts that people are racially subjugated because they are racially different—whether due to improper reactions of white people or the white structural design of institutions. In the logic of exclusion that governs these justifications, there is a perverse movement where the racial other, their difference, is held responsible for their own subjugation. This is possible due to the erasure of colonial expropriation as raciality transforms "mechanisms of expropriation into natural defects (intellectual and moral) signaled by physical, practical, institutional differences, etc." (Ferreira da Silva 2019, 178). This framework, however, is inadequate for addressing forms of racial subjugation, such as police terror, which do not require the explicit invocation of race to operate. For instance, in "The Scene of Nature" (2017), Ferreira da Silva demonstrates how the statistical likelihood that Diallo was a criminal—based on his place of residence and death in the Bronx—was taken as sufficient evidence to absolve police officers and justify the murder of Diallo as a lawful act. Race did not need to be explicitly invoked; instead, statistical data, which "seem to prove only what everyone already knows," acted as a socio-scientific justification because "what-is-known" functions as a reservoir of racial knowledge.

While different, Brazilian and US-American texts produce similar effects. However, understanding the profundity of these differences, and more importantly, the production of this difference articulates "insurgent counter-discourse." In her first published work, "The Death of Mãe

Menininha" (1986), Ferreira da Silva highlights how *Candomblé* and other manifestations of African heritage were adopted by the Black Movement in Brazil to represent a distinct black identity. However, she questions whether emphasizing cultural resistance is sufficient, noting these cultural elements have been appropriated to reinforce the thesis of racial democracy. Even in the later article, "Facts of Blackness" (1998a), Ferreira da Silva observes how Zumbi, chosen by the Brazilian Black Movement to represent a separate identity, was being appropriated by the racial democracy discourse, though the discourse did not have widespread acceptance, since it presented Brazil as a country lacking racial consciousness. Reading this lack as *excess* enables Ferreira da Silva to indicate that beyond exclusion, the logic of obliteration plays a central role in racial subjugation. In the logic of obliteration, racial others tend to disappear in the presence of the white/European.

Ferreira da Silva not only identifies mechanisms of subjugation, but also assembles black feminist poethics as both a critical and an imaginative praxis that wanders toward the *end of the world as we know it*, towards decolonization, or the return of the total value expropriated from captive bodies and Native lands. In her later works, Ferreira da Silva (2016) locates the onto-epistemological pillars—sequentiality, separability, and determinability—and descriptors that sustain modern knowledge. Black feminist poethics violates Understanding and its pillars contemplating existence beyond the ordered world, without the separations between subject and object, and without control over time. This praxis is assembled from the perspective that the feminine subaltern subject needs to fit neatly into the categories of Understanding. The possibility that opens when the racial feminine body cannot be resolved "as a woman" within the patriarchal economy is the poethics crafted from excess. It is evident in the possibility indicated by Venus: the ungendered female flesh, which, as Hortense Spillers (1987) observes, was not only torn, mutilated, and displayed but also subjected to scientific intervention.[8] She is simultaneously marked by knowledge and rejected by it. Ferreira da Silva points out that the creative capacity of blackness lies in its ability to comprehend total violence by abandoning the notion that everything that exists does so strictly within the confines of space and time. Beyond space and time, decolonization can be articulated: the total return of value expropriated from captive bodies and native lands, walking towards the end of the world as we know it. This invites the contemplation of other ways of knowing and doing, ones that resist accusations of irrationality, mysticism, or futile fantasy (2019, 108).

---

[8] Here, I am thinking of Sarah Baartman, also called Venus.

Anastácia's Freedom

In the previous section, I highlighted how, unlike in the United States, the racial has operated in Brazil without relying on the recognition of a fundamental separation between racial groups (i.e., miscegenation). However, as Ferreira da Silva argues in "Zumbi & Simpson, Farrakhan & Pelé," it is crucial to avoid rigid dichotomies, such as segregation versus miscegenation: "These narratives do not run in parallel but intersect at a crossroads" (1999, 93). Ferreira da Silva demonstrates that, while understanding the construction of each country's specificities is necessary to interpret how these figures are portrayed, they "cannot be conceived as possessing fixed and unalterable identities" (1999, 93). Instead, these figures themselves are also the context, the specificities of these societies, which "can be constructed and reconstructed based on the possible strategies within a given political conjuncture and the discursive elements available" (1999, 93). Ferreira da Silva's analysis of soap operas reveals a significant shift in Brazil's racial discourse. The inclusion of black characters in these productions marked an important moment of change, aligned with the demands of the Black Movement and its authors who employ the discourse of modernization and a more faithful depiction of reality.

Anastácia's emergence occurred during a period of restructuring within the Black Movement in Brazil, which gained renewed momentum in the 1970s.[9] This was a time marked by Brazil's democratic opening, struggles for decolonization in Africa, and the Civil Rights movements in the United States. The Brazilian Movimento Negro revitalized political protest and introduced ideals of "ethnic identity" and anti-racist resistance (Dias de Souza 2001, 80). However, Anastácia's narrative was not fully embraced by this movement, as it originated within the Catholic Church—an institution that, in the 1930s, had been rejected by the Frente Negra Brasileira in favor of uplifting African-derived religions, a trend that continued in subsequent years (Dias de Souza 2001, 80). Yet Anastácia has a rebellious existence and was not fully accepted by the Catholic Church. By the late 1980s, the curia officially prohibited her cult. This prohibition was largely based on a 1987 newspaper article by Monsignor Schubert, in which the priest sought to scientifically disprove Anastácia's existence. He argued that Escrava Anastácia originated from a lithograph in Etienne Arago's book *Voyage Around the World*. Schubert also contended that it was improbable for an enslaved person to be subjected to the combination of two punishments

[9] This led to the creation of the Unified Negro Movement (MNU). Before that, other national movements existed. For example, in 1931, the Frente Negra Brasileira (FNB), a mass movement with around sixty thousand members. Also, local movements such as the 1954 Associação Cultural do Negro Brasileiro were founded in São Paulo with the goal of establishing an ideology for Black Paulistas.

depicted in her imagery and asserted that the figure portrayed was not a woman but had masculine features.[10]

Indeed, Anastácia has an uncertain existence. From Monica Dias de Souza's (2001) dissertation we learn it is likely Anastácia is a derivation of a drawing Victor Etienne Arago made during one of his journeys to Brazil in the early nineteenth century as part of a scientific expedition. Over two centuries later, this painting was exhibited in the 1970s at the Museu do Negro, housed in the Church of the Irmandade do Rosário e São Benedito dos Homens Pretos—a church built by enslaved people. It was during this period that Anastácia gained a name, a cult, and a narrative. At the same time, the museum, though housed in a church, was not an official site of worship. Its activities often clashed with the preferences of the higher Catholic hierarchy. The museum contained objects considered sacred by visitors, including items brought by enslaved individuals, among them instruments of torture. The material nature of the cults practiced there—such as the offering of gifts—unsettled the Church hierarchy. The Irmandade (Fraternity) managing the church supported Anastácia's cult at least until its official prohibition (Dias de Souza 2001).

Yet, the prohibition did not suppress Anastácia's existence. Dias de Souza traces how this prohibition ignited discussions about racism within the Catholic Church and fueled a "struggle for her legitimacy" among many of her devotees. Anastácia began to be featured in various newspaper articles and even inspired a miniseries that incorporated multiple versions of her story. Moreover, her cult expanded beyond its original location, spreading to other parts of the city and beyond. It persisted within "popular Catholicism" and spiritual practices such as Umbanda. Her worship continued to move and inspire devotees, many of whom attested to miracles attributed to her intervention (Vilela Berbel 1987). Interestingly, even the critical priest did not outright deny the occurrence of these miracles. Instead, he contested their source, attributing them not to Anastácia herself but to the faith and inner conviction of her followers.

If, until then, Anastácia's existence had been marked by the torture devices she received at the end of every story told about her—whether as a martyr or as an emblem of the horrors of slavery—in 2019, she appears for the first time without the mask in Yhuri Cruz's art installation *Monument to Anastácia*. Through a process of digital manipulation, Cruz removes the mask and gives her the mouth of an African saint. The large image, Anastácia

[10] Cruz asserts the openness that it has meant to him: "If before, the image of a liberated Anastácia could already encompass so many people, nowadays I can say that I literally see myself in the image, and I see my mother in that mouth, I see my grandmother in that gaze, Jade, Caju, Yago ... In short ... I feel that this is an image that becomes plural and diverse in ways that we have no control over, and it is an image that has traversed the narrative of my life" (Cruz and Hartman, 2020).

Livre (Free Anastácia), is displayed alongside the word "Voz" ("Voice") written in bold letters. Holy cards featuring the Anastácia Livre image and a prayer on the reverse side were distributed as part of the installation.

Cruz explains that the idea for Anastácia Livre arose from an invitation (Caê 2022). In 2018, he created *Monumento à Presença*, an art-denunciation piece about the "inhabited unsafe spaces" within an art institution in Rio de Janeiro. Using data, the work critiqued the limited presence of black individuals in that space. When asked by a friend to replicate the work in another venue managed by black people, Cruz declined, reasoning that it would not make sense in that context. Having lived with the image of Slave Anastácia in his home for many years, he realized the next project would center on her. Cruz recalls that his mother was a devotee of Anastácia, and he saw her image daily. Today, the Anastácia Livre image is displayed on his refrigerator (Muro Pequeno 2019).

Initially known in a more restricted circle, in 2022 Anastácia Livre became famous when the singer Linn da Quebrada entered the reality program *Big Brother Brasil*, one of the most widely watched television programs in Brazil. Linn wore on the show a shirt designed by Yhuri Cruz featuring the image of Anastácia Livre. Linn's participation marked a departure from the usual portrayals of trans bodies on Brazilian television, which are often reduced to caricatures—a point Linn herself highlights in interviews. Extending beyond the screen and into the streets, the shirt grew in popularity.[11] Since 2023, her image has also been prominently featured in a large mural by Cruz on the wall of Gentil, located in the open-air market of Saara, Rio de Janeiro. With each exhibition, the mask that confines Escrava Anastácia is destroyed once again. However, it is also a risky move. For example, the misuse of pronouns was exploited exhaustively by the program, and Linn herself expressed some weariness about this. Moreover, the show has, in recent years, included more black participants. However, incidents of racism frequently recur, and while they seem to just depict reality, these scenes ultimately boost viewership and online engagement and ironically, even from those who oppose such incidents, as their reactions feed into the program's metrics.

Although we are in a different moment, this dynamic strongly resonates with what Ferreira da Silva describes in her analysis of soap operas. It can be understood as the logic of inclusion/exclusion functioning as a tool of subjugation. In "Bahia Pêlo Negro" Ferreira da Silva asserts that in multiculturalism, where "new voices" enter the scene of representation, "even as the subaltern position gains visibility, it remains firmly confined within the realm of affectability" (2005). The self-determined and autonomous subject remains assumed when we imagine that voices can be recuperated and reintegrated into the universal reservoir of humanity. The

[11] Cruz himself does not sell the shirt, which he trades for participation in his performance, as noted above. However, an unofficial version of the shirt also circulates.

dynamic of engulfment, as mentioned above, continues to operate, with all its violent consequences. However, in "Bahia Pêlo Negro" we see an alternative possibility when the question of self-consciousness is rejected, and when we remain in the space of affectability. Here, Ferreira da Silva offers a constructive response to the question posed in "Can the Subaltern Speak?" This is not because Olodum's lyrics merely express or embody a black or African spirit, but because they emerge from a space of contention. These lyrics arise from a political relationship,a struggle against oppression, legal domination, and economic dispossession/exploitation. Ferreira da Silva argues that these lyrics use blackness and Africanity as signifiers of shared material conditions of existence. Similarly, Anastácia's freedom can be understood not as an abstract attribute of the modern subject but as a movement of material release that simultaneously represents a transmutation. As Linn states: "I understand that being free also means freeing oneself from something, and it can—and should—mean freeing oneself from oneself." In Anastácia's case, freedom is a form of material release.

What moved me in this text was the realization that if Anastácia's emergence is largely connected to the mask, removing it does not negate her existence. It merely exposes her secret, since without the mask, what appeared to define her, her suffering and martyr-like resistance to it, also fades away. We now know less, not more, about Anastácia. A mystery has always existed, as the plethora of stories makes apparent. That realization gives image for the black feminist poethic task of releasing blackness as a category. If it emerged largely due to colonization and its scientific framework, releasing it from the clutches of knowledge does not eliminate blackness but opens its creative potential. When translating Anastácia into this text, I also realized that, in English, "Free Anastácia" can be read as a demand. Another opposite possibility posited by Anastácia's freedom was the question, "What if we are already free?" If so, our freedom/liberty (two words that have no difference in Portuguese) has not eradicated the colonial violence. In that case, Anastácia points to the fact that no effective abolition can happen without restoration. Indeed, she is demanding her tongue back.

Recently, Cruz created the scene "Negrotiation: my tongue is in your mouth, and I want it back." In this performative art scene, people receive the shirt in exchange for signing a contract with fingers printed in blood-red ink, authorizing the filming and use of images of their tongues. They read the following text to the camera:

I awoke with blood on my hands
and red eclipsed the color of my skin.
Where do I trade the blood for a new image?
I have lived a story with my voice confined
within the tomb of a portrait.
Where do I trade the silence for a new voice?

> I sleep every night with a restless, quivering tongue,
> Between the life and death of language.
> Where do I trade the tongue of war for the tongue of the body?
> My tongue is in your mouth, and I want it back.
> My voice is in your throat, and I want it back.
> My image is in your memory, and I want it back.
> (Cruz 2023)[12]

We are called to pay attention to the dismemberment behind the mouth. Just as Ferreira da Silva asks what the wall where Dana's arm is stuck might reveal to us, we can ask the same about the mask (2022). In *Unpayable Debt*, Ferreira da Silva suggests that, without time, Dana's traversings from the 1970s to the antebellum period are not impossible, "that can be imagined and that happens (actually, possibly, and virtually) when that which exists is approached elementally" (2022, 289).

Without time, Ferreira da Silva also re/de/composes historical materialism into raw materialism. Against the erasure of colonial productivity, labor is understood as the transmission of matter-energy. Seen this way, there is no doubt that, "the horses, the soil, the rainwater, and the sunrays," just as "the body of the Slave, as well as her mind, [is] transduced into cotton, sugarcane, tobacco, or any other commodity that her labor brought into existence as such" (2022, 24). From this raw materialism, it is possible to reinterpret the flesh—the marked flesh as posited by Spillers—as the elements present in everything that exists:

> For if the flesh holds, as a mark/sign, colonial violence, the Dead's rotting flesh returns this marking to the soil, and the Dead, then remain in the very compositions of anything, yes, as matter, raw material, that nourishes the instruments of production, labor, and capital itself. That is how the dead slave/Native lives in/as capital.
>
> (Ferreira da Silva, 2020)

---

[12] Acordei com o sangue em minhas mãos
e o vermelho eclipsou a cor da minha pele.
Onde negrocio o sangue por uma nova imagem?
Vivi uma história com minha voz trancafiada
dentro da tumba de um retrato.
Onde negrocio o silêncio por uma nova voz?
Durmo toda noite com a língua inquieta, tremulante
Entre a vida e a morte da linguagem.
Onde negrocio a língua da guerra pela língua do corpo?
Minha língua está em sua boca e eu a quero de volta.
Minha voz está em sua garganta e eu a quero de volta
Minha imagem está em sua memória e eu a quero de volta.
(Cruz 2023)

From *corpus infinitum*, where each thing is a singular expression of an elemental entanglement, there is no fundamental difference between the tongue, the soil, and the iron and what is demanded is the return, as that which has never left (Ferreira da Silva 2019).

In *Anastácia as Venus*, Zimbra contends that engaging with the archive involves confronting an impossible space marked by vestiges. She emphasizes facing the vestiges as a confrontation with emptiness, involving the "decomposition of matter that is sensorially strange" (Bezerra 2020, np). Reflecting on the void, she recalls the new moon, explaining that it is new because it precedes the empty sky. But this void, pointing to the infinite possibilities to exist otherwise, can be mobilized and indeed it has been, as the Black Feminist Poethics wanders toward the end of the world as we know it, and as we continue to pray to Anastácia.

References

Assis, Machado (1906). "Pai contra mãe." *A Biblioteca Virtual do Estudante Brasileiro*. http://www.bibvirt.futuro.usp.br.

Bezerra, Caju, Iagor Peres, Yhuri Cruz, and Jade Zimbra (2020). "Anastácia como Vênus, uma cena de tradução." *Yhuri Cruz*, YouTube, September 25. https://www.youtube.com/watch?v=q4QmC-SJSTU&t=1826. Accessed December 10, 2025.

Caê, Rodrigo (2022). "CaêTalks #39 – Yhuri Cruz." YouTube, October 10. https://youtu.be/8009rmVVm50?si=5bpZnJQmi1pnPCZL. Accessed December 10, 2025.

Cruz, Yhuri (2023). "NEGROCIAÇÃO #1: Minha língua está em sua boca e eu a quero de volta, uma cena de Yhuri Cruz." *Yhuri Cruz*, YouTube, July 26. https://www.youtube.com/watch?v=m1B9kV4RvDU. Accessed December 10, 2025.

Cruz, Yhuri and Saidiya Hartman (2020). "Vênus em dois atos, de Saidiya Hartman – Tradução não-oficial para a cena *Anastácia como Vênus, Vênus como Anastácia*, de Yhuri Cruz." July. https://doceru.com/doc/xv5c0sc.

Dias de Souza, Mônica (2001). *Escrava Anastácia: construção de um símbolo e a re-construção da memória e identidade dos membros da Irmandade do Rosário e São Benedito dos Homens Pretos*. Master's thesis, Universidade Federal Fluminense, Instituto de Ciências Humanas e Filosofia.

Ferreira da Silva, Denise (1986). "A morte de Mãe Maneninha: cooptação ou resistência?" *Comunicações do ISER* 21.

Ferreira da Silva, Denise (1991). "O Reverso do Espelho: O Lugar da Cor na Modernidade – Um Estudo sobre Mito e Ideologia Racial nas Novelas da TV Globo." Dissertation, Instituto de Filosofia e Ciências Sociais, Universidade Federal do Rio de Janeiro.

Ferreira da Silva, Denise (1998a). "Facts of Blackness." *Social Identities* 4, no. 2: 201–31.

Ferreira da Silva, Denise (1998b). "Revisitando a 'Democracia Racial': Raça e Identidade Nacional no Pensamento Brasileiro." *Estudos Afro-Asiáticos* 16.
Ferreira da Silva, Denise (1999). "Zumbi & Simpson, Farrakhan & Pelé: As encruzilhadas do discurso racial." *Estudos Afro-Asiáticos* 33.
Ferreira da Silva, Denise (2001). "Towards a Critique of the Socio-logos of Justice: The Analytics of Raciality and the Production of Universality." *Social Identities* 7, no. 3: 421–54.
Ferreira da Silva, Denise (2005). "Bahia Pêlo Negro: Can the Subaltern of Raciality Speak?" *Ethnicities* 5: 321–42.
Ferreira da Silva, Denise (2007). *Toward a Global Idea of Race*. Minneapolis: University of Minnesota Press.
Ferreira da Silva, Denise (2016). "Sobre a diferença sem separabilidade." In *32a Bienal de São Paulo: incerteza viva*, edited by Jochen Volz and Júlia Rebouças. Fundação Bienal de São Paulo.
Ferreira da Silva, Denise (2017). "The Scene of Nature." In *Searching for Contemporary Legal Thought*, edited by Justin Desautels-Stein and Christopher Tomlins. Cambridge: Cambridge University Press.
Ferreira da Silva, Denise (2019). *A dívida impagável*. Translated by Amilcar Packer and Pedro Daher. São Paulo: Forma Certa.
Ferreira da Silva, Denise (2020). "Reading the Dead – A Black Feminist Poethical Reading of Global Capital." In *Otherwise Worlds: Against Settler Colonialism and Anti-Blackness*, edited by Tiffany Lethabo King et al., 38–51. Durham: Duke University Press.
Ferreira da Silva, Denise (2022). *Unpayable Debt*. London: Sternberg Press.
Ferreira da Silva, Denise (2024). *A dívida impagável: Uma crítica feminista, racial e anticolonial do capitalismo*. Translated by Nicolau Gayão, Nathalia Carneiro, Roger Melo, Jefferson Monteiro, and Vivine Nogueira. São Paulo: Editora Zahar.
Hartman, Saidiya (1997). *Scenes of Subjection*. New York: Oxford University Press.
Hartman, Saidiya (2008). "Venus in Two Acts." *Small Axe* 26, no. 2: 1–14.
Muro Pequeno (2019). "#Potências Negras 24: Yhuri Cruz." YouTube, November 28. https://www.youtube.com/watch?v=EU7_iGGJ1o4&t=2s. Accessed October 10, 2023.
Spillers, Hortense (1987). "Mama's Baby, Papa's Maybe: An American Grammar Book." *Diacritics* 17, no. 2: 65–81.
Vilela Berbel, Joatan (1987). *Anastácia Escrava e Santa*. https://www.youtube.com/watch?v=OeYZIO_d3ck

18

Towards a Different Future of Ethnic Studies

Maile Arvin

I imagine that, in any discipline, there is a lot of angst and stress among graduate students. Grad students want to prove themselves, to show themselves to be the smartest, the most likely to win awards or publish early. In Ethnic Studies, where the production of knowledge is often deeply personal and tied to genuine concerns about violence in and against communities of color, this often results in tension and conflict between different racial identities as graduate school pushes students to try to prove themselves and their topic's grand significance. Ethnic Studies is also a field with deep commitments to community engagement and activism. Accordingly, another common faultline is around the relative value of European theorists—i.e., why should Ethnic Studies students need to study and understand what are fundamentally racist philosophies?

As an Ethnic Studies graduate student at UC San Diego circa 2007–2010, I took classes with Denise and eventually she became my mentor and a co-advisor of my dissertation. Denise provided entirely different points of reference for these common debates of the field. In her classes, we read European philosophy in order to understand the genealogy of race in post-Enlightenment thought. Where many of us wanted immediate, actionable solutions to oppression, Denise asked us to trace the violence our communities were experiencing all the way back to the foundational formulations of the human. I am telling you, dear reader: this was not popular with Ethnic Studies graduate students. But if we stuck with it, following Denise's direction through Kant, Hegel, Herder, Marx, Foucault, and more, we found ourselves someplace different. Not all of us liked it, at first! When confronted with the ways that ideals of self-determination were bound up in an exclusive ideal of the human as a transparent, rational European man, always defined over and against his affectable others, we were confused (Ferreira da Silva 2007). What did that mean for Indigenous peoples and others' fights for recognition, for self-determination, for human rights? Denise was teaching us that the premises of all these hallowed words we use for freedom were, perhaps, set up on terms that would never serve us. Ouch.

I imagine that, in any discipline, graduate students have moments like this, where the rug is pulled out from under them and they start questioning the things they thought were "pure," or "radical," or "true." It is a hard moment, and easy to arrive from there at nihilism. But nihilism was never Denise's point, and she didn't let us stop there either. What I understand now, as someone who teaches graduate students, this not letting us off the hook—this making us sit with difficult, inconvenient, and inaccessible knowledge, of not telling us only what we wanted to hear—was an incredible gift. Denise taught us that we were all smart enough to read and analyze Derrida, and that it could have value even when—or especially when—we did not agree. She showed us, in ways that no other professor cared to take the time to, how to criticize the origins of things, how not to take anything for granted. And in doing so, she showed us a way out of our tired Ethnic Studies debates about the "four food groups" (a reference to the common subdividing of Ethnic Studies into Asian American, Native American, African American, and Latinx areas), about race defined only within the United States versus more globally, and activism versus theory. She would not let us get stuck in these places. She asked us to really think about where the knowledge that was structuring our ideals of justice were coming from, in order to be more clear-eyed about how to actually achieve it. I still marvel at what a gift that has been for me, in my own scholarship and activism.

In my first book, *Possessing Polynesians* (2019), I took Denise's lessons and applied them to mapping out a deeper genealogy of the concept of the "Polynesian race," as explicated in Western social scientific literature as a race that was "conditionally Caucasian," than I had seen anyone else do. It helped me explain some of the ways that whiteness works in settler colonialism in Hawai'i and other parts of Polynesia, as well as why some challenges to settler colonialism are more generative than others. It wasn't what I expected to write, and it forced me to confront the ways that Native Hawaiians can internalize and be complicit in the racist ideal of Polynesians as almost white. It was and still is hard to sit with this; and also, I would not want it to be any other way.

In my current research, which examines the history of industrial schools in Hawai'i, Denise's critiques have helped me insist on addressing this history as not only one that happened to and is relevant for Kanaka Maoli (Native Hawaiians) but for the many Asian and other immigrant communities in Hawai'i. It would be, in some ways, easier in contemporary discourse and expectations about racial and ethnic identity to make more of a singular claim—to not acknowledge the relations we Kanaka Maoli have with others. But both because of Kanaka Maoli forms of knowledge that are inclusive and relational, and because of the ways that Denise's work relentlessly upends the expectations that Ethnic Studies work should focus individually on one ethnic group, I have embraced the more complicated fact and framing.

As part of that framing, I argue that Kanaka Maoli often seek and gain knowledge that brings a collective fullness (physical and spiritual satisfaction) through the action of noho. "Noho" is defined by Pukui and Elbert in the Hawaiian dictionary as "to live, reside, inhabit, occupy (as land), dwell, stay, tarry, marry, sit" (1986). R. Keawe Lopes Jr. adds that noho "is reflective of one who has made a commitment to establish a relationship with a place or a person" (2016: 32). While this is a Kanaka Maoli practice of learning and relation, it is not exclusive to those who are Kanaka Maoli. It is simply open to anyone who will noho, who will commit to a long-term relationship. This sitting in and tarrying with place also aligns with Katherine McKittrick's approach to geography as a method to "dislodge crude identity politics, to cast the net beyond the individual and to emphasize that *where* we know from—rather than what we already know about our seemingly authentic selves—is a more generous and difficult political project that takes into account interhuman geographies" (2021, 108).

I can speak with confidence about Waiale'e, for example—the site of a former industrial school for boys on the island of O'ahu—because I commit to spending time there (to noho), not because I am Kanaka Maoli with some mystical connection to it. I understand but am weary of the debates about what to call each other, including the debates in reference to Asian settler colonialism (Fujikane and Okamura 2008). Kanaka Maoli forms of knowledge have always been open to those willing to make a lifelong commitment to be in good relation, to be humble and patient, to practice and learn. To set Kanaka Maoli against those we make our kin diminishes us and our connections to the world. Kanaka Maoli feed whoever is hungry. "Land back," one popular slogan for Indigenous movements today, is not an eviction notice to non-Indigenous people. The point of dismantling our current modes of capitalism and settler colonialism is to be able to feed everyone: to re-establish interdependence for everyone living on and with '*āina* (the Hawaiian word for land, which literally means "that which feeds").

To put it another way, Kanaka Maoli are not Kanaka Maoli because of our "identity" or "cultural difference" but because we want to be good relatives and have ancestral and ever-evolving knowledge that can help us do so. I am saying that Kanaka Maoli knowledge is more than local knowledge or perspective; although it is always in relation to place—it is not stuck in place. Thus, Kanaka Maoli forms of knowledge are distinct from many forms of post-Enlightenment thought that depends, as Denise teaches us, on an ideal of human "separability," which she defines as a principle that: "Considers the social as a whole constituted of formally separate parts. Each of these parts constitutes a social form, as well as geographically-historically separate units, and, as such, stands differentially before the ethical notion of humanity, which is identified with the particularities of white European collectives" (Ferreira da Silva 2016, 63). We do not have to presuppose that difference is premised on separability, Denise says. Instead, we can approach difference as "not a manifestation of an unresolvable *estrangement*, but the expression of an elementary *entanglement*" (2016, 65). The future, for all of us in the world, depends on realizing that entanglement, of refusing to be unresolvably estranged. Kanaka Maoli placemaking shows us one way (not the only way) to do so. Denise taught me how to see and value this, how to be confident that the premises of Kanaka Maoli knowledge are fundamentally different from the premises of dominant understandings of life and humanity in the Western world, and therefore to be confident that this knowledge can be potentially revolutionary for all of us. I am eternally grateful that her work shows us all a different way to do Ethnic Studies and related critical scholarship about and against racial violence.

References

Arvin, Maile (2019). *Possessing Polynesians: The Science of Settler Colonial Whiteness in Hawai`i and Oceania*. Durham: Duke University Press.

Ferreira da Silva, Denise (2007). *Toward a Global Idea of Race*. Minnesota: University of Minnesota Press.

Ferreira da Silva, Denise (2016). "On Difference Without Separability." In *32nd Bienal de São Paulo–Incerteza Viva*, edited by Jochen Volz and Júlia Rebouças. São Paulo: Fundação Bienal de São Paulo.

Fujikane, Candace and Jonathan Y. Okamura (2008). *Asian Settler Colonialism: From Local Governance to the Habits of Everyday Life in Hawai'i*. Hawai'i: University of Hawai'i Press.

Keawe Lopes, R. (2016). "Ua Noho Au A Kupa I Ke Alo" In *Kanaka 'Ōiwi Methodologies*, edited by Katrina-Ann R. Kapā'anaokalāokeola Nākoa Oliveira and Erin Kahunawaika'ala Wright, 30–41. Hawai'i: University of Hawai'i Press. http://www.jstor.org/stable/j.ctvvn2v3.7

McKittrick, Katherine (2021). *Dear Science and Other Stories*. Durham: Duke University Press.

Pukui, Mary Kawena and Samuel H. Elbert (1986). *Hawaiian Dictionary: Hawaiian-English, English-Hawaiian*. Honolulu: University of Hawaii Press.

19

Four Notes on Black Art

Authority, Criticality, Subjectivity, and Separability

Denise Ferreira da Silva

Introduction

> There is not a single central message. This uses language as a means among many, but its meaning cannot be compressed into language or exhausted by language. You have to go in, walk around, look, listen, read and smell. If you are patient, willing to receive in various channels and keep thinking about it later, eventually everything will come together. (Adrian Piper 2018)[1]

What if, instead of approaching the work in search of its intrinsic, unique, or deeper meaning, the public came to it the way Adrian Piper instructs? What if the visitor or the viewer approached the work of art as something that exists, something to be heard, looked at, read, and smelled? And instead of trying to apprehend, understand, or explain it, after taking it in, one just gave

[1] This was said in an interview, as a comment on the exhibition related to Adrian Piper's awarding of the Kathe Kollwitz Prize in 2018 (https://contemporaryand.com/exhibition/adrian-piper-kathe-kollwitz-prize-2018/). https://www.frieze.com/article/i-still-do-believe-they-want-me-dead-interview-adrian-piper

in and waited for/with it, waited for its meaning to arrive or not, eventually? What if... Whatever it is called, if a name is needed, the approach does not fit very well into conventional descriptions of (aesthetic/art) criticism and (theoretical) critique; it does not immediately mobilize or easily recall any critical theoretical orientation. As such, it does not fit very well with/in other common and relevant uses of the term critical. For if the critical—critique or criticism—refers to the task of identifying and exposing the foundations, the rational principle guiding a particular apparatus and deployment of knowledge, and if criticism is the task of evaluating creative works according to a rational principle, combining the two becomes a simple exercise, if one ignores that both are based on the assumption that the terms "rational," as used in both, means or refers to the same procedure.[2]

Now this departs from these other senses of the task precisely because it challenges what holds them together, which is the type of mental gesture said proper to aesthetic, analytical, and theoretical statements. This mental gesture, evaluation or judgment, both presumes and institutes meaning, as well as a context and something like its production and tools for its presentation, apprehension, and understanding. More explicitly, this gesture—which constitutes the context, target, and material for the works that inspire this proposition—presupposes the figure of the I think, that is, the *transparent* I (in its many guises, as human, humanity, subject, and subjectivity), as an object of aesthetic, scientific (analytical or theoretical), or ethical (moral) judgment and, together with it, the onto-epistemological regime that has prevailed over the last two hundred years or so.[3]

"Four Notes on Black Art" gathers musings inspired by artworks, in which I identify formal interventions, against this presumed authority, as their work explicitly or implicitly refuse to signify blackness in the prescribed ways. Here I am interested in how these moves, their rebellious formal gestures confront the notion that organizes post-Enlightenment representation, namely cultural difference, in its historic and scientific rendering. For this notion—everywhere cultivated prevails in the sensibility that, like the subject-position to which it corresponds, the appreciator, cannot accommodate work that confronts the colonial, racial, cisheteropatriarchal matrix of the transparent I as properly aesthetic, that is, it consistently reads them as ethnographic specimen.

Each of these notes also consists of an experiment with rehearsing a mode of approaching art, I call it a reading of art, which does no more than

---

[2] Incidentally, the same applies to the many versions of critical theory and supports its confidence in its own ability to explain and intervene in "social life." This footnote is important because my proposal is relevant to critique, art criticism, and critical social theory.

[3] Here I am obviously referencing to the Kantian notion of judgement as presented in Immanuel Kant, *The Critique of the Power of Judgement* (Cambridge: Cambridge University Press, 2000).

to register a thinking with artists and their work, which here I exemplify in three different ways. The first set of notes, my annotation on the Simone Leigh's work, *Sovereignty*, featured in the US Pavilion at the 2022 Venice Biennial, simply maps the terrain and describes the artist's engagement with the appreciators. In the second, I report on a conversation and comment on aspects of black British feminist dancer, filmmaker, and performer Zinzi Minott's work. Here, I focus on how her treatment of the first-person singular statement, through themes such as history and memory, disturbs subjectivity, that is, the figure at the core of the aesthetic field. The third, my reading of the Brazilian artist Paulo Nazareth's work, identifies a formal gesture, literality, a mode of figuring that results from trans-forming critical tools into raw material. Finally, the fourth set of notes, speculates with the Brazilian dancer, sculptor, and writer, Iagor Peres's experiments with materials and concepts. From reading the work, I derive a term, uncategorical, which is a possible descriptor under which one can study such interventions collectively, as well as the form of my engagement with Peres's proposition. Another way of describing what I do in this chapter is a call and response structure as my engagement with each artist moves with and takes from what they invite me to think.

I

I've seen some preliminary thoughts on the Biennial and concerns about radicality. I need to say that if you haven't read, not a single thing written by Saidiya Hartman or Hortense Spillers. And if you have no knowledge, never heard of Negritude or how it's related to surrealism. If you don't know who Senghor is or why he would have anything to do with art. If you never spent anytime figuring out who was and wasn't at FESTAC 77. If you have no idea what critical fabulation is. If you didn't know what I meant when I said In The Wake. If you never studied Independence architecture. If you don't know why Pauline Lumumba walked through the streets of Kinshasha bare breasted. If you have no idea who Katherine Dunham is or her scholarship, but yet you consider yourself well versed in the work and contributions of the woman she hired as a secretary, Maya Deren. If the words Black Feminist Thought bring absolutely zero concepts to mind. If the words "Dave the Potter" mean nothing to you. If you didn't ponder the significance of Sharifa's unruly kitchen when she embodied Uhura in my video and you don't even know what a kitchen is. If the words "Dogon statuary" conjures nothing. If the only thing you know about Benin bronzes is that Europe stole them. If you casually use words like ethnic, exotic and tribal and you still think those are useful words. If you don't know what story I'm referring to when I talk about

FIGURE 19.1 *Simone Leigh, Venice Biennale page: https://simoneleighvenice2022.org, March 2024, available at https://simoneleighvenice2022.org/wp-content/uploads/2022/04/Simone-Leigh-Venice-Schenck-DSC_9600crop.jpg*

> A Question of Power. If you thought I was being weird when I told you I was too busy sharpening my oyster knife. If you've never heard of the Herero Genocide. Then you lack the knowledge to recognize the radical gestures in my work. And that is why, instead of mentioning these things, I have politely said black women are my primary audience.
>
> —Simone Leigh, Instagram, @simoneyvetteleigh

Reading Simone Leigh's artwork against her critical statement on the contemporary art appreciator reproduced above, I find a formal rendering of refusal both in the artist's statement (the art critic lacks the critical-intellectual tool for understanding her work) and in that which (black feminist critical tools) she brings into the contemporary art scene, as her aesthetical forms do in the "sensible" (in that corner shared by the senses and the imagination) what the theoretical tools deployed by black feminist thinkers inspiring her, Hortense Spillers, Saidiya Hartman, and Christina Sharpe, perform in the "intelligible" (the corner shared by the imagination and the understanding). That much was already evident to me the first time I considered Leigh's work, the first time I stopped to think about what to say about her exquisite forms, the only word that seemed an appropriate guide was *how* (Ferreira da Silva 2019). How not, however, as a question but as the beginning of a description for something that seemed to refuse, that aptly sidestepped and undermined anything that would suggest an answer for a question of what or why, any questions that would render the work datum, that is, an unmediated, *natural* expression of black women's experience, histories, or identity.[4]

"If you don't know ... ", the artist tells critics, who insist on ignoring interventions both theoretical and aesthetical, "do not even bother because the work, my work, this work does not address you." Not because of any distinctive, unique feature of the work itself, but because of the knowledge apparatus shared by critics and the public (and questioned by the artist and the intellectual tradition of which she is part) does not comprehend her work and its conceptual reference among that which is properly and immediately taken as artistic. "If you don't ... you can't" is as much about a not-knowing as it is about a kind of knowing. What Simone Leigh's statement, as well as her work and those of the two other artists with whom I think here does is to challenge precisely the presupposition of authority that accounts for both the presumption (of knowing already, that is, without having to study) and the arrogance (to then move onto a critical commentary that is nothing more than the recounting of anthropological common places about black or African cultural forms). Though it may be called upon explicitly, for the most part that authority operates within the terms and statements deployed in descriptive or reflective (critical) commentaries. This is so because it rests on two components of the context set up by the commentary itself: on the one hand, it is housed in the lexicon, the vocabulary available for critique is constituted as such that it cannot but yield a black subjectivity (of the black artist and of a postulated black public) within the confines of the anthropological and sociological knowledge that have produced it; on the other hand, it is housed in the institutions, which do not count the black artist as a typical presence in their domain (see Moten 2003). It is as if the black artist is a special guest, one whose interest in dismantling black subjugation is an exotic addition, which may add (ethical) value, but is not supposed to have an impact; it does not or I should say, it cannot reconstitute the aesthetic field and its institutional arrangement because it does not really belong to it.

In Simone Leigh's artwork, I find a formal rendering of refusal both in the artist's statement and in that which she brings into the contemporary art scene. However, I am not proposing that Leigh's artworks are formal in the sense of being conceptual tools. To use the typical distinction, it can be said that her aesthetical forms do in the "sensible" (in that corner shared by the senses and the imagination) what the theoretical tools deployed by black feminist thinkers inspiring her do in the "intelligible" (the corner shared by the imagination and the understanding).

---

[4] This statement needs to be read considering Tina Campt's comment on Leigh's "capacity to actively create our own gaze—a Black gaze that demands active forms of engagement, rather than passive acts of watching or consumption—that requires the work of witnessing from its viewer. It is the work of enduring discomfort and facing it head on" (Campt 2021, 153).

Let me elaborate on this statement by commenting on some of the pieces included in *Sovereignty*, that is, her commission in the US Pavilion for the 2022 Venice Biennale.[5] My focus here is on her expressed intention that her artwork contributes to the creation of an audience for black feminist thought. I highlight how, in her attempting to do so, the work unsettles, because of how it exposes, the presumed position of the appreciator, that is, that of the transparent I as it performs in the aesthetic field. Hers is a demand—an imperative interpellation ("if you haven't ... you don't")—that the appreciator (public, critic, curator, and other artist) reflects on what is a basic tenet in the field of aesthetics. Put differently, hers is a refusal of the critic's and the public's lack of interest in considering black forms (theoretic, aesthetic, historic), one which recalls the presumedly *transparent* position of the appreciator. In doing so, she invites us to consider how the subject of disinterested (aesthetical) judgement,—the one which is available to the critic, the artist, the viewer, the curator or gallery or museum director—is thoroughly mediated by distorted "meanings" of blackness and africanity found in the anthropological, historical, and aesthetical archives.

Leigh's confrontational borrowings from the archives combines both a refusal to simplistic attribution of identity and representability to her work and the effort of making visible black women's history, labor (including intellectual), and aesthetics. How she does so, formally, can be grasped from her own comments on her work. For instance, in "Super Nature," a short text published in 2008, Simone Leigh provides us a key for reading her intervention in contemporary art. When describing her installations, she says, that "[m]aterials are collected, decorated, scarred to amplify or designify the ethnographic object of its Orientalist markings" (121). Key here is obviously the verb to "designify" the object, to strip it off the scientific ("ethnographic") signature. How this happens is something the viewer is compelled to attend to precisely because of how the works gather and recompose materials (clay, cowrie shells, and raffia) and (architectural [African] and physical [black]) *forms*, which is something most critics and mainstream media commentators consistently miss. For instance, "Leighs' 7m-tall bronze sculpture based on D'mba headdresses in the shape of a female bust," says a critic about Sentinel, towers over visitors as they arrive. The critic continues to say that "Leigh's work explores the black female body and imagery from the African diaspora—how it has been portrayed and used by other people. But while here the object takes on that *familiar imagery*, Leigh gives it her own spin, blowing them up in scale" (Cole et al. 2022). Nothing in the remainder of the text returns to Leigh's description

[5] The images mentioned here can be found at Leigh's website titled Sovereignty at https://simoneleighvenice2022.org/sovereignty/.

of the task, which is to designify these images. All the reader can conclude is that Leigh's "own spin" is given in the making of the "familiar" object (like the black female bust) bigger!

Leigh's artistic intervention consisting in expressions of a black feminist sensibility (inseparability of the sensible + intelligible) can be grasped if one attends to how her work (the actual work of creating and the creations) is not only the undoing but a re-doing of "meanings" that are in fact determinative (anthropological) products. It is an intervention in the archives of art (African art), of knowledge (anthropological knowledge), and of history (colonial and postcolonial references): as she said at the opening of the 59th Venice Biennale, "to invent what might be missing from the archive, to collapse time ... to formally move things around in a way that reveals something more true than fact" (Leigh qtd in Golden 2019). For precisely these familiar "meanings" constitute the materials onto which she applies a designifying technique, these anthropological (the cultural ones) and sociohistorical (the stereotypes) are altered in the creative work which, Leigh tells us, is inspired by Saidiya Hartman's notion of critical fabulation (Golden 2019). In her version of critical fabulation, Leigh's work on the archives of knowledge and of history combines material and mental forms, in a gesture that also requires that the viewer do some (critical, reflective) work on her own sensibility, when confronted with the stereotypical representations of blackness and Africanity, with *familiar* "meanings" that lie deep in her or his imagination.

What is her move? That which happens in the artwork, as the artwork, transformation that occurs not through discourse, not through recasting (changing form) but by changing them into raw material, through the use of media, materials, and form. For instance, it happens in *Façade* (the pavilion itself is rematerialized, with the use of with wood, raffia, etc.) as it does *The Last Garment* (rematerializes a racist image of Jamaica that was in postcards—the washing woman) as a bronze sculpture. The other sculptures perform further re-materializations that occur inside the rematerialized US Pavilion, acquire the meanings conveyed by sovereignty, which in this context is about control at the level of meaning creation, signification. Take the watermelon, for instance, which is part of the repertoire of symbolic violence (stereotypes) against black people: in Leigh's sculpture, it is transformed into a mold for oversized cowrie shells, which are part of the repertories of economic violence (slavery) against black people.[6]

To be sure, in the case of the inside sculptures, the formal gesture is the similar obverse of *Façade*, which is the first necessary transformation of the

[6] As Nicole J. Caruth, says, in sculpting and building up the shapes, instilling in each her own views and aesthetics, they are totally transformed and offer up new frames of reference. See Greenberger (2020) at https://www.artnews.com/feature/simone-leigh-who-is-she-why-is-she-famous-1234574361/.

master's house into the sovereign domains of black feminist thought, which enables the others. It is as if when the figure of the woman washing clothes is cast in bronze this is an expression of *Sovereignty*, which is exercised as a critical (formal intellectual) treatment of the historical or personal archive in which that postcard is or could be found. Furthermore, Leigh's sculptures comment on the limits of that very context's (the Venice Biennale) definition of what belongs, what is art (sculpture in bronze) and what does not, that is Leigh's materials: ceramic, raffia, cowrie shells, clay, and the forms of black feminism and the black femme. As she puts it, in a 2019 interview, "I would describe the cowrie shell as a stand-in for the female body, or a body in general, or a representation of an absence as well as a presence" (Leigh qtd in Kennedy 2019). This absence, I find, is not so much of content; this is not about exclusion of African and Black forms from the art scene. For, as Leigh comments, Western (mostly white, European, cis man) artists have drawn inspiration (as well as content and forms) from African art for over a century now. Hence, the absence here is not really material (content) but formal, both conceptual (lack of acknowledgement of black feminist critical tools) and aesthetical (the African forms and materials are not considered properly artistic). That is, as the commentary reviewed above shows, when before "familiar" Black or African forms, today's "politically educated" appreciators (critics, artists, publics, or gallery and museum directors)—that is, the ones that have a sense of interventions that confront the colonial, racial cisheteropatriarchal matrix—are not yet ready to see these as something other than *datum* (anthropological or historical specimen), those the inclusion (or repatriation) of which would attend to and correct a colonial or racial wrong, whether theft or mis-representation.

II

> Ancestral interference is the feeling of rage or anger bigger than your own rage, pain bigger than your own pain, it is the feeling of being tired of a fight you have only just begun. It is the feeling of being on the march forever, of screaming from a place deep inside that does not belong to you. It is the feeling of being frightened for your life, fighting for your life. It is standing on the edge of the sea and hearing screams, it is being begged by them not to give up. It is being on your portion of a walk that has been ablaze for centuries, and feeling the weight of every foot that has walked. It is being strengthened by the ability for your ancestors to lose everything, and build something, again, and again and again.
>
> (Zinzi Minott, Fi Dem III, Ancestral Interference, Spike Island at https://www.spikeisland.org.uk/programme/digital-commission/zinzi-minott/)

FIGURE 19.2 Fi Dem III, *Ancestral Interference, Spike Island*
© 2025 Zinzi Minott. All Rights Reserved, DACS.

A constant feature of the work of contemporary black artists, one which has been generative in my point of view (and which resonates with Rizvana Bradley's (2023) thesis on black aesthetics) has been how it is a speculative opening driven by a sometimes explicitly but most time only implicitly staged direct confrontation with modern representation. Along with, and inseparably from its aesthetical characteristics, as I highlight in my comments on Simone Leigh's work, the work also contains disruptive theoretical elements, which refer immediately to the metaphysical and ontoepistemological context in which art itself, as we know it, comes to be.

Let me expand this observation by commenting on Zinzi Minott's work; in particular on the ways in which the work engages with concepts such as subjectivity, temporality, history, and memory.

When Minott asks, "What kind of Slave would I be?," blackness (in its categorial and historical modes) sustains the speculative exercise, despite the presumed irreality of time reversal. In a conversation we had back in 2020, she highlighted how this im/possibility, time travel, however, is available to the artist for speculation, precisely because of how blackness functions as an historical referent (https://www.youtube.com/watch?v=5-nr1JrDfmw).[7] As many have indicated, the person (in the juridic-ethic sense) to which blackness refers historically, that is the slave, is a mode of existing as human

[7] "In Conversation: Zinzi Minott, Denise Ferreira da Silva, and Joan Anim-Addo," November 10, 2020. Available at https://www.youtube.com/watch?v=5-nr1JrDfmw (accessed January 2, 2024).

which is not contemplatable as subjectivity (see Ferreira da Silva 2022). The "I" in Minott's question is in the archives and—as Hortense Spillers and Saidiya Hartman have reminded us—it is always already occupied because pre-positioned by (the actuality and threat of) total violence. Historically, the Slave in so far as she is a Negro, a commodity, is an economic thing; as chattel (property), she is a juridic thing; it is as such that she is present in the records—newspapers, title documents, wills. That, of course, extends to her poems and novels, memoirs and essays, as well, because whether she is an enslaved or a freed writer these do document the political (juridic-economic) conditions under which they were written. For this reason, subjectivity is not to be demanded from or imposed on them. Nor is its unavailability, it is important to add, to be lamented, which is something Minott's speculation gifts us. Would I be a slave or had I been a slave, as a speculative first-person statement, does not differ from *had I not been one*; both indicate what has not happened, in one case because the *I* is positioned ahead in the line of time and in the second case because the *I* is positioned without the condition of enslavement. In both, it is the violation of sequentiality, which is key to any representation of consciousness or self-consciousness—Descartes, Kant's, Hegel's, and even Deleuze's—that delimits the work.

When, in our conversation, we talked about "What kind of Slave would I be?," Minott highlighted precisely a connection between these two possibilities when referring to wonderings about those called "jumpers"—the captured persons who managed to jump off the slave ships and died in the Atlantic Ocean. Those whose remains (as particles), Christina Sharpe (2016) recalls, are still part of the planet's waterscapes. What becomes thinkable if one pursues a line of inquiry suggested by Minott's work and intention? What happens when the jumpers are claimed by those of us who descended from those who completed the crossing, and were enslaved? When blackness recalls the captive as dead, as a ghost and as a molecule, as/in one of the atoms that composed the body or in the elementary particle that composes everything? Whatever else becomes thinkable, and as such takes part (at the level of the symbolic) of this, our now, will certainly exceed what is made available by the archive of violence, the one which supports the claim to transparency, in which silence is the only answer to Minott's question, that is, when the question hails a person who would reply from the position of enunciation the artist occupies, as a black first person singular. Fortunately, as Minott's artworks offer, the artist is not detained by the archive's holdings: the historical and the anthropological archives and their records are also but raw materials available for re/de/compositional intervention.

The *Fi Dem* series give a sense of the kind of re/orientation being invited, which would be at the core a mental (ethical and analytical) shift, in regard to temporality. In *Fi Dem*, *Fi Dem II*, *Fi Dem III*, and *Fi Dem IV*, figured as material movement—as the references to the dead captive and blood recalls re/de/composition—I find a reference to ancestrality that invites the image of reversibility and not the unfolding sequentiality given by linear time. If, as an historical referent, blackness cannot yield that which is the condition of possibility for the aesthetic experience, subjectivity, precisely because of how it presents the Slave—who, as a first person singular is pre-positioned, juridically and economically—as a material referent of that particular juridic-economic entity; blackness as an attribute of a body (not of a type of body, which it does categorially) but of a solid organic composite, recalls the long dead, the ancestors of such a person, both the ones who would not become, who could not have been (jumpers) and those who would and did (ghosts).

Foregrounding pre-position, in particular—because Subjectivity can only emerge if protected with/in the arche-form (that is, the figure of the patriarch, as the husband, father, owner, settler) of the juridic-economic subject—in Minott's artwork I read blackness as reclaiming what for the transparent I is immediately given as/in memory and history. Recalling, claimed and claiming an ancestrality that does not rely on kinship—bloodline or cultural heritage, no DNA, no organic/biological inheritance—Minott's work refers to and inheres the body itself/her body, the ancestrality of its raw material (many of which are 13 billion years old) and also as always already a re/de/composition of other raw materials, that is, existents, that both constitute and sustain it, the body that would have been that of a slave does this work, as a still or moving image that distorts the historical record.

III.[8]

When artist Paulo Nazareth said "All immigrants are political exiles" in a 2014 interview to *Keen On Magazine*, he was addressing directly what was then, before, and remains unquestionably one of the most significant global issues of our times (Tam). While here he directly speaks about this situation in his artwork, the same theme is presented in such a way that it renders bits and pieces of critical statements and formulations, that is, criticality itself, into raw materials. For instance, when commenting on this displacement of populations—black and brown people—from their homes in the former colonies of Europe, in Latin America, Africa, Southeast Asia, and the island-countries of the Pacific and the Caribbean. He recalls its juridic-economic—and not simply ethical, humanitarian—significance when he says that "if these countries [the US and Europe] do not want to let in illegal immigrants

[8] This section was previously published as part of the essay: Ferreira da Silva, "After It's All Said," in Alex Ganterfeld and Gean Moreno (eds) *Paulo Nazareth:* Melee (Munich: Hirmer Verlag GmbH, 2021).

FIGURE 19.3 *"All immigrants are political exiles," Paolo Nazareth, 2014.*

and refugees, please do not promote political instability and oppressive economic policies in the peripheral countries" (Tam 2014). Straightforward, and yet far from simple, however, is how Nazareth's artwork comments on this (including today's refugee crisis) while at the same time recalling its historical precedents and global reverberations.

Here I am interested in the work's direct confrontation with a critical sensibility, which is held by cultural difference (a tool of raciality)—that of the transparent I—the prevailing one, the one that cannot accommodate anti-colonial and anti-racist expressions as properly aesthetic, that is, which are consistently read as ethnographic specimen. Nazareth's mode of presentation, his compositional strategy comments on these currently political circumstances by confronting and undermining attempts at reading both his work and its intention as just another operation of cultural difference. Through repetition, humor, and healthy dosages of weirdness and urgency, Nazareth's performances, photographs, sculptures, and installations request a sensibility that presumes and anticipates what lies beyond all that has been said and done about colonial and racial violence and the works they perform for global capital.

Each one of his artworks is a composition of elements that registered total and symbolic violence against black and indigenous populations and their strategies of refusal and survivance. Through pieces collected (in international and trans-continental walks) or created (sculptures, videos, or drawings), Nazareth's performances and installations collapse the distinction between the ephemeral/casual and the monumental/formal, in a way that renders the use of explicit elements of critical racial, anti-colonial, or anti-capitalist discourse unnecessary and, even, I dare say, unhelpful. An exemplary work is his piece for the Latin American pavilion at the 56th Venice Biennale, *Indigenous Voices*, led by the curator Alfon's Hug.[9] With a focus on the regions' endangered indigenous languages, the exhibition displayed the work of artists from sixteen countries, including Nazareth's sound installation, in which he and Guarani-Kaiowá children repeat words in Portuguese and Kaiwá. Reading Nazareth's description of this particular piece (quoted above) in the context of his comments on his artwork in general, I wondered how the critics and audience at the biennale responded to these straightforward but apparently disconnected pieces, both in form and content: On the one hand, the sound piece, in which one hears his and other voices repeating words in two different languages, without any commentary or indication of how it relates to the larger theme of the pavilion. Mere presentation, juxtaposition, without any maker of a hierarchy or dominance between the two languages, the indigenous children and Nazareth speak in both languages. On the other hand, the description retells recent, past, ongoing colonial (total) violence against indigenous persons and populations.

Pure denunciation without any analytical or interpretive device, Nazareth writes about the ongoing attempt at obliteration of indigenous peoples, of his people, throughout the continent. There is no reason to think that the audience did not connect the dots. However, I am not sure if it did more than to read in it a culturally (Latin American, Brazilian, indigenous, black) determined mode of expression. That the very mode of presentation of the Venice Biennale, with its national pavilions, invites such reading is and is not besides my point here, incidentally. What I find in this work (and also others) by Nazareth is precisely a response to such likely (because overdetermined by the form of the Venice biennale itself) reading. Juxtaposing two languages, an image of the children posing like the members of the Brô Mc's, a popular indigenous-Brazilian rap group, and the recounting of the ongoing total violence against indigenous populations and person in the Americas, without analytical or interpretive operators to signal a critical stance, the parts of Nazareth's sound piece stand for what they are, each presenting an aspect of indigenous existence, of survivance in the face of ongoing colonial violence: languages (Kaiowá and Portuguese), musical forms (hip hop), and state (perpetrated or authorized) violence.

[9] Sound and text available at https://universes.art/en/venice-biennale/2015/tour/latin-america/paulo-nazareth-text.

What I read here is a refusal to deploy the available signifiers of the ruling critical racial discourse in the presentation of colonial and racial violence. How it is rendered, how does the work try to resist the comprehension of the artist's intention as an expression of his/her/their cultural difference? It does so, I find, because, in his work, both his body (in the films and performances) and objects (collected and created) do not stand for anything other than themselves, that is, neither of the usual descriptors for the artwork's mode of signifying, metaphor nor metonymy, captures how his material (his body and objects) refigure colonial and racial subjugation and possible tools, methods, and strategies for its destruction.

Literality, I find, is a more suitable descriptor for a mode of figuring that is self-referential, that is, one that does not recall something else in form (metaphor) or as content (metonymy). I use the term to name a compositional strategy—and as such a highly formal procedure—that creates a lapse in the movement of signification (the refusal to mean beyond what is said because it [the said] is already the meaning) through which the artwork is released from the demands of any specimen of modern discourse. This occurs because literality (counterintuitively, I must add) allows Nazareth to present anti-colonial and anti-racist statements that escape the grips of representation precisely because they do not rely on its modalities of figuration (namely, metonymy and metaphor) or deploy analytical or interpretive devices or terms that appeal to (and please) the audience's (for its) critical literacy. Literality works, I find, because the artwork takes the form of a *fractal* assemblage that indexes simultaneous operations of colonial and racial violence as well as of survivance at many scales: language, juridical violence, the person's body, and, in the case of this particular piece, including collective modes of expression shared with other (black) populations subjected to total violence, such as rap music.

IV.[10]

From the invisible to the unspeakable, the moments when attention to what is not seen blossoms the perception of other densities that permeate us. That is, looking at the invisible helps critical reflection on how other layers also act in our everyday. Densities that reformulate and emphasize the environmental spheres in which are (or were displaced?). Relations

[10] A longer version of this piece was published in the PIPA Prize Catalogue 2023, which is available at https://www.pipafoundation.com/wp-content/uploads/2023/12/catalogo_2023_para-web_compressed.pdf (accessed January 24, 2024).

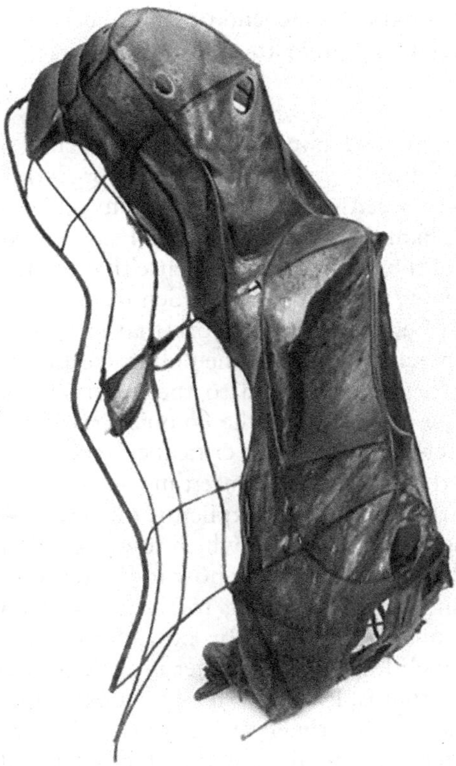

FIGURE 19.4 *Screenshot of* No Title #3, *2019, materialskin. (synthetic and organic components) and iron. https://ehcho.org/en/content/there-among-us-something-invisible-and-obliterating-iagor-peres.*

with the invisible much more complex than any logical organization of the order of the world. An exercise that forces comprehension of these bodies as also life agent and modifiers of our relations.

(Iagor Peres, n.d.) https://ehcho.org/conteudo/ali-entre-nos-um-invisvel-obliterante

To think about the continuity of something that I position in space in a certain way and it ceases to be only what I positioned when it repositions itself. When it exerts this transformation, it is itself in the world and re-situates itself with another place, other than the space I placed. Maybe they are not even my extension anymore. There is no formulate between what it is, when, when it ends, or when it becomes something. We are always in a relational field. Depending on the perspective, this object, or this living thing, changes in relation to me.

(Iagor Peres 2021)

When I first encountered Iagor Peres's work, when I saw the photos of *Pelematerial*, included in his online exhibition, *Ali Entre Nos Um Invisible Obliterante* (there between us an obliterating invisible), at the EhChO.org platform and then, many months later, when I saw and touched one of the pieces that is part of the series, I had the sense that the things before me did not invite a what, why, what for, or by which means kind of consideration. Instead, once again I encountered artwork that unapologetically requested that the critical appreciator—that is, the public, curator, the critic, who may praise themselves for being attuned to the questionings presented by an apparatus of critique that address the colonial, racial cisheteropatriarchal matrix of the subject—set aside their critical certainties and attended to the experiment before their eyes. A first unsettling moment in it is that the work refuses—and the artist, even more explicitly, obviously—to be caught as a matter for knowing, something with which to become familiar, as an object for the understanding, or one to learn how to appreciate.

At the same time, when attending to the work, I am arrested by the same wonderings, musings inspired by how the work renders blackness. To that *how*, by which I mean the manner in which the work does what it does, the procedure, that is, I will give here the name of uncategorically: the work renders blackness experimentally, and as such without attributing it definition or definiteness. How this manner does what it does—and as I say that I am aware of the fact that that saying, Peres would say, has become not part but the work—has to do with how it treats what we understand under terms such as body, object, and thing. Having been hailed as an accomplice by the artist, I find it important to have Iagor Peres be part of this commentary on the work. As it may be obvious by now, I do so not to use the commentary as evidence but as itself an aspect of Peres's artwork. As for me, I write this in movement, that is, on the fly, as they say. Trusted into the position of appreciator by the gallery, museum, biennale or the art publication, I find relief accepting the work's invitation to speculate.

Looking at images of Peres's work over the past nine years, it is not difficult to find the resonances between the performances and the sculptures. What does not come about, at least not to me, is a term that would comprehend either or both. That neither the performances nor the sculptures lend themselves to naming, to categorization, indicates something that Peres has commented on recently. Nonetheless, the fact that blackness suffuses the work both as a form (a term) that captures the context of its reception and as its material also renders the performances and sculptures as commentaries on the very context of colonial, racial, and cisheteropatriarchy in which we encounter them. Precisely this tension, I find, works through the work as each piece transfigures body, object and thing precisely as it invites the public to attend to how it exists, to how its conditions of existence—which was the phrase used as a synonym for life in the nineteenth century—are constitutive of it as an existent. And those include the artist, as Peres insists on reminding us. The "continuity of the gesture in the space" might as well be another name for existence when considered in the register of movement.

What if these "relations with the invisible" were to become that by which we understand existence? The artist tells us that much when commenting on the work itself, on the relation between the artist and the work but also on how that "continuity" that occurs in space renders the work also and always unfinished, in existence—as it is modified by temperature, air pressure, humidity, noise, light, neutrinos and dark matter, and so on—or to use Peres's word, alive. Body, object, and thing are nothing more than the continuity of a gesture, both of the artist who first per-formed/pre-formed it and of the later per-formance/formation of everything else visible and non-visible with which it shares space. How to write about the work when knowing that the artist has already claimed anything anyone has to say about it? The continuity of a gesture in space is a call for attention to inseparability also in regard to the mind, the subject, and the person. In Peres's work implicancy does not come as a message to the appreciator (public, curator, interviewer, critic) in the first-person. Instead, it comes out of the manner through which the artist turns us into accomplices in what happens to the materials that compose the object of art. It is the artistic object, as it gives continuity to a gesture in space, as affected by its condition of existence—that is, as it shifts and changes in space/in time—that establishes how the appreciator becomes part of it.

Two thoughts become unavoidable to me once I start to think of continuity in this manner, in Peres's manner: On the one hand, one cannot but wonder about whether or not when looking at/touching something, even if not consciously so, one (the human thing) is also touched by that which has been part of the thing-in-existence. On the other hand, and consequently, one must wonder if her sensing (seeing, touching, smelling, hearing, tasting) of the thing-in-existence, the artistic object, commits the thing to the continuity of a gesture in the space in which it exists. Both questions, of course, also then request a consideration of how then the thing-in-existence, in so far as it comments on the workings of the colonial, racial, cisheteropatriarchal matrix, also affects the latter continuity, as also a gesture in space.

Slowly but surely, I hope, I have moved this commentary on Peres's work, which now is another component of its in-existence, towards that which it unsettles, which is precisely the two defining relations in the aesthetic field, the one between the artist and the work and the one between the appreciator and the work. How that is done, the manner that obtains the singularity of Peres's experimental art, that is, art that intervenes by confronting (and in doing so exposing) the colonial, racial, cisheteropatriarchal matrix, I find, exemplifies something that, perhaps because of the protected place it has enjoyed throughout its 200 year-old trajectory, the aesthetic alone seems able to afford. That how, as the work itself, does not allow for categorization, it insists and persists in its refusal of a name. And, it is precisely because it does so by dismantling that which is at the core of categorization—body, object, and thing—by rendering it without form, without solidity, within extension, that is, as movement or, in Iagor Peres's words quoted above, a continuity of the gesture in space.

Conclusion

How to inhabit the exhibition space, walk through the corridors of the exhibition without immediately finding yourself in the position of the connoisseur? However, when this position is exposed, when its reservoir of meanings, its grammar, lexicon, and significators, are evident, something else occurs, a dis/orientation, which resonates, reverberates, the artist's intervention because it halts any immediate grasping of the meanings of the work; resolution in/as representation.

For it is precisely because coloniality and raciality consolidate the position of appreciation, the place of enunciation available to the artist, curator, the public, critic) aggregates a reservoir (terms, formulations, meanings—as well as images and sounds) of racial (categorial and historical) meanings that enter into the composition of the aesthetic text, in the twentieth century. A complex and complicated positioning because, in addition to the Kantian subject of aesthetic judgment, which has the same basis as the scientific subject of experience, it also houses the subject of social critique, who may or may not be Marxist, and who may or may not be literate in the critical social text, that is to say the critical arsenal that targets coloniality, raciality, and the cis-hetero-patriarchal matrix. Much complexity and many complications result from this co-inhabitation. For example, the subject of criticality can—and I'm pretty sure, does—present itself as a non-Kantian or even anti-Kantian appreciator. However, at the same time, his/her/their inclusive/decolonial/diversity-wise statements about works or artists bears a Kantian orientation, even when not as explicitly as when she rests her claims on his notion of cosmopolitanism. Regardless of its manifestation, this presentation indicates one of the ways in which raciality operates in the intrastructure of subjectivity, which is the writing of the *transparent* subject of reflection who cannot objectify itself because it engages the world as its own and of *affectable* subjects to whom reflection is always already pre-occupied by a *world* that is constituted by representations built according to the tools of racial knowledge and the workings and configuration of political architecture they helped to build.

My focus here is in the gestures of refusal—of authority, subjectivity, criticality, and separability—that confront this construction. Thinking with Simone Leigh's exposing and challenging a presumed authority, when she states that the majority of those occupying the position of the appreciator in the contemporary scene do not have the conceptual tools for grasping her work, has inspired questions about the aesthetic which, I hope, help to outline, without apprehending or in any other way limiting or confining, what lies beyond the challenge brought by the artworks that confront the colonial, racial, cisheteropatriarchal matrix. Though it seems unavoidable not to approach these artistic interventions without assuming that they express or actualize particular histories, experiences and subjectivities, it is not impossible to read them as such, that is, as artistic statements that not so much seek the inclusion of formerly absent perspectives but which in their very existence already threaten a shift at the core of the field of aesthetics.

Another way of saying the same thing is that Minott's and Peres's artworks intervene at the metaphysical and ontoepistemological level—through two crucial notions, subjectivity and separability—in ways that refuse the very grounds of our thinking through gestures that unsettle the space of their occurrence. That gesture is precisely to trust the work to that which composes it and to that which is already in play, where it will exist. My wonderings with their artwork were only possible because I could not resist the artist's invitation to try, to experiment. Once there, where the artist and the appreciator become just another existent that is also part of the artwork's conditions of existence, is where it may be possible to speculate about thinking of existence without violence. Here, at the threshold, which is also the surroundings, the outskirts of modern representation and the authority that manifests onto-epistemologically, it is possible to contemplate a sensibility that is not nourished by the proper (transparent, presumably a-cultural because universal and transcendental) subject of disinterested appreciation, and everything else modeled after him.

References

Bradley, Rizvana (2023). *Anteaesthetics*. Stanford: Stanford University Press.

Campt, Tina (2021). *Black Gaze*. Cambridge, MA: MIT Press.

Cole, Allison, et al. (2022). "Venice Biennale 2022: The Must See Pavilions in the Giardini." *The Art Newspaper*, April 19. https://www.theartnewspaper.com/2022/04/19/venice-biennale-2022-the-must-see-pavilions-in-the-giardini.

Ferreira da Silva, Denise (2019). "How." *E-Flux* 105, December. https://www.facebook.com/efluxeflux/videos/denise-ferreira-da-silva-how-e-flux-journal-105-december-2019-deniseferreiradasi/905054416637607/.

Ferreira da Silva, Denise (2022). *Unpayable Debt*. Berlin: Sternberg.

Golden, Thelma (2019). "Zendaya and Simone Leigh Are Going Beyond Beauty." *Garage Magazine* Issue 17, September 7. https://garage.vice.com/en_us/article/9kebk3/zendaya-garage-simone-leigh-style.

Greenberger, Alex (2020). "How Simone Leigh Sculptures Centering Black Women Brought Her to the Venice Biennale." *Artnews*, October 19. https://www.artnews.com/feature/simone-leigh-who-is-she-why-is-she-famous-1234574361/.

Kennedy, Nancy (2019). "Interview with Simone Leigh: Simone Leigh, Now on the Spotlight, Contemplates the Theme of Invisibility." *The Art Newspaper*, April 29. https://www.theartnewspaper.com/2019/04/24/simone-leigh-now-in-the-spotlight-contemplates-the-theme-of-invisibility.

Leigh, Simone (2008). "Super Nature." *Small Axe*, February 25, 12, no. 1.

Moten, Fred (2003). *In the Break*. Minneapolis: University of Minnesota Press.

Peres, Iagor (n.d.). https://ehcho.org/conteudo/ali-entre-nos-um-invisvel-obliterante. Translation Da Silva.

Peres, Iagor (2021). "É preciso que você seja um corpo frequentador de um outro corpo." *Monica Coster, Revista Desvio*, October 4. https://issuu.com/iagorperes/docs/_preciso_que_voc_seja_um_corpo_frequentador_de_o.

Piper, Adrian (2018). "Interview: Kathe Kollwitz Prize." https://www.frieze.com/article/i-still-do-believe-they-want-me-dead-interview-adrian-piper.

Sharpe, Christina (2016). *In the Wake*. Durham: Duke University Press.

Tam, Lumi (2014). "To Represent and to Serve," interview with Paulo Nazareth, *keen on* 2. https://www.pipaprize.com/2020/05/read-the-interview-with-paulo-nazareth-from-mendes-wood-dm/

CONTRIBUTORS

Carson Cole Arthur is Lecturer in Criminology at the University of Law, London, UK. He received his doctorate from Birkbeck, University of London. His work has been published in the *British Journal of Criminology*, *Crime, Media, Culture*, and *Rhizomes*.

Maile Arvin (Kanaka Maoli) is Assistant Professor of Ethnic Studies at the University of Hawai'i at Mānoa and the author of *Possessing Polynesians: The Science of Settler Colonial Whiteness in Hawai'i and Oceania* (Duke University Press, 2019).

Katucha Bento is Senior Lecturer in Race and Decolonial Studies in the Sociology Department at the University of Edinburgh, and an honorary chaplain in Candomblé. She also serves as Associate Editor of *Identities: Global Studies in Culture and Power*. Her research interests are Black Feminist, queer, and decolonial approaches to community worldmaking, and word-crafting, including the art of translation.

Danielle Bouchard is Professor of Women's, Gender and Sexuality Studies at the University of North Carolina, Greensboro and author of *A Community of Disagreement: Feminism in the University* (Peter Lang Publishing Inc., 2012). Her work focuses on postcolonial and cultural studies, queer theory, critical militarization studies, and film/media.

Long T. Bui is Professor of Global and International Studies at the University of California, Irvine. He is, most recently, the author of *Viral World: Global Relations during the COVID-19 Pandemic* (Routledge, 2024).

Nathalia Carneiro is a PhD candidate in the Department of Spanish and Portuguese at NYU. She holds a PhD and an MA in Political Theory from the University of São Paulo. She is a member of Coletiva Gira, a counter-colonial and antiracist study and intervention group, with whom she co-translated *Unpayable Debt* by Denise Ferreira da Silva into Portuguese.

Pedro João da Silva Bisneto is a PhD student in Philosophy at the Federal University of Rio Grande do Norte (UFRN), Natal, Brazil.

Alexandro Silva de Jesus is Associate Professor in the Department of Anthropology and Museology at the Federal University of Pernambuco and is known for his works *Corupira: Bad Encounter, Translation and Colonial Debt*, and *Notes on the Current State of the Colonial Wound* (Titivillus Editora).

Agnes Oliveira Costa is a PhD student in Philosophy at the Federal University of Rio Grande do Norte (UFRN), Natal, Brazil.

Denise Ferreira da Silva is Samuel Rudin Professor in the Humanities in the Department of Spanish and Portuguese at New York University.

Julietta Hua is Professor of Gender, Sexuality and Women's Studies at the University of California, Davis, USA. She is the author of *Trafficking Women's Human Rights* (University of Minnesota Press, 2011) and co-author, with Kasturi Ray, of *Spent Behind the Wheel: Taxi Drivers in an Uber Economy* (University of Minnesota Press, 2021).

rashné limki is Senior Lecturer in Race, Decolonial, and Organization Studies at the University of Edinburgh, UK. Her academic thinking and writing focus mainly on the role of coloniality in the world as is, and the possibilities for decolonization.

Thuani Queiroz holds a PhD in Anthropology from the Fluminense Federal University (UFF, Brazil) and has dedicated her academic career to studying gender and sexuality.

Cecilia M. Rivas is Associate Professor of Latin American and Latino Studies at the University of California, Santa Cruz, and the author of *Salvadoran Imaginaries: Mediated Identities and Cultures of Consumption* (Rutgers University Press, 2014).

Federico Sanguinetti is Professor of Philosophy at the Federal University of Rio Grande do Norte (UFRN), Natal, Brazil.

Sara-Maria Sorentino is Associate Professor in the Department of Gender and Race Studies at the University of Alabama. Her research and teaching excavate philosophical connections between anti-black violence, real abstraction, and social reproduction, focusing on the methodological and political challenges involved in routing German Idealism and Marxism through the problem of slavery.

INDEX